PARAPSYCHOLOGY
IN
RETROSPECT

MY SEARCH FOR THE UNICORN

Books in the Same Series

by

R. A. McConnell

ENCOUNTERS WITH PARAPSYCHOLOGY
(1982)
(ISBN: 0-9610232-1-X)
(LCCCN: 81-90032)

PARAPSYCHOLOGY AND
SELF-DECEPTION IN SCIENCE
(1983)
(ISBN: 0-9610232-2-8)
(LCCCN: 81-90464)

AN INTRODUCTION TO PARAPSYCHOLOGY
IN THE CONTEXT OF SCIENCE
(1983)
(ISBN: 0-9610232-3-6)
(LCCCN: 82-99945)

PARAPSYCHOLOGY
IN
RETROSPECT
MY SEARCH FOR THE UNICORN

R. A. McCONNELL

Editor & *Publisher*
Research Professor Emeritus

BIOLOGICAL SCIENCES DEPARTMENT
UNIVERSITY OF PITTSBURGH

The front cover shows Galaxy M81 as photographed through the 200-inch Mt. Palomar telescope by Milton Humason in 1952 and published in *The Hubble Atlas of Galaxies*. This galaxy, located in Ursa Major, is distant 9 million light-years. The light that made this photograph had traveled most of the way toward Earth before conscious man came into being.

International Standard Book Number 0-9610232-4-4
Library of Congress Catalog Card Number 86-90590
Copyright 1987 by R.A. McConnell. All right reserved.
Manufactured in the United States of America.
Printed on alkaline-buffered archival paper.
Book design by R.A. McConnell.

CONTENTS

PREVIEW

This is a book about people and parapsychology as seen through the eyes of the editor-author. It is a collection of essays, memoranda, and research reports concerning parapsychology as a science in an irrational world. The work is divided into two parts: *Light*, which deals with the discovery and dissemination of parapsychological knowledge, and *Shadow*, which explores the social borderland of parapsychology.

How could a young physicist, who had just completed a PhD in electronics after enjoying nine successful years in engineering research, suddenly give it all up for a lifetime in parapsychology? The answer appears in Chapter 1, which is an autobiographical lecture delivered by the editor to his University of Pittsburgh colleagues upon the occasion of his retirement in 1984.

This is followed by a report of the editor's recent attempt to lift parapsychology by its bootstraps by giving 4800 copies of parapsychological books to scientists and teaching libraries in sixty countries. Drawing upon his own experience, the editor has added an appendix on self-publishing in parapsychology.

In a chapter titled "View from Mount Nebo," the editor juxtaposes his views on parapsychology with those of his colleagues from other areas of science in an effort to understand the reality perception gap separating them from him.

The scientific centerpiece of the present volume is a report of the influence of wishing upon falling dice. To gather and analyze the data of this report took seven years in a span of twenty-six. The editor and his co-author, Thelma K. Clark, see this experiment as a precursor to the theoretical understanding of psychokinesis.[1]

In the course of a long career in parapsychology a parapsychologist makes many casual personal contacts. In "Excursions from the Laboratory" the editor tells of worthwhile ideas he gained from psychic persons who came to him for help.

Under "Unintended Psychokinesis" the editor explores the possibility that a well known psychologist may have unwittingly been

---

[1] "Psychokinesis" is the name given to this and other mind-over-matter effects. "Psi" is a generic expression for all parapsychological phenomena.

doing psychokinetic research with rats over a period of several years.

The editor closes the cheerful half of this book by examining the possible relationship of biofeedback to parapsychology and to psychosomatic medicine. He expresses modest hope for an experimental solution to the mind-body problem. In an appendix to this chapter he offers some parapsychological ideas about hypnosis and Ego-State Therapy.

Under the rubric, *Shadow*, the editor has assembled parapsychological documents of a sociologically illuminating kind. Detailed case histories illustrate how, in parapsychology as in life generally, by loose symbolism and false logic, all of us distort the real world for our individual gain and to our collective disadvantage. Chapter titles suggest topics covered: Editorial Logic, Books in Review, On the Academic Custody of Research Money, A Festival of Self-Deception, Forces of Darkness.

To minimize the embarrassment his revelations may cause to others, the editor has refrained from using names except where the activities discussed are already a matter of public record. No other effort has been made to conceal identities.

In his final chapter, "A Wild Card against the Ace of Spades," the editor re-examines his 1982 predictions for the year 2000. He closes with the hope that parapsychology will eventually guide us toward nonsuperstitious moral principles.

The editor is the author of this book except for chapter 4, of which he is co-author.

A warning disclaimer is in order. This book presents ideas of interest to its editor and, hopefully, to others. It is not a survey of the field. Nor does it describe the current literature. At this time in the USA there are perhaps a dozen fully committed experimental parapsychologists who are making substantial contributions to progress in eliciting and understanding psi. Experimental work by the editor and his co-workers is reported herein, but its importance for progress in the field remains to be determined.

PARAPSYCHOLOGY
IN
RETROSPECT

Part I: LIGHT

1

ESCAPE FROM BOREDOM:
AN AUTOBIOGRAPHICAL ACCOUNT

A lecture dedicated in gratitude to the Department of Biological Sciences and to the University of Pittsburgh by Professor McConnell, and delivered to departmental colleagues and other friends, 17 May 1984, on the occasion of his appointment as Research Professor Emeritus.

STUDENT

What determines a scientist's choice of his area of specialization? Why, for example, would a physicist, already well-launched on a successful career, suddenly, at age 33, throw aside the skills he had learned and set sail on the uncharted sea of parapsychology? Rather than try to answer this question, I shall give a thumbnail sketch of a physicist who took that course of action.

I was the middle child among five siblings. My father died when I was eight, leaving us dependent upon a small inheritance and the unobtrusive charity of relatives and neighbors.

Among my earliest memories is the building of a solid-state radio receiver using a bit of mineral lead sulphide clamped in a tiny metal cup and touched by a fine wire called a ''cat's whisker.'' Tuning was by means of a sliding contact on wire coiled around a Quaker Oats box.

Later there was a single vacuum tube, whose filament I heated with a six-volt lead-acid battery kept on trickle charge under a living room table. I remember clearly my sudden introduction to chemistry when I crawled under the table and lit a match to see if the battery needed water.

The town of Emsworth, Pennsylvania, could not afford a high school; so I commuted by railroad daily to Allegheny High School in Pittsburgh. From our teachers we learned such ideas as these: That the value of the dollar depends upon how many are printed. That the Constitution of the United States means whatever the Supreme Court says it means. That the USA, in the course of its history, had engaged in some very questionable military adventures. Also, these teachers made us read from the great literary works that preserve the past and illuminate the future, and they required us to practice the art of precise verbal communication on paper. I sometimes think that a high-school diploma then was worth more than a college degree today.

Was there anything in my childhood that foreshadowed my career in parapsychology? Perhaps the following was a clue. By age 12 or so, I had discovered that the thinking of most people is logically defective. No one with respect for rationality would complacently endure the unending barrage of deceptions to which we are subjected by society. I decided that, if I wanted to know reality, I must abandon all belief in authority—except in the natural sciences where authority is supposedly derived from unbiased observation. Interestingly enough, over the years since then, I have been forced to re-admit to my belief system many of the timeless truths that I had ruthlessly cast out in adolescence.

Nevertheless, I still agree with all of you that the world is mad beyond comprehension. To control the intrusion of madness into our home, the loudspeaker in our television set is connected to a little switch box by a long cable. A touch on the lever at the other side of the room and heavenly silence is restored. We would not want TV without that switch.

While in high school I was a radio amateur and, in due time, achieved the ultimate goal of direct communication with Australia. Later, I earned a professional operator's license and spent one college summer as an assistant operator at KDKA's 50,000 watt transmitter. The main, water-cooled vacuum tubes stood almost as tall as I, while the tuning inductors and capacitors were the size of an elephant. One day, seated at the master console, I could not resist throwing the incoming telephone switch to cut the program off the air momentarily and thus convince myself that such a tiny lever was really so powerful. The senior operator thought something was wrong and came running. He seemed to understand, for he did not say much except, "Don't let it happen again."

I studied physics at Carnegie Mellon University when that school was still called Carnegie Institute of Technology. Along with other physics students, I helped build Carnegie Tech's first amateur radio station. We grandly promised a 300-watt voice transmitter and were allocated several hundred dollars from departmental funds. We constructed two large steel racks and began to fill them, but we ran out of money and had to settle for a simple, code-sending station. Our faculty adviser scolded us for not staying within budget.

With a bachelor's degree in hand, I came to the University of Pittsburgh, hoping to become a scientist. The country was still in the midst of the Great Depression. I lived at home and thus was able to survive on $50 a month as a graduate assistant, teaching elementary physics laboratories. I grew to detest the correcting of laboratory reports. To be fair to the students, I found that I was spending most of my hours grading their work, with too little time left for my own studies. Also, I had not yet gained a comfortable grasp of thermodynamics and quantum mechanics, even though I had been taught to manipulate the equations. After a year and a half, I decided to postpone my academic career to get some industrial experience.

PHYSICIST

Following a few weeks training in shallow seismology at Gulf Oil Corporation at Harmarville, Pennsylvania, I was told to drive a five-ton panel truck loaded with seismic equipment to south Florida where I would meet a crew being shipped in from Oklahoma. I had never driven anything larger than a Model-A Ford sedan, but the company decided that the truck must get there fast. My supervisor said, "Take it home with you and get an early start tomorrow morning."

For the next six months, working as an assistant interpreter, I converted seismic wiggles into slopes and depths, looking in vain for a salt dome. We were based in Everglades, a town of 500 people on the western tip of Everglades National Park. Our explorations were to the north in Big Cypress Swamp. The Fort Myers–Miami Highway was the only paved road. There were fish, water moccasins, alligators, mosquitoes, and water birds in magnificent abundance, but very few people. I did not imagine how much this wild and beautiful country would be changed in the next 45 years by immigration, tourism, drug smuggling, and the need for water in Miami.

When no oil was found in Florida, I was returned to Pittsburgh and placed in charge of the construction and maintenance of radio equipment for 35 field stations. Dissatisfied with my salary of $150 a month, I took a Civil Service examination and in 1939 accepted employment in aircraft testing at the Philadelphia Navy Yard.

Two ominous events remain clear in my memory. Sometime in 1940 we were asked to measure the vibrations caused by the firing of a .50-calibre machine gun mounted in the wing of a fighter plane. An ordnance expert requisitioned a gun and installed it on its prepared bracket in the aircraft, while we mounted our measuring equipment. When the plane was rolled out to the firing range and the gun trigger pulled, a round or two went off and the gun jammed. It took two weeks and several more full-scale attempts before we could get enough shots for a measurement. The war in Europe had already begun and our Navy expert could not get an old-fashioned machine gun to fire. That I found frightening.

A few months later they brought in a Messerschmidt 109 that had been captured undamaged. It was disassembled on tables in a hangar so that we could inspect it. That was even more disturbing. The engineering and workmanship were superb. It was clear why Hitler expected to win. I knew then that it was going to be a long war.

The Navy, true to its tradition, had me working under senior civil servants who knew less than I did. Our entry into the war was, at most, only months away. Unless I got out of the Navy Yard, I would be locked in for the duration, doing nothing useful, or I would be shipped off in uniform as a technician. Already it was impossible for a defense-employed worker to negotiate with another employer, but it was still allowable to quit and look for another job—if you were willing to take the chance of being snatched by your draft board.

Rumor reached me that Massachusetts Institute of Technology was the place to go. I gave notice of termination to the Navy Yard, and, seven weeks before Pearl Harbor, my wife and I packed our pots, pans, and music into two old sedans and drove north to Cambridge. So desperate was the manpower situation that all I had to do was walk in the door at M.I.T. and say, "When do you want me to start?" Within a year they doubled the salary I had been receiving at Philadelphia.

The M.I.T. Radiation Laboratory was an exciting place to be. We spent our time designing and building microwave radar for all the armed services. Eventually, I found myself in charge of a group, including doctors of philosophy who were older than I. They knew more physics than I did, but their practical knowledge of electronics was limited. Worse than that, they had never learned the basic rule of engineering—which some years later acquired the name "Murphy's Law."

ADVENTURER

In the middle of the war, in 1943, I happened to read a few paragraphs in *Time* magazine in which a man at Duke University by the name J. B. Rhine was said to have found in the laboratory that some people could affect the fall of dice merely by wishing. I knew that the world is full of people who will believe anything, but this case was unusual because Rhine claimed to have experimental proof.

Even in war, one cannot work day and night; so I spent some recreational time at Harvard's Widener Library. I soon discovered that, even though at that time I did not know much statistics, the critics of Dr. Rhine knew even less. Also, it was evident from their writings that most of the critics were more concerned with their own emotions than with objective reality.

In the library, along with accounts of Rhine's laboratory work, I found sixty years of the the the British *Proceedings of the Society for Psychical Research*. Much of these volumes was devoted to well-documented cases of spontaneous, anomalous transfers of information. After a few months I became certain that there were strange but real phenomena awaiting investigation in this field.

My opinion today is what it was then. There is so much evidence from scientists and laypersons, offered in the tradition of Western science, that any competent scientist who will take six months to study the literature, who can lay aside his cultural preconceptions about the possible range of mental phenomena, and who is skilled at inductive thinking—as opposed to linear-logical thinking—cannot fail to be convinced of the reality of an extrasensory perception of some kind or other.

After the war ended in 1945, everyone who had worked at the Radiation Laboratory in a position of responsibility had many employment opportunities. I was no exception. AT&T said I could have a job in any area I chose. They especially wanted to place me in the development of fiber optics, which they rightly foresaw would become the communication channel of the future. I regretfully said *No*.

Nobel Prizewinner I. I. Rabi called me into his office at M.I.T. He pulled out a desk drawer within which, lying in solitary splendor, was a small sheet of green glass formed at Alamogordo under the first nuclear bomb. His only comment was, "It's radioactive." Then he asked me if I would like to do a doctoral dissertation under him at Columbia University.

I had already made up my mind. By special pre-arrangement I had gathered data at M.I.T. for a University of Pittsburgh dissertation under the aegis of physicist E. U. Condon, who had been employed in Pittsburgh at Westinghouse Corporation. Now, I wanted to get my degree as quickly as possible so that I could go to work in parapsychology. Playing tricks with vacuum tubes had been great fun during the war, but it did not relate to the question that interested me most, namely: What are we? What is the role of consciousness in the universe?

After three more semesters at Pittsburgh, I received my doctoral degree in physics. Before finally committing myself to a new career outside of physics, I thought it might be well to gain additional acquaintance with parapsychologists and their critics. I spent the summer of 1947 in search of people who might have opinions about J. B. Rhine's work. At Duke University, where I lived for a month in a dormitory, my questioning included the president of the university and everyone else on campus who I thought might have feelings, pro or con, about parapsychology. I learned a lot of history, but nothing that cast doubt on the validity of Rhine's experiments.

In New York City I visited Bell Laboratories where I talked with Thornton C. Fry, whose textbook, *Probability and Its Engineering Uses*, is in my library. He said that he had examined Rhine's statistical methods and found them adequate for the purpose for which they had been used. He told me also that he knew of unpublished experiments by a close colleague that confirmed Rhine's work. He said he would *not* give Rhine public support. He was not sure that mankind needed the kind of knowledge that Rhine was seeking. In my wanderings that summer and subsequently, I have occasionally encountered similar fears of the unknown.

PROFESSOR

In 1947 all universities were short of teachers; so the University of Pittsburgh was willing to offer me an assistant professorship. Beside doing parapsychological research, I taught elementary physics. Because of my background I was asked to set up an applied electronics course. One of the experiments was a string-

and-sealing-wax demonstration of nuclear magnetic resonance. I did not imagine that, 35 years later, MRI would be revolutionizing medical diagnosis.

After five years in the Physics Department I was denied tenure because my work was not contributing positively to the department's growing reputation in nuclear physics—a judgment with which I could not disagree.

Fortunately for my wish to continue parapsychological research, a new Department of Biophysics was about to be started under Dr. Max Lauffer. He was agreeable to my entering his department as a research assistant professor without tenure if outside financial support could be found. I think it highly probable that, without his sponsorship at that time, as well as his continuing support throughout the years, I would not have stayed at the University of Pittsburgh or would not have been able to remain full-time in the field of parapsychology. I am pleased to acknowledge my indebtedness to him for the survival and success of my program.

There are many others who have given me indispensable help over the years at the University of Pittsburgh. These include Deans Herbert Longenecker, David Halliday, and Jerome Rosenberg, as well as faculty members, A. Ciocco, H. S. Frank, R. S. Craig, A. E. Fisher, L. A. Jacobson, C. C. Li, and R. A. Patton. All of these colleagues served at one time or another on a special advisory committee created to assume responsibility for my work and thereby to protect the reputation of the Mellon Trust supporting my research—just in case I did something foolish. Henry Frank, a physical chemist of some reknown, developed a strong interest in parapsychology and gave me encouragement and wise advice from 1953 until his retirement in 1974.

Beyond these special names there were all of you, as well as others now gone, who gave me a friendly home in your department, without which I could not have done creative work.

Outside the University there were other people to whom I am indebted. I shall mention now only my three major sources of financial support. These were the Rockefeller Brothers Fund, Chester F. Carlson (the inventor of Xerox), and the A. W. Mellon Educational and Charitable Trust. The contributions from the Mellon Trust over the years amounted to more than $840,000.

Let me get back to my story, which I shall briefly conclude since it is well known to most of you.

In the Biophysics Department I taught fluid dynamics for eleven years. After classical mathematical analysis went out of fashion in biology, I had no teaching duties until 1973, when, at the invitation of the Dean of the College, and by the request of undergraduate students, I began a course in parapsychology. That course was given for eleven years and culminated in the publication of three books in 1982 and 1983.

What, if anything has been accomplished in the 37 years I have worked in parapsychology? There is no doubt that the acceptance of parapsychology by scientists has grown continuously, although very slowly, throughout the academic world. The founding of a professional society, its subsequent affiliation with the American Association for the Advancement of Science, an ever-increasing number of parapsychological courses offered for credit in psychology departments at small colleges, and the open-minded treatment of parapsychology in most introductory textbooks of psychology—all of these have happened in the last three decades. Forty years ago, at the end of World War II, they would have seemed an impossible dream.

What about experimental progress as distinct from academic acceptance? Has there been any scientific progress at all? For a satisfying answer you must go to the literature of the field. To encourage you to do so, I shall mention two ideas that strike me as significant.

In the last 15 years a large and convincing body of evidence has been gathered, pointing to the importance of mental dissociation for the production of extrasensory perception and psychokinesis. It now seems probable that, for these phenomena to be intentionally produced, one must loosen or partially lose one's normal sense of identity. One must abandon to some degree one's command over one's cognitive processes. This is a condition that can be experimentally produced in many ways.

The second significant idea is alarming—so much so that it seems never to have been seriously discussed prior to the publication of my *Introduction to Parapsychology in the Context of Science*. In chapters 15 and 16 of that book I present some evidence for a hypothesis concerning the nature of hypnosis. As you know, hypnosis has been intensively investigated for the last forty years by hundreds of psychologists—most of whom would not care to be associated with parapsychology. It is my belief, based largely on the work of Russian physiologist, L. L. Vasiliev, done in Leningrad in the years 1933 to 1938, that hypnosis is the psychokinetic control of one brain by another. This conception opens a Pandora's Box of questions that no one seems willing to consider. What is needed is a spirit of adventure.

2

PROBING THE ELEPHANT
OF SCIENTIFIC OPINION

TOOLS

At present, political, economic, and intellectual leaders have no choice but to ignore parapsychology because of the adverse advice and even ridicule they receive from the majority of psychologists and physicists when the topic arises. Under other circumstances, these same leaders might welcome parapsychology as a possible key to the long-range solution of certain social problems. Thus, a rapid increase in institutional and governmental support for parapsychological research might come from a synergism between a shift from opposition to neutrality by scientists generally and a modest increase in the number and courage of the few favoring scientists.

Several years ago I asked myself: What might be accomplished in this direction by the widespread distribution of scientifically sound parapsychological information to scientists and teaching libraries? In seeking an answer to this question, I have gathered some interesting data bearing upon the image and acceptability of this field which I would like to share with the readers of the *Journal*.[1] To interpret these data, one needs a familiarity with the three parapsychological books whose free distribution I undertook in this project. For those who have not read my books, I give the following brief descriptions:

Encounters with Parapsychology (EWP) is a collection of critical, nontechnical essays by professional scientists and other intellectually competent persons who encountered parapsychology in the course of their careers and who eventually became advocates of research in this field. The book offers no strongly convincing evidence for the reality of parapsychological phenomena but is intended to help dispel the aura of incompetence, credulity, and

---

[1]This paper appeared as ''An Educational Effort in Parapsychology'' in the *Journal of the American Society for Psychical Research*, 78(1984), 341–354.

fraud that parapsychology has acquired by being mis-associated with the occult. Hopefully, the imaginative skeptic would have his curiosity aroused by this book. Presumably, any adverse reactions would reflect, not the inoffensive content of the book, but prior attitudes toward the field.

Parapsychology and Self-Deception in Science (PSDS) includes several case studies of reality-avoidance by self-deception which are drawn from diverse fields of science. These studies encompass two original experimental papers that show complex patterning in parapsychological data. In physics, such patterning has classically been used for theory building. In parapsychology, it offers hope for a unified explanation of "scoring declines" and "target missing." Such an explanation might, in turn, lead to a dependably repeatable experiment and to practical applications.

In the final chapter of the book I speculate on the role parapsychology may play when society can no longer deceive itself about the ecological ruin that is upon us.

Introduction to Parapsychology in the Context of Science (IPCS) is intended for students and teachers. It presents:

1. A condensation of current knowledge in parapsychology, including some recent, evidentially strong experiments.

2. A physicist's assessment of parapsychology, offered for scrutiny by professional scientists.

3. A defense of orthodoxy in science, written to fill a gap in present-day high-school and college-science curricula.

4. Documented studies of fraud in, and of prejudice against, parapsychology.

5. New insights suggesting experimental linkages of parapsychology with other fields of science.

6. A short history of parapsychology in England and the USA since 1882.

7. A bibliography of important papers in parapsychology.

The message of this book is that each of us is many persons in one body. We all have subclinical multiple personalities. Mental dissociation and other forms of self-deception are essential for survival, although often pathological. Examples drawn from scattered areas of science and technology illustrate that self-deception is universal and that human beings are inescapably intellectually corrupt. In this situation, the consensual authority of scientists offers the nearest possible approach to reality. In a field such as parapsychology, where consensus is lacking, the individual in search of truth can rely on no judgment save perhaps his own.

Originally, I had planned only a textbook and a supplementary collection of essays, suitable for students, age 16 and up. When the first book, *EWP*, was judged unacceptable by trade publishers and university presses, I became my own publisher. In retrospect, this was a fortunate decision. Normal-channel publication feeds books only to those already interested in a topic. What parapsychology needs is the critical attention of competent minds from outside the field. Ideally, one might hope for a dialogue between our scientific leaders and young, professionally uncommitted students who still have time for intellectual adventure. Neither of these groups would be likely to see my books were they offered solely for sale. The logic of the situation dictated direct distribution to the outside readers whose attention is required.

In time, my two books grew to three and my plans for distribution expanded beyond the easily manageable. In 15 months I gave away 4,800 books. The project is summarized later in Table 1. For its interpretation some procedural description must first be provided.

OBJECTIVES

The objectives of this distribution of books were:

1. To accelerate scientific progress in parapsychology by bringing a comprehensive survey of the field to the attention of leading scientists everywhere, with particular emphasis on scientists in fields closely related to parapsychology.

2. To lay a basis for the future growth of parapsychology by placing scientifically sound material in libraries of excellence throughout the world.

3. To make scientific information about parapsychology available in foreign lands where money-exchange restrictions discourage the importation of books.

4. In the event of nuclear war, to preserve somewhere in the world the knowledge we have so far gained in parapsychol-

ogy as a key to the eventual scientific understanding of human consciousness.

5. To present new theoretical conceptions (Chapters 14 and 15 of *IPCS*) that might change the direction of parapsychological research.

6. To offer for the consideration of interested scientists my views about parapsychology in relation to society.

One purpose of the present report is to provide information by which others may help me discover how well these objectives have been achieved. This report also tries to assess the direct responses I received to the book distribution for the light they may throw on the attitudes of scientists, librarians, and countries toward parapsychology.

POPULATIONS SAMPLED

The books of this series were made available as gifts to 1,973 scientists and scholars and to 1,831 libraries as follows:

428 members from the 1982 *Directory* of the Society for Neuroscience, living in 41 countries but excluding the USA and Canada. (This society has no members in the USSR and its satellite countries.)

368 editors, associate editors, consulting editors, and editorial advisers of the following journals, which were selected because they are among the best of their kind: *Behavioral and Neural Biology, Brain and Cognition, Brain Research, Cognition, Cognitive Psychology, Integrative Psychiatry,* the *Journals of Experimental Psychology, Journal of Neuroscience, Memory and Cognition, Perception, Psychological Review,* and *Psychometrica.* (Twenty-nine percent of these persons live outside the USA.)

79 other U.S. psychological or brain scientists judged to be exceptionally creative by knowledgeable colleagues.

158 foreign scientists who had recently requested psychobiological journal reprints from a campus colleague of mine.

54 Nobel laureates in natural science and medicine still scientifically active and residing in the USA.

399 Fellows of the Royal Society of London young enough to be scientifically active (from among a Fellowship of about 900).

106 members of the Parapsychological Association living outside the USA.

 78 foreign national officers of the International Union of the History and Philosophy of Science.

194 foreign scientists and scholars from various fields who had expressed an interest, pro or con, in parapsychology.

109 miscellaneous USA scientists not included in the above.

588 foreign university and scientific libraries selected from the 1980–81 *World of Learning*.

327 undergraduate libraries of U.S. universities of more than 10,000 students and of smaller U.S. colleges with a reputation for academic excellence.

587 libraries serving all U.S. public high schools with five or more 1984 Merit Scholarship Semifinalists.

293 libraries of U.S. private secondary schools, including all those with five or more 1984 Merit Scholarship Semifinalists plus 81 chosen for academic excellence from the National Association of Independent Schools but too small to meet the Merit Scholarship criterion.

 36 libraries of foreign university preparatory schools selected for academic excellence.

METHOD

The offering of gift copies of *EWP* began with its publication in October, 1982. After the publication of the second book in April of 1983, *EWP* and *PSDS* were usually offered, and then mailed, as a pair, with *IPCS* following later. The mailing of all books was completed in February, 1984.

Thus, as it happened, most foreign mailing of the three books was done separately in three stages; whereas most USA mailing was a two-stage process as described above. The only important exceptions were the two-stage mailings to the Fellows of the Royal Society of London and to the (partly foreign) editorial advisers of brain-science journals, and a two-book distribution to U.S. Nobel laureates.

The first book or book pair was sent to individuals only after an offering letter had been marked by them and returned to me. With few exceptions, this procedure was also followed for all foreign university and scientific libraries. However, for some USA libraries the first book-pair was sent unsolicited, as shown in Table 2

The letter offering the first book by itself merely listed on its back the contents of the book, taken verbatim from the book cover. The other first letters, which offered books 1 and 2, or book 2 alone, appeared in slightly differing versions, depending on the groups to which they were directed. In all versions, a brief factual description of the offered book(s) was included.

Every copy of the first two books was accompanied by a transmitting letter in which the next book was announced or briefly described and was offered free if the recipient would request it by returning the letter with an indicating check mark. The form of this letter varied somewhat, depending upon the group to which it was directed.

For certain groups, as described later, those persons or libraries who failed to acknowledge receipt of their first book(s) were sent a letter re-inviting them to ask for the next book.

All copies of the final book were transmitted by one letter, which (1) asked that the letter be returned so that I might know that the book had arrived safely, (2) told briefly the purpose and scope of the book-distribution project, and (3) asked the recipient to indicate by a check mark whether or not he or she "would like to receive possible future information about the field of parapsychology."

Except in this last question, no overt attempt was made to discover the thoughts of the book recipients. To have requested self-descriptive information would, I believe, have been offensive to skeptical scientists and therefore counter-productive for my six objectives as listed above.

The books for this project were donated by me. Postage was paid from the residuum of research funds provided earlier by the A. W. Mellon Educational and Charitable Trust.

INTERNATIONAL BARRIERS

After a test mailing of books by surface ship to South America and Europe showed delays of up to four months, books were sent by International Postal Union airmail everywhere except to the USA and Canada. Even so, serious book delivery difficulties were encountered with the Soviet Union and Italy. From the repeated advice of my Italian correspondents that all mail be registered, I infer trouble in that country's infrastructure. For the Soviet Union, another explanation must be found.

Although I had sent offers of the first book (*EWP*) to 82 university and research-institute libraries in large cities throughout the Soviet Union, the only acceptances were from the Soviet Academy of Sciences and from the State University of Tomsk. For 60 offers of *EWP* to individual scientists, the response rate was a high 51%. However, of 45 copies of *EWP* mailed to these 31 individuals, only one was acknowledged to have been received. Repeated letters of inquiry from me brought continuing and sometimes plaintive expressions of interest, together with confident assertions that there are no barriers to the importation of scientific books into the USSR for use by individuals. This may well be true for the books of usual interest to these scientists.

By informal inquiry to knowledgeable U.S. Postal Service employees in Washington, I learned that my experience with the Soviet Union was not unusual when a book might be thought to have social significance, even though it contained nothing politically offensive. Those who find this situation difficult to imagine may wish to read an editorial in *Science*[2] dealing with the excision of articles from subscription copies of that journal coming into the Soviet Union.

After my initial experience, I mailed all books to the Soviet Union singly, at scattered times, and without transmitting letters (which were mailed later). Because letters travel more quickly and slip through censorship more easily than packages, this procedure generated requests for the second and third books without showing whether the previous book(s) had been received. The meager results of a major effort to reach Soviet Scientists appear in Table 1, in which replacement books are not counted. Most of the books listed there were mailed to scientists of obvious stature, including laboratory directors. I tried, with equally poor results, both home and work addresses. As of March, 1984, only seven books sent to the USSR are known to have reached their destinations. These were: a copy of *EWP* mailed to a scientist in Novosibirsk, copies of *EWP* and *PSDS* hand-delivered to scientists of Moscow and Leningrad, and copies of *EWP* and *PSDS* mailed to the Leningrad library of the Soviet Academy of Sciences—an organization that ranks in power with the KGB and the military.

---

[2]W. D. Carey, "Censorship, Soviet Style." *Science*, Vol. 219, 25 February 1983, p. 911.

Table 1

GEOGRAPHICAL DISTRIBUTION OF GIFT COPIES OF *Encounters with Parapsychology (EWP)*, *Parapsychology and Self-Deception in Science (PSDS)*, and *Introduction to Parapsychology in the Context of Science* (IPCS)

Countries	To Persons			To Libraries			Totals
	EWP	*PSDS*	*IPCS*	*EWP*	*PSDS*	*IPCS*	
Great Britain	134	124	90	47	44	23	462
West Germany	46	35	33	9	9	8	14
France	40	31	27	12	11	5	126
Switzerland	26	22	17	5	3	1	74
Belgium & Netherlands[a]	26	23	18	2	2	2	73
Denmark, Finland, Norway & Sweden	38	34	23	14	13	12	134
Other (8) West European	32	18	11	8	5	4	78
Soviet Union[b]	31[d]	10[d]	3[d]	14[e]	1	1[d]	60
Other (7) East European	39	34	29	24[f]	15	12	153
Israel	29	21	18	3	3	2	76
India	11	11	.9	11	9	8	59
Japan	21	18	16	5	4	3	67
Peoples' Republic of China[c]	7	7	6	9	8	8	45
Other (12) Asian	17	14	10	11	9	9	70
Australia & New Zealand	41	37	29	13	13	12	145
South Africa	4	4	4	6	6	5	29
Other (2) African	2	1	1	0	0	0	4
Canada	29	26	26	12	9	8	110
Central & South American (11)	43	39	27	17	14	11	151
Sub-Totals	616	509	397	222	178	134	2056
United States of America	147	156	117	924	924	509	2777
Totals	763	665	514	1146	1102	643	4833

[a] Offers of *EWP* were sent to 21 libraries in Belgium or the Netherlands.
[b] Offers of *EWP* were sent to 60 scientists and 82 libraries in USSR.
[c] Offers of *EWP* were sent to 13 scientists and 16 libraries in P.R.C.
[d] Sent but mostly unacknowledged. See text.
[e] Includes 13 unacknowledged copies of *EWP*, 12 sent by University of Pittsburgh's Library Exchange Program (5 unrequested and 7 requested through Parapsychological Association members).
[f] Includes 6 copies of *EWP* sent by University of Pittsburgh Library Exchange.

Although I have established from various sources, including news generated by the KGB,[3] that the Soviet government has a secret program for parapsychological research, I must conclude

---

[3] In 1977, Robert Toth, correspondent for the *Los Angeles Times*, was arrested and detained by Soviet Security Police (KGB) for receiving a parapsychological document from a laboratory chief of the Institute of Medical-Biological Problems (*New York Times*, 12 June 1977).

from my mailing experience that censorship of incoming parapsychological information to Soviet libraries and scientists is tight. The implications of this anomalous situation challenge the imagination.

In the Soviet Union, professional and popular science are rigidly segregated and separately promoted by the government. This makes possible disparate professional and popular treatments of politically hazardous topics such as parapsychology.

There is widespread public interest in parapsychology in the USSR—scarcely less than in the USA. Judging from the many Soviet news items that have come to my attention, there are no restrictions on the newspaper publication of amateur ESP experimentation of the kind that in the USA titillates the populace and maintains the contemptuous attitude of professional scientists. It must be presumed that, as a consequence of this Soviet policy of selective censorship of the parapsychological literature (publish the foolish and suppress the serious), secret government research is well supplied with genetically endowed psychic subjects recruited from the informationally cultivated worker class. Meanwhile, those who are educated well enough to discern possible ideological implications in parapsychological phenomena are kept in contented ignorance of the true state of the field. If this is the objective of the KGB, it is hardly surprising that my books have been stopped at the border, even though—or especially because—they were addressed to competent scientists.

One is reminded of the decade after World War II, when Soviet politicians publicly condemned Heisenberg's quantum mechanics as contrary to dialectical materialism—even while Soviet scientists were using it to understand the nucleus of the atom. Evidently the ideological fear of parapsychology has not abated since 1949, when three eminent Soviet psychologists accused American parapsychologist, J. B. Rhine, of fostering a "thoroughly rotten bourgeois ideology . . . trying to darken the minds of the toilers in order to forestall or at least postpone the inevitable collapse of capitalism."[4]

---

[4]*New York Times,* 19 October 1949, I, p. 10.

4,800 BOOKS TO SIXTY COUNTRIES

In Table 1, I have counted by country or geographical region all scientists / scholars and libraries that were sent books in this distribution project. Copies sent for journal review or to laypersons are not included.[5]

All books to persons in Table 1 and (with few exceptions) all books to foreign libraries were sent only upon request. Of the Table 1, United States library totals, 694 copies of *EWP* and *PSDS* were sent in pairs, unsolicited, as shown in Table 2.

It may come as a surprise to the critics of parapsychology that, from Table 1 as a whole, there is evident a worldwide interest in this field among scientists and scholars sufficient to lead to requests for these books.

In Table 2, I have chosen for detailed examination the response records of book recipients belonging to several identifiable populations. To allow ready comparison between groups despite differing conditions in the mailing of the first two books, I have presented actual numbers of books in the first four columns and percentages in the last three, where 100% is the number of copies sent of the second book.

The most evident feature of Table 2 is the drop in number of requested books in progressing from the first to the third book and the paucity of recipients who ackowledged the third book. One would expect a declining response when selling books sequentially by mail, but perhaps not when books are offered as gifts. In presenting some explanatory speculation about the matter, I shall discuss persons and libraries separately.

In Table 2, the drop between offers-to-persons and first-book(s)-sent, documents the busy scientist's lack of curiosity about, or, as the case may be, his hostility toward, parapsychology-in-the-abstract. In contrast, the respondents lost between *EWP*-sent and *PSDS*-sent may be those who were bored by the bland historical content of the first book. The persons remaining, who requested *PSDS*, might be expected to have a more robust curiosity that could be tested by the last two books.

PSDS has two chapters (4 and 5) that could challenge a statis-

---

[5]Since the distribution of books reported in this paper, I have sent as gifts 5400 copies of these books to an additional 2160 USA high school libraries that responded to an offering letter.

Table 2

SELECTED GROUPS RECEIVING GIFT COPIES OF *Encounters with Parapsychology (EWP)*, *Parapsychology and Self-Deception in Science (PSDS)*, and *Introduction to Parapsychology in the Context of Science* (IPCS)

Recipient Groups	Preceding offers	EWP sent	PSDS sent	EWP sent with PSDS	IPCS sent[j]	IPCS answered[j]	Future interest[j]
Foreign members of the Society for Neuroscience[a]	428	170	118	—	68%	39%	31%
Editorial advisors to brain science journals[b]	368	—	—	94	55%	33%	26%
US creative brain scientists[c]	79	—	—	28	68%	32%	32%
Nobel laureates residing in the USA[d]	54	—	13	—	38%	15%	0%
Fellows of the Royal Society of London[e]	399	—	—	96	72%	45%	23%
US college libraries[f]	none	—	—	327	57%	43%	25%
US public secondary school libraries[g] (preceding offer)	411	—	—	183	72%	40%	33%
US public secondary school libraries[h] (no preceding offer)	none	—	—	176	46%	24%	24%
US private secondary school libraries[i] (preceding offer)	102	—	—	47	70%	40%	19%
US private secondary school libraries[i] (no preceding offer)	none	—	—	191	41%	25%	20%

[a] Excluding Canadian.
[b] *Behavioral and Neural Biology, Brain and Cognition, Brain Research, Cognition, Cognitive Psychology, Integrative Psychiatry, the Journals of Experimental Psychology, Journal of Neuroscience, Memory and Cognition, Perception, Psychological Review, Psychometrika.*
[c] Not in the editorial advisor group.
[d] Currently active in natural science or medicine.
[e] Having pre-emeritus professional status in a total Fellowship of circa 900.
[f] Colleges selected for size or academic reputation.
[g] Public schools with 5 to 8 1984 Merit Scholarship Semifinalists.
[h] Public schools with 9 or more 1984 Merit Scholarship Semifinalists.
[i] Private schools selected for academic excellence.
[j] Percentages are in relation to the number receiving *PSDS*.

tically sophisticated reader, but the book also contains considerable sociological material that could be distasteful to scientists more interested in science than in people. Those who sur-
vived *PSDS* and requested *IPCS* would, I hoped, be emotionally
and intellectually open to the philosophically disturbing ideas of
that final volume.

Among those who received all three books, there could be many
entangled reasons for not acknowledging the last. Dominant
among these, I surmise, was a frequently given-and-then-
forgotten self-promise to return my letter later—after the book had
been examined and the question of a possible future interest could
be more reasonably entertained. In any case, from those who did
acknowledge the arrival of the final book, there were many pencilled expressions of thanks—even from those who indicated no
desire for future information. Such politeness suggests an absence of hostility in the acknowledging group.

The factors affecting library responses to this book-distribution
project are undoubtedly different from those governing individual
responses. Because the annual cost of shelving a library book is
often more than its purchase price, teaching libraries tend to
restrict their acquisitions to instructional materials and to areas of
special interest. A university library may receive several
thousand old books each year, given by alumni or their survivors
as charitable tax deductions. New books arrive unsolicited every
week as the unsuccessful author's last hope for fame. Because
most libraries lack the personnel to handle this flood, the arrival
of one more gift book is not an event likely to brighten a
librarian's day—a fact not evident in the beautifully printed letters
of thanks that are routinely sent to donors. Under these circumstances, the final-book request rate (57%) of U.S. college
librarians after they had received an unsolicited gift of the first
two books cannot be regarded as an indirect measure of opposition to parapsychology or to the books.

At the secondary school level, however, the fact that more than
half failed to respond in those groups that were sent first an offer
of *EWP* and *PSDS* may provide an upper limit and rough measure
of the disapproval of parapsychology among high-school
librarians. This speculation rests upon the following syllogism:
High-school librarians (1) are generally eager to encourage student interest in science, (2) are aware of avid adolescent interest
in ESP, and hence, (3) would be glad to inspect gift copies of

scientifically intended books on parapsychology if they believed that the subject was respectable.

To examine the question of librarian interest in parapsychology near the top of the academic ladder, a casual list of great U.S. universities was made and divided into those whose libraries did or did not accept my invitation to receive *IPCS* (after having received the first two books and, where necessary, a second invitation to respond). Those who did not ask for *IPCS* were: Columbia, Harvard, Johns Hopkins, Massachusetts Institute of Technology, Princeton, Stanford, University of California (Berkeley) and Washington University (St. Louis). Those on the list that did ask to receive *IPCS* were California Institute of Technology, Cornell, University of California (Los Angeles), University of Chicago, University of Illinois (Urbana), University of Michigan (Ann Arbor), University of North Carolina (Chapel Hill), University of Wisconsin (Madison), and Yale. This 53% acceptance rate is close to that of college libraries as a whole (57%).

To my final question about possible future interest, one would expect that a professional librarian's response would normally be *no* for any stray topic such as parapsychology. The number of *yes* responses suggests that many high-school and college librarians or their advisers are personally interested in parapsychology.

To gain some feeling for the number of persons and libraries that failed to request later books because of postal nondelivery or because of time pressure and limited interest rather than hostility, a repeated invitation was sent after a suitable delay to 189 foreign individuals (excluding editorial advisers and Fellows of the Royal Society) who had failed to request *PSDS* after being sent *EWP*, to 204 U.S. college libraries that had failed to ask for *IPCS* when sent *EWP* with *PSDS* and to 369 U.S. high-school libraries that, likewise, had not responded to *EWP* sent with *PSDS*. The requests for the next book that were received in response to these follow-up invitations were 51%, 31%, and 26%, respectively, of the re-invitations. These additionally requested copies correspond to 25%, 35%, and 30%, respectively, of all copies of that book sent to each of these groups.

From the few claims for lost books I conclude that, for most countries, postal delivery did not present a significant problem and that the observed decline in book requests was a direct, human response. So large a favorable reaction to the follow-up invitations supports the hypothesis that most busy people—be they scientists or librarians—have, at best, a mild curiosity about parapsychology. Likewise, the overall pattern of the book distribution in Table 2, as shown by the weak initial response and the all-group mailing-to-mailing decline in response to both gentle and forceful books, suggests to me, not so much an adverse reaction to the books, as a minor and easily exhausted prior interest in parapsychology, which was not strengthened by the books' pessimistic presentation of the difficult scientific task that lies ahead of us.

CONCLUSIONS

What generalizations might be drawn from this book-distribution experiment as a whole?

As shown in Table 2, 33% of brain scientists, worldwide, who were offered parapsychological books accepted at least one and thereby showed an interest in the claimed evidence for parapsychological phenomena. In all likelihood, most of these scientists are to some degree receptive toward the possible reality of such phenomena. The percentage was remarkably uniform among the scientifically more advanced countries and tended to be slightly higher among the scientifically less advanced. The corresponding figures for scientific leaders in other fields were: U.S. Nobel laureates (24%) and Fellows of the Royal Society (also 24%).

Seven percent of the brain scientists and scientific leaders solicited, as shown in Table 2, admitted to a continuing interest in parapsychology after receiving my third book. Those scientists may reasonably be supposed to have, on the average, a considerable degree of openness toward parapsychological phenomena. These, I suspect, are scientists who have themselves experienced such phenomena spontaneously or who have been told of spontaneous experiences by persons in whose probity and observational competence they have full confidence. I surmise that no other explanation can account for so large and uniform a degree of scientist interest in phenomena whose reality would threaten the Neo-Cartesian world view upon which Western civilization was built. It would be too much to ascribe this degree of interest to the experimental investigations of J. B. Rhine and his few followers—and it is certainly not the result of diligent study of the earlier, more qualitative literature.

The offer-first data of Table 2 allow comparisons of *(initial responses)* ÷ *(initial offers)* and of *(future interest)* ÷ *(initial offers)* for three groups: editorial advisors (26% and 6%), creative brain scientists (35% and 11%), and high-school librarians (45% and 14%).

The no-offer-first data of Table 2 permit comparisons of *(number requesting third book)* ÷ *(number to which first books were sent)* and of *(number expressing future interest)* ÷ *(number to which the first books were sent)* for three groups, as follows: college libraries (57% and 25%), public high-school libraries (46% and 24%) and private high schools (41% and 20%).

Regardless of motivational interpretation, the numerical results of this distribution project are compatible with the achievement of my goals as listed above. They leave to the future the question of the degree of that achievement.

Chapter Appendix
SELF-PUBLISHING IN PARAPSYCHOLOGY

For the benefit of parapsychologists who may have written a book and are wondering whether to publish it themselves, I shall outline some choices that must be made.

Anyone with time, energy, and money can write, edit, and design a book and have it typeset, printed, and bound. I shall say just a little about these easy steps. The real problem is distribution.

If you are publishing a scientific book, it is helpful to have prepared papers for professional journals and to have access to a style manual from your own or a nearby field. You will need to consult the University of Chicago Press: *A Manual of Style* or its equivalent and to learn printer's jargon. For your first book, pay a friendly editor to review your edited copy unless you are sending it to a publisher who provides this service.

Today, you will prepare your typescript on a word-processing computer. If you have access to a sufficiently flexible formatting program, you can make your copy ready for electronic typesetting. For high quality offset printing the typesetting machine should have a resolution of at least 1200 lines per inch.

Supposedly equivalent fonts with similar names from different companies may differ significantly in design. Even the same typesetting machine may use non-identical fonts with the same name. A font that is proportioned well for 10 points (for text use) will look ridiculous when enlarged to 18 points (for display use). Compromise fonts may not be fully satisfactory for either purpose.

You will have to learn about papers and binding. For most purposes any acid-free paper (pH > 7.0) will do. You will have to choose the weight, thickness, and finish of the paper. Do you want to pay for a hard binding? Of what kind? Paper binding is cheaper and saves mailing costs as well, Among paper-back bindings, "perfect" binding will do for many purposes, but, if you wish to give libraries the option of rebinding, you must use glued "Smyth-sewn signatures." Probably you will want plastic lamination on the outside of the cover. It costs little and prevents scuffing.

Printing prices vary regionally over the USA. You may be able to save several thousand dollars if you are willing to travel 500 miles. Printing quality varies, but not always with price, even in the same city. Ask your university press for suggestions. Visit the printer. If you don't know printing presses, you can still judge shop morale—which correlates with workmanship. Inspect a sample book using the exact binding machine and method you will be getting.

Some photographs can be difficult to reproduce. (The cover on this book required the two-plate, "duotone" process.) Do not hesitate to pay for press proofs if you have critical half-tone illustrations.

The foregoing are some of the trivia you must master if you decide to be your own publisher. Before you make that decision, you will have answered many questions, including the following: Why have I written this book? For whom is it intended?

If your purpose is to make money, my experience will be of little help. Let us suppose, however, that you have written a book that you believe may just pay for itself. Who is going to publish it? Publishers in the USA today divide along two axes, size and specialization, with university presses in a class by themselves.

The large publishing houses whose names come first to mind will no longer take a book unless they think they can sell 20,000 copies. They know the readers they reach, and their judgment is generally sound. They distribute to large bookstores through sales representatives and to libraries and small stores through large distributors. Large distributors will not handle books from a small publisher unless they think they can sell 500 copies of that title per year.

High quality, specialized publishers (e.g., for scientific monographs) do not require so large a potential sale, but their list prices begin at $30, and the publisher must believe that a market exists. Some parapsychological books have been sold this way, but the customary direct-mail and journal-display advertising goes to the wrong people and the price is too high for the casual buyer.

University presses publish high quality, short-run books at the lowest possible prices. However, even if a press specializes in psychology books, one's chances of getting a parapsychological book past its academic consultants is slim unless one is a senior faculty member at that university. My innocuous and scholarly *Encounters with Parapsychology* was refused by thirty-two university presses. One press editor explained: "My advisors in philosophy of science feel that a broad, nontechnical introduction to any controversial scientific subject—while it has its place—is not appropriate for us."

Small publishing houses scratch a living out of books that have narrow but definable markets among the general public. They have their own professional organization, and exist almost to spite their large competitors. They use small or specialized distributors to get into book stores. Their promotion is mostly direct-mail, aimed at a particular public sector. Their reach is very limited. A lone parapsychological book, if published by such a company, would be lost in the noise.

In the USA there is one, small, hardback publisher who handles a few parapsychological books, along with books on unrelated topics in the middle range of prices. He reaches parapsychologists but probably few others who might buy serious parapsychological books.

This leaves subsidy, or contract, publishers. They exist in all varieties. Some will do an honest and serviceable editing and manufacturing job. Most of their business is in hard bindings. Some will give a little promotion, but not of a kind that will help a serious parapsychological book. If they share cost with the author, they will require ownership of the book—as do all commercial publishers. Subsidy publishers have no distribution systems worthy of the name. They are not publishers but contractors for book making, starting with your manuscript. If a parapsychologist wants a book published, has money, is short of time, energy, or book-making courage, and is willing to worry about distribution by himself, subsidized publishing may be the right choice.

The final possibility is to become a publisher and to take responsibility for everything, including copyright, Library of Congress cataloging, International Standard Book Number, listing in *Cumulative Book Index*, *Forthcoming Books*, and in *Books in Print*, storage, advertising, contracting with a small distributor, arranging for at least one dependable retail outlet, mailing review copies, and keeping financial records for the U.S. Internal Revenue Service.

In every enterprise there are unexpected obstacles. Here are two that I encountered.

I had hoped that my books could be sold through college bookstores, of which there are 2700 in the USA. *Books in Print* (and *Paperback Books in Print*) categorize parapsychological books under "occult." As a result, such books are inevitably shelved under "occult" in bookstores. No self-respecting student or professor would care to be seen browsing among "Occult Books." Hence, parapsychological books are rarely noticed in bookstores except by occultists.

My second surprise was complementary to the first. University, high-school, and public libraries cannot, in general, pay cash in advance for a book. Scientific book publishers set prices high enough to sell single copies on credit to libraries and professors. General trade publishers, distributors, and bookstores, on the other hand, cannot sell low-priced books on credit except to regular customers who have formally established credit and who buy enough books to cover the accounting overhead. To fill this gap, there is a cottage industry of book dealers who extend credit to libraries and offer to deliver books at list-price-plus-postage. These dealers have enough business to establish credit with one of the several large distributors who stock books from all large publishers.

When a library sends an order to its dealer for a single copy from a small publisher, the dealer, in turn, sends an order directly to that publisher, asking for shipment of one copy, on credit, and at a discount (which is his profit). However, no publisher can afford to ship a single copy at a discount, let alone extend credit to an unknown dealer. My response is to return such orders with a printed notice telling the dealer how to buy a single copy from the

University of Pittsburgh Book Center at list-plus-postage, cash-in-advance.

If the dealer orders the book at list price and adds a markup to cover his costs, the library perceives the dealer's service to be too costly. On the other hand, if the dealer passes my purchase information along to the library, the library discovers that the dealer is unnecessary. In this no-win situation the dealer may be tempted to reject both alteratives and to tell the library that the book is "not available."

3

THE VIEW FROM MOUNT NEBO

For forty years I have wandered in the wilderness of parapsychological data. When, in January, 1985, we completed the main analyses of the falling-dice experiment reported in the next chapter, I was reminded of Moses sighting the Promised Land. For the first time in my mind, hope was replaced by an inner certainty that the phenomena of parapsychology will some day be understood by the method of science. Beyond that, I could now believe, as I had long suspected, that psi occasionally affects the outcome of ordinary scientific experiments.

The time will surely come when, with further understanding, we shall routinely take steps to ensure that psi does not interfere with investigations in other fields. Like Moses, I do not expect to live to enter that promised land.

PSI AS AN IMPROBABLE ODDITY

My thoughts turned next to the opinions of other scientists. I wondered how they would regard our findings. Here was a carefully done experiment that fitted into the logical chain of earlier research in a satisfying manner. Moreover, we did not claim to have demonstrated "walking on water," but merely a weak, sporadic departure from ordinary physical expectation—a departure that might easily have been missed if it had occurred in physics experiments of the past.[1] How would competent experimental scientists look upon such an experiment? Or would they?

My past experience in attempting to attract the interest of scientists at large had not been encouraging. Perhaps a more personal approach would prove effective.

* * * * *

---

[1] If, on the other hand, an experimental physicist (or psychologist—*see* chapter 6) had the rare gift of controlled psychic ability, any clearly anomalous psychic effect that he created would not be reproducible by his colleagues; he would be regarded as "mistaken"; and, under duress, he would probably lose his ability to produce the anomaly.

A friendly colleague for whom I have high regard as a neuro-scientist readily agreed to examine and comment upon the McConnell and Clark paper. He subsequently reported that he had read the abstract and the introductory review of the associated literature, which he felt was enough for him to form an opinion. His comment was that the physical effects reported were too small to hold his attention. He explained as follows:

- He had no previous exposure to parapsychology, and he wel-comed this opportunity to be able to make a tentative judg-ment of the field, or at least of that part reflected in this paper.

- His experience as a scientist, beginning with his training un-der Neal Miller, had led him to the working conviction that, to deserve his attention, a biological effect should be strong enough to be seen without the aid of statistical analysis. He is not averse to using probability theory to assess and con-firm his findings.[2]

- The number of trials in his own research is likely to be five or ten rather than several thousand. He has no feeling for large-number statistics. Consequently, he is not prepared to decide whether or not there might be something real behind parapsychologists' claims for small effects.

- He would never have considered working in parapsychology because there are many interesting scientific problems in which one can obtain large experimental effects.

I gave the classical answer to my colleague's reason for neglect-ing parapsychology: In the history of science many important dis-coveries were initially seen as weak and barely discernible ef-fects. In playing the game of science it is reasonable to be guided

---

[2] This prepossession against small effects is understandable. The experimen-tal literature of psychology consists largely of studies showing small but statis-tically significant correlations among observables. These studies are valued by their authors and by scholars but receive little attention otherwise. Typically, these correlations are real but (1) without intrinsic theoretical interest, (2) too weak to be promising as guideposts to further research, and (3) too weak to be of clinical or industrial value.

Experiments in parapsychology fail on the last two counts, but not on the first. For an example of an evanescent effect believed to have theoretical inter-est, see *Neal Miller's Rats* in the chapter titled "Unintended Psychokinesis."

by the mathematical expectation of net gain (defined as the product of the probability of success and winnings, minus the product of the probability of failure and its cost). In parapsychology, if the a priori probability of success seems small, the importance of the phenomena, if real, is enormous.

My colleague accepted the logical proposition, but could not see the possible importance of parapsychology. He asked, "Has there been any recent progress toward practical application?"

I tried to explain in the following few words why I think parapsychological research is potentially important:

> This world's desperate problems are ultimately psychological rather than physical or biological. None appears to be beyond solution if we can agree upon an appropriate set of universal objectives and find the will to pursue them. It is my assumption as a scientist that our lack of unity stems, either directly or remotely, from a lack of knowledge about ourselves: our origin, our destiny, our natural relations to one another, and, hence, about our obligations to ourselves and to others. Parapsychology, which is the study of the relationship of consciousness to the physical world, includes, by inference, these broad philosophic questions. That is the reason why I, and probably why most parapsychologists, think our field is important.

My colleague replied: "You evidently feel deeply about this. Would it be correct to say that your interest in parapsychology is a religious one?"

I replied: "If so, it is completely unstructured. I have no religious beliefs whatsoever."

I did not ask, although I would like to have done so: "What are your hopes and fears for mankind? In what philosophic framework do you relate your professional activities to the future of Homo sapiens?"

I would also like to have had his reaction to the following: "It is understandable that you have no wish to devote much time to parapsychology at this stage in your career. But shouldn't you feel a professional obligation to make a tentative technical judgment as to the scientific soundness of a field that is conceptually close to your own and that will surely impinge upon your interests if its claims prove to be true?"

That, of course, is the complaint of parapsychology: It cannot attract the critical attention of the leaders from related fields who have the technical competence to make an authoritative judgment as to whether real anomalies of the purported kind possibly or certainly occur. If that judgment were made, society would then be in a position to decide how vigorously this research should be pursued. As it stands, none but emotional misfits will take time to criticize this field.

* * * * *

I sent this colleague the foregoing inter-asteriskal account of his inspection of our paper, telling him that I might like to publish it and that he could read, ignore, correct, annotate, or expand as he wished. He chose to annotate as follows:

- By "religious" he meant "that it proceeded more on the basis of belief than on the basis of strong and tangible evidence."

- He said that he would be happy to answer my question about his hopes and fears for mankind—meaning, upon another, suitable occasion.

- With regard to any professional obligation to judge para-psychology, he said: "My answer here is that I would prefer to wait until after the claims prove to be true. I am too oc-cupied with issues of more immediate concern and relevance to my own work to take time to study something so far removed."

These comments complemented in a personal fashion the ex-perience I had gained in distributing parapsychological books to scientists worldwide as reported in chapter 2 of this book. From that educational experiment I had learned that exceptionally com-petent scientists are likely to have a slender and easily satisfied curiosity about parapsychology, a curiosity having to do with the technical nature of the purported phenomena rather than with the evidence for their reality or with their possible, larger sig-nificance. I am now confident that I know the reason for that limited interest: Our scientific leaders, to the extent that they are open-minded in this area, think of extrasensory perception and psychokinesis as improbable oddities and nothing more.

INVITED CRITICISM

By now I knew that most scientists would not be interested in our dice experiment, but I hoped that perhaps a few might find it challenging. To test this idea, I mailed our paper[3] to more than 500 scientists and scholars, including the 92 outstanding scientists who, as shown in the first five categories in table 2 of chapter 2 of this book, had indicated that they "would like to receive possible future information about the field of parapsychology."

I asked my recipients to help me find any "flaw, weakness, or possible weakness in our paper that could call into question our conclusion." I explained, "If we have erred, as scientists we want to know it. If, on the other hand, you find our conclusion inescapable, we would like to know that, too . . . ."

The conclusion to which I referred was this: "Either the outcome of this experiment represents a rare chance event, or the behavior of the dice was directly affected by the conscious thinking of the subjects and / or experimenters."[4]

From these 500+ recipients I received no criticism of our conclusion. Nor did anyone write to say that they found our conclusion inescapable. From many persons friendly to parapsychology, I received noncommittal acknowledgments and thanks. Only three persons sent letters with substantive comment. Two of these letters, with the permission of their authors, appear in Appendixes *A* and *B* to this chapter. The third came from a Fellow of the Royal Society in the Neurobiology Department of the Australian National University. He said, in part:

- On the face of it, the statistical design and analysis seem satisfactory. However this was also true of more famous experiments, such as those of S. G. Soal, which were later shown to [be fraudulent].

- One suspicious feature of the paper is that there are four references to papers by J. B. Rhine, who was completely dis-

---

[3] Essentially as presented in the next chapter.

[4] Making a choice between chance and causation requires a subjective judgment. One would not expect to make such a choice without considering the evidence available from other experiments. I did not, of course, ask our recipients to make this choice for our experiment.

credited. [There was no mention of when, or by whom, Rhine was discredited.][5]

– If the effect is real, I do not think it has any philosophical or theological relevance. [We had not suggested theological relevance.]

Puzzled by this nearly null response, I speculated that perhaps I had offended some skeptics by offering so controversial a topic matter-of-factly. To explore the effect of a more diffident and personal approach, I sent the following letter to the twenty-five faculty members of the Psychology Department of Carnegie Mellon University:

UNIVERSITY OF PITTSBURGH
Department of Biological Sciences
Pittsburgh, Pennsylvania

Dear CMU Psychologist:

It is appropriate for scientists to take an occasional look at properly presented claims of anomalous discoveries relating to their field. With that thought, I am enclosing for your consideration two, recent papers describing anomalous experimental results in cognition and volition.

The first paper, titled "Psychology and Anomalous Observations" by Professor Irvin Child of the Yale Psychology Department, reviews the ESP dream research done at the Maimonides Medical Center in New York City. (*American Psychologist, 40,* 1219–1230, November, 1985). I hope you will find time to read at least the abstract.[6]

The second paper, of which I am co-author, is titled "Anomalous Fall of Dice," and reports an experimental search for a direct effect of wishing upon falling dice. Please scan this paper to determine the quality of the presentation without regard to the plausibility of the hypothesis under test. If our paper meets your standard of technical excellence, I would be most grateful if you would search seriously for a

---

[5] See chapter titled "A Festival of Self-Deception."

[6] The abstract will be found later in this book under *Unscholarly Brokers* in the chapter titled "Forces of Darkness."

flaw, weakness, or possible weakness that could call into question our conclusion.

Broadly speaking, the hypothesis under test in parapsychology is that human consciousness has a direct physical reach beyond our bodies. It has been my experience in 39 years largely devoted to parapsychology, that many competent psychologists say they are not interested in experimental evidence because they know this hypothesis to be untrue.

Sincerely yours,

R. A. McConnell
Emeritus Research Professor
 of Biological Sciences
CMU alumnus, Physics, '35

It is now ten months later, and no response of any kind has been received. My letters were hand-deposited in the CMU campus postoffice and their safe delivery can be assumed.

From experience I conclude that most scientists will not take time from their own work to examine the case for and against parapsychology because they do not see the matter as sufficiently important. If parapsychology is to gain scientific acceptance, it will have to be by some means other than doing experiments to impress those who are too busy to read them.

In the next chapter we report a carefully done experiment, providing "strong and tangible evidence" for the occurrence of a psychokinetic effect. I think it safe to predict that, like all the other strong experiments in this field, it will not be read by those who are most competent to judge it, and will be ignored or misrepresented by that handful of professional skeptics who are dedicated to the disparagement of parapsychology.[7]

PERCEIVING THE IMPORTANCE OF PSI

Why do scientists not perceive at once the potential importance of psi? I shall approach this question indirectly by answering another: Why did I foolishly suppose that they should?

In 1943, I chanced upon a news report of a claim by J. B.

---

[7] See chapter titled "Forces of Darkness."

Rhine that he had found experimental evidence for "psychokinesis." Prior to that, I had heard of Rhine's research on extrasensory perception but had discounted it as surely spurious. Psychokinesis seemed even more bizarre than ESP. Perhaps it was this fact that led me to stop at nearby Harvard's library.

I was immediately struck by the extent of the scientific literature in this area, beginning with the founding of the (British) Society for Psychical Research in 1882. After sampling this literature in depth and breadth, I concluded that at least some of the purported phenomena must be real.

The editorial management of the Society's journals formed an unbroken network of credibility, reaching back from the present and involving scientists and scholars known for their sincerity and sophistication. No conspiracy of uneducated zealots could account for the spontaneous and experimental evidence accumulated in these journals. To have rejected the findings in their entirety, would have been easy for a theologian but impossible for an engineer.[8]

In the years that followed, my conviction as to the genuineness of some psi phenomena was strengthened by further study of the literature, by my own experiments, and by talking to parapsychologists who had performed successful experiments.

My initial conviction had been strong enough to cause me to decide at age 30 to abandon a well-paying and intellectually satisfying profession for which I had been preparing for fifteen years. It should perhaps be made explicit that, unlike many who accept parapsychology, I had never had a spontaneous psychic experience and had never known a person who claimed to me that he had.

With time, my conviction has become complete—in the sense that one fully accepts any established scientific phenomenon, whether or not one sees it every day. My belief-consolidation process differed somewhat from the strengthening of a religious faith. From World War II up to the present, I have actively

---

[8] Even today there are parapsychologists who are not fully convinced of the reality of psi (McConnell & Clark, 1980). Future generations will judge this as reflecting, not upon the adequacy of the evidence, but upon the scientific competence of these skeptics. (References are at end of chapter.)

urged, not the acceptance, but the criticism, of parapsychology, and I have, myself, continually re-examined the evidence for psychic phenomena in the light of my growing understanding of abnormal psychology and of human behavior in general. I have assigned an increasing probability to the more incredible phenomena of the field (such as gross psychokinesis) only as my detailed study of the mounting evidence seemed to warrant.

Thus it was that a young, relatively inexperienced, experimental physicist of modest academic attainment decided in a matter of months that some parapsychological phenomena were both real and important.

I assumed as a matter of course that, if I had evaluated the situation so easily, other physicists would surely follow if only I would bring the matter to their attention. As illustrated above, I have not succeeded in persuading scientists to examine the evidence, let alone agree that the purported phenomena are real—or even that they would be important *if* they were real.

To assess the evidence for psi requires, among other things, an intuitive grasp of the fundamentals of physics and an active curiosity about one's self. By the time physicists have acquired the former, most have suppressed the latter. With or without the aid of religious belief, they have barred from their attention all questions about life's meaning. They have become, not philosophers, but puzzle solvers.

Any educated person who is not a scientist will readily agree that, if the physical reach of human consciousness beyond our bodies (which has been an element of belief in every great religion) could be shown experimentally to occur and could be studied scientifically, it would alter modern man's self-image more than any other discovery of science.

Scientists, however, are a breed apart. If you say to a scientist that parapsychology offers evidence of a direct, outward, physical reach of the mind, the answer may be: "Has there been any recent progress toward application?"

What moves scientists in this regard is a fear unknowable by laymen. Scientists fear that their cozy philosophical workplace, which they have hacked out of the jungle of ignorance over the last 500 years, will be invaded by the beasts of superstition which they thought were fenced out forever. They fear that the barrier between the physical and spiritual domains will dissolve and that they will become, not happy puzzle solvers, but anxious philosophers.

If asked directly, scientists as well as laypersons will readily admit the importance of the question with which parapsychology purports to deal: What are we human units of consciousness? Whether that is a theological or a scientific question depends only upon the methods used to try to answer it.

Chapter Appendix A
LUIS ALVAREZ ON PARAPSYCHOLOGY

In response to my above-described mailing of our dice paper, I received a telephone call from a Nobel laureate in physics, which, in turn, led to the following correspondence:

UNIVERSITY OF PITTSBURGH
Department of Biological Sciences
Pittsburgh, Pennsylvania

26 March 1986

Dr. Luis W. Alvarez
Lawrence Berkeley Laboratory
One Cyclotron Road
Berkeley, California, USA

Dear Luis:

After some editing by both of us, this has become the joint letter we agreed to write about my psychokinetic experiments. It was good to hear your voice again after so many years and to reminisce a bit about the exciting times we shared at the [M.I.T.] Radiation Laboratory.

I am pleased that you were willing to telephone your reaction to the falling-dice experiment that I recently sent you. Because your opinion is unfavorable, I can understand your reluctance as a friend to summarize in a letter, even at my request, the gist of our conversation.

However, I think it is important that people working in parapsychology know how a physicist of your stature regards our work. If nothing else, it should sober our enthusiasm to have your opinion as to the nature of our scientific folly.

I am therefore accepting your kind counter-offer to allow me to summarize my understanding of what you said and to send it to you for approval or correction. I shall confine my summary to what you said about our dice paper, inasmuch as your comments thereon seemed to reflect your opinion of the field generally.

I expect to publish our experiment in book form, along with other essays mostly of a historical nature. With your permission, I propose to publish this letter, together with your comment or corrections, in a chapter summarizing such other comments as I may receive concerning this dice experiment.

Let me record, first of all, your statement that you will have no difficulty accepting psychokinesis if it can be demonstrated by a simple, well-controlled experiment before suitable witnesses.

As an example of a good experiment you suggest trying to move a torsion pendulum in a vacuum with an amplitude greater than that expected from Brownian motion. In your thinking, the important requirement is that any effect be strong enough to leave no doubt as to its reality, i.e., the signal-to-noise ratio must be moderate to large. Such a pendulum experiment would have the advantage of direct visual feedback, so that learning could occur.

Starting at this point, Luis, you had so many suggested changes to my original version that I'll let you begin anew with what you were telling me over the phone: (Everything you write will be indented, to let the reader know "who is talking.")

> If the psychokinesis you believe you have observed is a real effect—and I have no problem believing that PK could exist—then it will be *an addition to*, rather than a substitute for, our present knowledge (in the way that General Relativity added something to Newtonian gravitation, but didn't change the calculations of NASA experts on planetary dynamics, using Newtonian laws to make rendezvous with the outer planets). So I am confident that, if dice respond to your thoughts, it will be because your thoughts cause forces to be exerted on the dice at the proper times and in the proper directions. I am sure you will agree with me on this point. What I am saying is that I have no problem in believing that thoughts could give rise to forces that moved or tilted dice, but I would absolutely rule out the possibility that thoughts could move dice without first producing forces.
>
> And again, I would have no problem in believing in the existence of such thought-induced forces, if you can demonstrate them in a quasi-stationary experiment, such as the torsion-pendulum experiment I mentioned earlier. Cavendish understood that gravitational forces between ob-

jects in the laboratory would be exceedingly small; so he used the most sensitive device he knew—a torsion pendulum—and increased his signal-to-noise ratio by making use of its resonant properties. You should similarly wish the torsion pendulum to go alternately to the left and right at the period of the pendulum, the way you make your eyes follow a tennis ball at Wimbledon. And you have an ability Cavendish didn't have; you can buy all the liquid helium you need to drop the absolute temperature of the pendulum and its fiber support by almost a factor of 100, to decrease the amplitude of the "noise" from Brownian motion.

Since you know all about signal-to-noise ratios and the enhancements one can get by resonance and / or cryogenic cooling, I can't understand why you have spent so many years looking for PK in situations [e.g., with falling dice] where you were denied these enhancements in S / N ratios. And even more surprising to me is your use of experiments that you couldn't possibly expect to succeed, even if you were given perfect observations and perfect measurements of the actions of the dice, and error-free means for exerting variable and controllable forces on the individual dice. You will agree that either of us could draw a block diagram of a system that used optical or magnetic sensors (of the orientation of a die), and an electronic computer to decide what forces or torques should be applied magnetically to the die, and what currents should be sent through the coils, in what strengths, to produce those forces and torques to get the die to perform any action you had programmed the computer to demand.

I used to amuse myself by inventing practical combinations of "sensors and torquers," to control a bat that could hit a home run every pitch when facing the best pitchers in the major leagues. I am sure you would have no trouble in re-inventing my machines, which were quite possible even before modern computers were available. The reason we don't need modern high-speed computers is that a good baseball player comes within a factor of 100 of being able to do this; so we only need to give the machine 100 times better sensors and torquers than the man's eyeball-brain combination, and his brain-muscle system, respectively. The most important factor in this analysis is that the trained human computer system is very nearly able to do the job unaided.

But if you think of what would be needed to do the job you were testing for, you can quickly see that it is far beyond the capacity of a computer built of "squishy things," (soft tissue) whose signals are severely restricted in speed by the need for chemicals to diffuse through the walls of nerve cells. Computers were thought to be fast when they reached 1 MIPS (million instructions per second), and they are now operating in the 100 MIPS range. Contrast that with the brain, which can't see the flicker in a TV picture which is changed either 30 or 60 times per second. That rate, corresponding to something like .0001 MIPS, is fast enough to let a good batter get 0.3 hits per time at bat, but certainly not fast enough to permit a brain to sense the rapidly changing positions of the dice, calculate what to do on the basis of those observations, and then do what has to be done to accomplish the wished-for result. You will notice that I make no judgment as to the chance that PK might exist, but only on the cerebral bandwidth required to influence falling dice *if* PK exists. I claim that the cerebral bandwidth required to move the torsion pendulum exists in the brain as a computer, but that the job you are asking it to do is far beyond the capacity of anything built of squishy things, but trivial for a computer made of silicon chips.

Let me remind you of a standard parlor trick. You dangle a new dollar bill between your thumb and forefinger, and you ask your friend to place his thumb and forefinger on either side of the bill, even with its lower edge. You then bet that he can't stop the bill when you drop it without giving a precursor signal. This is a fair bet, because, by the time the bill starts to drop, till the time it falls below the friend's fingers is 0.18 seconds, which is the average time for a person to sense that the bill is falling and to clamp his forefinger to his thumb. Most people will miss the catch on the first attempt, but after "getting on hair trigger," they can just barely stop the bill in mid air on later tries. You will agree that if one designed an experiment in which cerebral sensing, computing, and torquing had to be compressed into a time of 50 milliseconds, the human brain could not possibly accomplish it. (That corresponds to catching the dollar bill when it has fallen half an inch instead of the usual six inches.) But the most sluggish electronic computer could easily handle it. I don't know what reaction time your dice-rolling experiment demands, but it is certainly less than the clock time of the brain. A good sized die might be 1 cm on a side; so the time it takes to fall that distance (starting from rest, to make the time longest) is 40 milliseconds. As I said at the outset, I have no problem with believing in psychokinesis, so long as the brain doing the psyching is not a human one, but rather one that uses faster "active elements," or, conversely, a real human brain doing a much less demanding job.

And, more importantly, why do you design your experiments so that the demonstrably small MIPS rate of the human brain will certainly mask any real PK effect that might be there? The torsion-pendulum experiment that Cavendish would have done, had he been interested in parapsychology, places no such demands on the brain's MIPS rate, and should it be successful, then you could go on to PK experiments that would measure the PK MIPS rate, as you "gradually pushed it to the limit." And the "Cavendish experiment" has the advantage that it would be a teaching device, in which the experimenter would learn to increase his PK forces as he saw the effects they produced. Without such a teaching device, what you are trying to do seems to me like asking Helen Keller to compose the "Moonlight Sonata." Beethoven did it when *he* was stone deaf. but he had years of good hearing, when he could teach himself to imagine the sounds he was later unable to hear. Your experiment doesn't permit any teaching experience to enhance the effect. In my opinion, that is a very serious defect, but a minor one compared to the demonstrable lack of computing speed in the human brain.

The brain is capable of lots of "parallel processing," which is a substitute for computing speed in a simple computer, but it doesn't help a bit if we are trying to do things faster than the individual active elements permit. As an example, suppose we want to count all the words in the Bible. If we have all the words encoded on a tape, and run that tape past a sensor, the total time required is the basic sensor time multiplied by the total number of words. If we have N such sensors (one per page, for example) we can run the N page-tapes past the N sensors, and get the answer N times faster. With N equal to 1000, that is a big speed-up. But we are always limited by the basic active-element time that is the same, no matter whether we use one sensor or 1000. So the brain's remarkable parallel-processing ability lets us see our surroundings as well as they can be produced on TV, with its 4 MHz bandwidth. (Four MHz of bandwidth is comparable to, but not equal to, 4 MIPS, and enormous compared to the brain's basic speed.) Similarly, our hearing makes use of parallel processing to overcome the narrow bandwidth of the brain, or expressed slightly differently, its very low MIPS rate. The pitch of sounds is sensed by the thousands of "hairs" in the cochlea, and each hair, in turn, feeds signals into the parallel fibers in the acoustic nerve, just as the rods and cones in the retina feed their signals down the optic nerve. So our senses work with surprising apparent bandwidth, when connected so beautifully in parallel to a *very* slow computer. That inherent slowness has made it impossible for you to detect PK in dice-rolling experiments, even though it might be an easily observable effect if detected by a torsion pendulum.

I hope these thoughts will let you see that I am not faulting you for spending 40 years in a search for PK. I'd be absolutely delighted to have you show it to me in an experiment of the general type I have described, and that would certainly demonstrate PK if it existed. My strong criticism of your career in parapsychology is based on the fact that you have spent your time doing experiments that your extensive background in communication theory should have told you could not possibly show positive results, even if PK were an easily demonstrable effect. In my opinion, you have, in effect, been trying to send a TV signal over a telephone line, even though you *know* that a TV signal demands a bandwidth 1000 times that which can be passed over a telephone line. The fact that such an experiment can't possibly work only proves that there is an enormous bandwidth mismatch, and has no bearing at all on the possibility of transmitting a picture over a telephone cable. The AP and the UP have been sending photographs to newspapers all over the world for 60 years—long before TV was invented. They started out by using a transmission time per picture of one minute—1800 times slower than the 1/30 second needed for TV broadcasting. If they had tried to send their pictures in 1/30 second, they would have failed dismally, and that failure wouldn't have constituted a proof that picture transmission was impossible. Similarly, I believe that your failure to obtain dice-control experiments with respectable signal-to-noise ratios has no bearing on the existence or nonexistence of PK; it merely shows that you were doing a badly conceived experiment that was doomed to failure because of the bandwidth or MIPS rate of a computer built of "squishy stuff" instead of silicon chips.

I thought I had explained my thoughts to you ten or fifteen years ago, when I suggested that you start over again with a

Cavendish-type experiment. But obviously, I didn't make myself clear. I hope I finally have in this letter. You still have plenty of time left to do the definitive experiment on PK without "lousing it up" with a "computer" [the human brain] that has excellent parallel processing capabilities but a very poor "clock rate."

I'll now pass this letter back to you, for your concluding remarks.

(sig) Louie

Luis W. Alvarez

In our telephone conversation you expressed regret—or at least puzzlement—that, after a brilliant start at the Radiation Laboratory, I had wasted the next forty years of my life in parapsychology. You say you are convinced of my honesty; for otherwise I would not have worked so many years with so little to show for it.

All of your comments were offered in a forthright and friendly manner and were gratefully received by me. As I told you then, I am delighted that you are willing to express your opinion. As I see it, the main problem in parapsychology (apart from the difficulty in producing the phenomena) is that very few competent scientists like yourself are willing to examine the evidence to whatever extent they feel necessary and then to express a public opinion.

I firmly believe that the fastest way to get to the root of the parapsychological puzzle (or to find that it has no demonstrated root, as you believe) is to discuss the matter openly among top-level scientists—and the blunter the language, the better.

If I have misrepresented in the slightest degree what you said, or if you believe that more must be added to fairly represent your opinion, please feel free to correct or comment.

Sincerely yours.

(sig) Bob

R. A. McConnell

P.S. This letter now expresses my thoughts concerning your experiments. I am pleased to have the opportunity to

cooperate with you in putting down on paper my reactions to
your search for PK. As I have told you before, my willing-
ness to do so derives entirely from my admiration for your
conception of, and reduction to practice of, moving-target indication radar. I have always considered it to be the most
remarkable technical tour-de-force in World War II.[9]

With warmest regards,

(sig) L.W.A.

I regard the foregoing letter as historically significant, and so,
no doubt, does Dr. Alvarez. For the reader's convenience, I
summarize his argument in the following paragraph, which appeared in my original letter to him, but which he replaced with
his own beautifully lucid, five-page elaboration:

> [You believe that ours] is a foolish experiment because it
> was foredoomed to failure. From all that we know in
> science, it is impossible that the human brain should compute
> which face on each of the falling dice is about to turn up and
> then send out the necessary energy to move the dice
> [laterally] in the desired directions. Alternatively, it is im-
> possible for the brain to know, by ESP or otherwise, the
> [lateral] direction to which the falling dice are individually
> tending and then to send out energy to cause dice to turn up
> favorable faces accordingly [thus horizontally separating the
> dice according to face when they came to rest]. You base
> your judgment upon the fact (with which I certainly agree)
> that the informational bandwidth of the electromagnetic
> energy transmissible from a soft-tissue brain is just not wide
> enough for that kind of discrimination.

I think Dr. Alvarez' argument is irrefutable if one begins with
his assumption about the nature of PK—a matter to which I shall
return presently.

First, however, I want to comment on the fact that Dr. Alvarez
argues that falling-dice psychokinesis is theoretically impossible,
but he does not criticize our paper as evidence for PK except indirectly by referring to our "failure to obtain dice-control experi-

---

[9] It was my privilege to lead a group of imaginative and diligent scientists
and technicians —RAM

ments with respectable signal-to-noise ratios.'' Because Dr. Alvarez does not say why our statistical evidence is not respectable, I can respond only in general terms.

Although most physicists are not accustomed to using the null-hypothesis test for small effects with a large number of data, such a test, when properly executed on suitable data, is capable of allowing conclusions of the form: ''an effect as large as that observed would occur on the average by chance alone once in $(1/p)$ such experiments.'' From a practical point of view, such a conclusion based upon a small p can lead to certainty that a real, non-chance effect exists when that effect has been found in many well-done experiments.[10]

It is proper to criticize such a statistical conclusion by impugning either the data or their treatment, and in the present experiment, to go further and deny the claimed psycho-physical implication of the effect, if real.

Dr. Alvarez ignored these scientific matters. Instead, he gave his personal belief about how strong and dependable a PK effect must be before he will be convinced of its reality. Some readers may wish to make this subjective judgment for themselves but would have been grateful for an expert's assurance that the dice report's logical conclusion is technically inescapable.

My regret that Dr. Alvarez did not dispute or accept our experimental conclusion was offset by my pleasure with his theoretical argument concerning the detection of PK with falling dice. His is, in fact, the only sophisticated discussion I have heard from a physicist concerning this topic. Dr. Alvarez conclusively showed, not that falling-dice PK is impossible to detect, but that, since it has been detected in many experiments, the nature of PK must be incompatible with the unmentioned assumption upon which he based his argument.

What Dr. Alvarez assumed is that PK would be transmitted from the brain through three-dimensional space in a manner analogous to electromagnetic radiation, i.e., as an amplitude or frequency, changing serially in time. Admittedly, this is the only kind of spatial transfer of information otherwise known to science (unless, perhaps, one considers recent experiments conforming to J. S. Bell's theorem in quantum mechanics).

---

[10] The possible importance of small effects was discussed near the beginning of this chapter.

What Dr. Alvarez has done is provide one more line of argument showing that PK, if real according to the claimed evidence, operates outside our familiar space-time continuum. Parapsychologists, who have had more time than Dr. Alvarez to study the parapsychological literature, have long accepted this conclusion as applying to all psychic phenomena. It is useful, nevertheless, to have the argument couched in physicists' language and applied to a specific experimental situation where it can be conveniently scrutinized.

After reading this chapter a colleague urged that I respond to Dr. Alvarez's recommendation to abandon dice as a research tool in favor of the torsion-pendulum balance.

Since the founding of the Society for Psychical Research in 1882, the mental movement of balances has been tried innumerable times but never, to my knowledge, with the sophistication envisioned by Dr. Alvarez. In any case, the results were never convincing except to those who were present at the test. Although he did not say so, Dr. Alvarez is evidently hoping for a demonstration repeatable upon demand. The methodological issues raised by his proposal are complex. For this book, the best I can offer is an answer in allegory.

> Many years ago, after hearing reports of unicorn sightings in northern Australia, I mounted a two-year expedition and came back with a faint but clearly identifiable photograph of a unicorn.[11] To my puzzlement, no one would look at it.
>
> Ten years later, I organized a second expedition, hoping to learn why unicorns are such elusive creatures. Again, all I could bring back was a faint but unmistakeable picture of a unicorn.[12] My hope at this point was, not to convince, but to encourage further search. However, all the zoologists to whom I showed my photograph have had nothing to say about it.
>
> A wise friend, who has studied two-horned vertebrates all his life, was sure that Australia would be too dry for unicorns, whereas Borneo should have a more suitable climate. He does not believe photographs, but he has

---

[11] McConnell, Snowdon, & Powell, 1955; also, chapters 4 and 5 in McConnell, 1983.

[12] Chapter 4 of this book.

promised that, if I bring back a live unicorn from Borneo, he will look at it.

Where should I send my next expedition?

Chapter Appendix B

J. S. BELL ON PARAPSYCHOLOGY

Because some theoretically inclined parapsychologists have given attention to the possibility that psi phenomena may eventually be explained in quantum-mechanical terms, it seemed desirable to seek an authoritative answer to the question: What implications, if any, for parapsychology are to be found in present-day quantum mechanics?

This question assumes its most poignant form in response to a cloud hanging over the world of quantum mechanics since the publication by Einstein, Podolsky, and Rosen in 1935 of a paper setting forth what has since then been called the "EPR Paradox."

Most physicists, including Einstein, had been content to accept the fact that our intuitive grasp of reality fails at very small distances. For example, a single photon behaves as both a particle and a wave, even though these are not compatible conceptions. Perhaps the most appealing way to explain this contradiction is to concede that our language, for which each of us has created private meaning based on our immediate sensory experience, loses its meaning at very small distances where we have had no immediate experience. Thus, we must say that a photon is neither a particle nor a wave, but something else for which we have no language.

Fortunately, the world of the tiny was saved from chaos by a mathematical formulation called "quantum mechanics," which accepts Nature on her own terms and provides, so far as we know, a full representation of all possible physical observations.

In their paper, EPR devised an imaginary experiment in which, according to quantum mechanics, apparent violations of common sense would appear even at human-sized distances. Rather than doubt the quantum predictions, EPR argued that quantum mechanics must be incomplete, and that in a more complete theory, giving a fuller account of what goes on behind the observations, the quantum predictions would become intelligible, and be seen to respect "local causality."

In 1964 J. S. Bell demonstrated that this hope could not be

maintained. He showed that no picture could be devised compatible both with the quantum predictions for observations and with the principle of local causation.

Since then, the theoretical argument has been deepened in various ways, and a series of experiments (Robinson, 1982; 1983), which are increasingly good approximations to the ideal EPR experiment, have continued to verify the "inexplicable" predictions of quantum mechanics, rather than the consequences of local causality.

What does this mean for parapsychology? Explicitly, nothing at all—at least for the present—but it does affirm that physical intuition cannot be depended upon to tell us what is possible in any unexplored area of human experience. I believe it is a fair extrapolation to say that the lesson of Bell's theorem for parapsychology is that even so absurd an idea as precognition must be approached with an open mind.

Because my knowledge of these matters is, at best, thirdhand (Mermin, 1985; Zukav, 1979), I wrote to J. S. Bell, sending him a copy of the McConnell and Clark dice report and saying, in part:

> It would be helpful if someone like yourself were to review in nonmathematical language the present status of experiments bearing upon the idea that quantum-logical effects should be observable at the macro level. I would like to see you spell out the broad implications of this for choosing mental strategies for trying to grasp the nature of the universe—or rather, for trying to take our next step forward in conceptualizing it. . . .
>
> I am not in a position to suppose any connection between psychokinesis and quantum mechanics, and perhaps no one else is either. Moreover, you cannot comment on the validity of the evidence for psychokinesis unless you have spent more time on it than I think likely.

Of course, Dr. Bell did not accept my suggestion to give methodological advice to the world at large. Instead, he sent me the following gracious and informative letter:

CERN
Geneve
Switzerland
20 May 1986

Professor R. A. McConnell
Biological Sciences
University of Pittsburgh

Dear Professor McConnell:

Thank you for your letter and paper of April 13, and for the material on parapsychology that you had sent previously. I have read all with great interest.

As I understand your letter, you would like me to express an opinion on the relevance or irrevelance of quantum nonlocality for parapsychology. Of course it is easy to see why people have felt there might be some connection. What has been brought out in the theoretical and experimental study of quantum nonlocality is that nature is much more curiously connected up than could have been envisaged by classical physicists, and more so even than was realized by many quantum physicists. But it must be stressed that what has been brought out here is just a feature of orthodox quantum mechanics—which fully predicts the classically inexplicable correlations which experimenters have found. Now while orthodox quantum theory is less well formulated theoretically than I would like, it is rather unambiguous in practice. And it implies rather clearly that these queer correlations do not enable us to act at a distance, for example to signal faster than light. So it seems to me that, strange as quantum mechanics is, and strange as psychokinesis is, the first does not help to explain the second. Such phenomena would require, I think, the revision of quantum mechanics as well as of classical physical theories.

So much for my opinions in an area where I might claim some competence. You guess quite rightly that I am not at all competent to judge the quality of the evidence for parapsychological phenomena. But perhaps you will allow me to express a personal impression, similar I expect to that of many, of what I have read on this subject, both in the material you have been distributing and before. In physics, as you know, they say that this year's discovery is next year's calibration. In parapsychology one does not seem to see any comparable cumulation of effort. I see that from time to time some person whose honesty seems transparent finds statistically significant effects in experiments that look sensible. Sometimes (but not always) I read later of how he was cheated by a collaborator—or by his own wishful thinking. What I do not seem to see is where one experimenter takes up the work of another, verifies it in a straightforward way, and carries it further. That is very frustrating.

But I remember how as a student in Ireland I was required to attempt experiments in electrostatics—and formed the opinion that electrostatics could never have been convincingly discovered in my home country—because of the damp. It may be that parapsychological phenomena are erratic only because of some factor analogous to damp which remains to be identified and controlled. However that may be, I would not think it sensible to ignore evidence simply on the ground that the phenomena in question would not be explicable, as far as I could see, in the context of contemporary physics and physiology. I am inclined to think that even physics is in its infancy, and that entirely new things will be found, if there is time.

Yours Sincerely,

John Bell

In requesting permission to publish his letter, I wrote, in part, essentially as follows:

Dear Dr. Bell:

I think you will be interested in my reaction to the penultimate paragraph of your letter, in which you give your impression of parapsychology. My own impression differs from yours in three ways.

To me it seems that there has been a great deal of "verification in a straightforward way." That, however, is not something dealt with in my books, in which I chose to emphasize selected experiments rather than debatable generalities. To illustrate my point, I enclose a paper by Radin, May, and Thomson (1985) given at the last annual meeting of the Parapsychological Association. These authors present a meta-analysis of 332 parapsychological experiments of one particular kind done between 1969 and 1984, namely, those that used an electronic, random-number generator to create targets.[13]

There has also, I think, been "accumulation of effort," but that is not likely to be evident to those outside the field whose attention quite naturally goes to evidence for and against the reality of the phenomena rather than to our tortoise-like progress in understanding.

My third disagreement is with your following two sentences:

> I see that from time to time some person whose honesty seems transparent finds statistically significant effects in experiments that look sensible. Sometimes, but not always, I read later of how he was cheated by a collaborator—or by his own wishful thinking.

These sentences convey the impression that the case for psi phenomena rests upon a few experiments done by a few experimenters, and that much, if not most, of the otherwise convincing work has been compromised by evidence of experimenter fraud or incompetence. Again, your impression is understandable. Outside attention is inevitably drawn to individual, newsworthy studies and especially to cases of fraud. As the above-cited meta-analysis shows, there is a large number of less pretentious supporting experiments of which the casual skeptic may be unaware. In the USA at present there are perhaps a dozen full-time experimental parapsychologists and several times as many part-time. Summing over the last fifty years, there have been many more.

The question of technical competence is a difficult one in any field. Conceptually, it is best dealt with, I think, on a probability basis.[14] No published paper is to be accepted as certainly mistake free. On the other hand, few peer-reviewed papers are to be discarded as totally worthless.

Undiscovered fraud by a subject undergoing parapsychological testing implies technical incompetence if the experimenter has designed the testing protocol and claims its outcome as evidence for a psychic phenomenon. In screen-

---

[13] An abstract of this paper appears as appendix *B* in the chapter titled "Forces of Darkness."

[14] *See* McConnell, 1982, chap. 16.

ing volunteer subjects, however, it is considered necessary to allow every claimant of psychic power to demonstrate his ability initially in his own way. The experimenter must then decide whether to continue and how best to progress toward scientifically meaningful experimentation. This renders the experimenter vulnerable to stage mentalists and others who might wish to enhance their prestige (or ridicule parapsychology) by claiming success under conditions that the experimenter does not consider adequate. This situation, coupled with the fact that professional psychics are usually impatient with scientific methods, has led in several cases to unfavorable publicity that reflected upon the field as a whole. Headlines proclaim the psychic's statement. The truth never reaches the casual skeptic.

Fraud by an experimenter is a separate problem. Offhand, I know of only two cases of fraud by prominent experimenters (Soal and Levy) in the last fifty years. In both cases the fraud was discovered by other parapsychologists. My impression after 39 years of dealing on a collegial basis with parapsychologists, is that they are as honest as the scientists I have known in more ordinary fields—either because of, or in spite of, the special pressures and temptations in parapsychology.

There must be many others who have your impression of the literature of parapsychology. If it is wrong, it will not be changed unless it is examined. For that reason I believe it is important that your ideas be published.

With appreciation for your kindness, I am,

Sincerely yours,

R. A. McConnell

REFERENCES

Bell, J.S. (1964). On the Einstein Podolsky Rosen Paradox. *Physics, 1,* 195–200.

Einstein, A., Podolsky, B., & Rosen, N. (1935). Can quantum-mechanical description of reality be considered complete? *Physical Review, 47,* 777–780.

McConnell, R.A. (1982). *Encounters with Parapsychology.* Pittsburgh, Pennsylvania: Editor.

McConnell, R.A. (1983). *Parapsychology and Self-Deception in Science.* Pittsburgh, Pennsylvania: Editor.

McConnell, R.A., & Clark, T.K. (1980). Training, belief, and mental conflict within the Parapsychological Association. *Journal of Parapsychology, 44,* 245–268.

McConnell, R.A., Snowdon, R.J., & Powell, K.F. (1955). Wishing with dice. *Journal of Experimental Psychology, 50*(4), 269–275.

Mermin, N.D. (1985). Is the moon there when nobody looks?: Reality and the quantum theory. *Physics Today, 38*(4),

Radin, D.I., May, E.C., & Thomson, M.J. (1985). Psi experiments with random-number generators: Meta-analysis part I. *Proceedings of the Parapsychological Association 28th Annual Convention, Volume I*, 201–233.

Robinson, A.L. (1982). Quantum mechanics passes another test. *Science, 217*, 435–436.

Robinson, A.L. (1983). Loophole closed in quantum mechanics test. *Science, 219*, 40–41.

Zukav, G. (1979). *The Dancing Wu Li Masters.* New York: William Morrow & Co.

4

ANOMALOUS FALL OF DICE

R. A. McCONNELL and T. K. CLARK

Biological Sciences Department
University of Pittsburgh

ABSTRACT[1]

Five-hundred, self-selected college students each separately donated an hour of his or her time to investigate the so-called psychokinetic effect in which the fall of gambling dice is supposedly influenced directly by the wishing of the player. The students were given the task of releasing by remote control six wooden dice while wishing those dice to tumble individually toward one side or the other of a scaled, playing table.

The faces of each die were marked in the usual manner with one to six circular spots. The direction of desired motion depended upon each upcoming die face. For the first six of twelve releases, the student was asked to wish the dice with low faces (1, 2, and 3) to go to the low-coordinate side of the table and dice with high faces (4, 5, and 6) to go to the high side. In the remaining six releases, the student was asked to reverse the direction of wishing.

Starting instructions were given by audio magnetic tape. The dice-releasing process was controlled by release-counting relays and monitored by a motion-picture camera, which recorded the dice throughout their time of travel. The field of the camera included a serially numbered card showing the student's name, a time-of-day clock, a high-speed elapsed-time clock, an automatically advanced display of both the release number and the wishing instructions, and a spherical-mirror image of the entire room.

Each student was supervised by one of two experimenters, A or M. After hearing the instruction tape, the student was given the choice of having the experimenter present in the room or absent

---

[1] This research was financially supported by the A. W. Mellon Educational and Charitable Trust.

from it while the dice were being released.

Before statistical analysis, the effect of wishing for faces 4, 5, and 6 was reversed by reflecting their transverse coordinates across the grand mean of the experiment using the equation: $Y' = 78 - Y$. In this way, all nonpsychophysical effects were cancelled.

Analyses of variance were based on the release means of transverse die coordinates, thereby ensuring independence and normality of the dependent variable.

Overall, the data showed statistical significance for Releases and for session Halves by Releases. When the data were broken down into experimenter groups, significant interactions were found between M-present and M-absent, and between M-absent and A-absent.

The overall ANOVA was verified by independent re-analysis of the data, starting with the motion-picture film and ending with a different ANOVA computer program. As an additional precaution, the smallest, single-group probability ($p = .0008$), which came from less than 20% of the subjects, was independently verified by hand calculator, starting with the raw data on magnetic tape.

Because of the controls employed, only one conclusion is believed to be possible: Either the outcome of the experiment represents a rare chance event, or the behavior of the dice was directly affected by the conscious thinking of the subjects and / or experimenters.

Moreover, the analyses suggest that different experimenters can affect the fall of dice differently even when those experimenters are absent from the dice room.

The extrachance scoring patterns of this repeated-trial experiment bear no recognized relation to the serrated decline of success that is sometimes found in synchronism with test-and-rest data-gathering patterns. The dual wishing task of this experiment has made possible both the elimination of adventitious physical causation and the demonstration of dice effects presumably caused by, but not conforming to, the conscious wishing of subjects and / or experimenters. This may imply a conceptually new class of psychokinesis.

INTRODUCTION

It is regrettable that gambling dice are out of fashion as a research tool in parapsychology. In the last twenty years the psychokinetic effect has been investigated by a variety of complex electronic devices. These have been convenient for exploring psychological variables but seem to have been of little value for discovering physical relationships. In electronic apparatus one can never know just where the supposed psychokinesis might have occurred—or even, in many cases, whether it could, instead, have been a form of extrasensory perception.

The following were some of our objectives in the present gambling-dice experiment:

1. To determine whether a psychokinetic effect as measured by the transverse location of fallen dice could be produced by relatively unselected college students handled by experimenters having no special psychic ability.

2. To record, reduce, and analyze fallen dice data under controls so rigorous that any statistically significant deviation from chance expectation could confidently be said to represent either a rare chance event or "psychokinesis." It was our intention to eliminate fraud, carelessness, and all possible ordinary physical explanations for any effects we might obtain. Our purpose in this was to avoid self-deception and to generate firm empirical facts upon which we and our colleagues could build.

3. To try to separate experimenter and subject effects by removing the experimenter from the testing room. This required that the experiment be fraudproof without the presence of an observer.

4. To discover whether subjects, simply by wishing, could spatially separate falling dice according to the faces that would appear on top when the dice finally came to rest. In other words, we planned to combine the original die-face experiments of J.B. and L.E. Rhine with the so-called "placement experiments" to which Haakon Forwald devoted his parapsychological career.

PSYCHOKINETIC MANIFESTATION

Psychokinesis, or the direct effect of thought upon matter, has been investigated in many ways. In this paper we are concerned only with repeated-trial experiments in which deviations from chance expectation can be quantitatively observed and statistically analyzed. Typical among such experiments are those in which gambling dice are thrown for pre-chosen faces (die-face experiments) and those in which falling objects are willed to move laterally in one direction instead of another (placement experiments).

On the basis of die-face experiments begun in 1934, Louisa E. Weckesser Rhine and Joseph Banks Rhine reported in 1943 that a total deviation from chance in the desired direction could sometimes be obtained with high statistical significance. Soon thereafter, it was found by a re-examination of past experiments that a statistically significant scoring-rate decline typically occurred over the data page or other unit of data acquisition (Reeves & Rhine, 1943; Rhine & Humphrey, 1944a). Such declines are now an expected feature of both psychokinetic and ESP experiments.

When does a scoring decline stop? If it were caused by a waning of "psychic power," the curve ought to approach the chance expectation axis asymptotically. Instead, it was found that the decline could pass through expectation. To explain this, parapsychologists have talked of a "sign factor" causing a reversal of the polarity of psychokinesis. Perhaps it would be better, instead, to use "opposing tendency" language (McConnell & Clark, 1983). This allows all degrees of unbalance and can describe a smooth transition between wished-for and against-wish psychokinesis.

Such a transition is illustrated in Figure 1, which shows the decline in scoring rate in a die-face experiment in which two dice were thrown and automatically photographed within a totally enclosing motor-driven cage (McConnell, Snowdon, & Powell, 1955). The three bars in the figure represent deviations of die-face counts from chance expectation $p = 1/6$) in the three data columns of the combined half pages of supplementary, handwritten records. After every half page the throwing was interrupted for a brief rest. The deviations from expectation of the first and third columns are both independently significant at close to the two-tailed, $p = .05$ level.

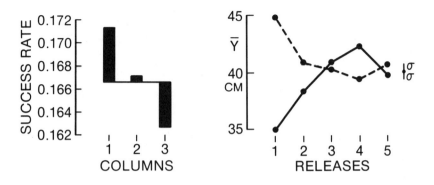

Figure 1 (On the left). A parapsychological "scoring decline." In this example, the rate of appearance of prechosen die faces declined linearly over a three-column group of data gathered between resting periods in the experimental testing session. The gambling dice were thrown and automatically photographed within a totally enclosing, motor-driven, rotating cage operated by the experimenter while college-student subjects (386, tested one at a time) wished for their single, target face to come up. The target face was varied from subject to subject in an effectively random manner. Each bar represents the success rate for 37,056 dice. The two-tailed chance probability of the difference between the first and third bars is .003. Notice that the scoring rate sinks below the chance expectation line: $p = 1/6$. (McConnell, Snowdon, and Powell, 1955.)

Figure 2 (On the right). Reversed-*J* "placement success" within a psychokinetic testing session. Shown are the mean transverse (Y) coordinates of the final resting positions of 16 mm, plain wood cubes, magnetically released to a table top by the Swedish engineer-psychic, Haakon Forwald. These curves represent the data of 50 self-testing sessions in which there were five releases per half session and six cubes per release. Thus, each point on the curves is the mean position of 300 cubes. The solid line shows the changing degree of success throughout the first half session in which Forwald wished the cubes to roll toward the low-Y side. In the second half session (dashed line) he reversed the direction of his wishing. The vertical bar is two standard deviations for any plotted point (McConnell & Forwald, 1968). The experiment of the present paper differs from this Forwald experiment chiefly by using ordinarily spotted dice, of which subjects were asked to spatially separate faces 1, 2, and 3 from 4, 5, and 6.

It was also discovered (Reeves & Rhine, 1943) that, although declines were most common, scoring-rate inclines could occur, especially near the end of the data-recording unit. Thus, *U*-curves or reverse *J*-curves came to be expected patterns for psychokinetic scoring in repeated-trial experiments.

The cube-placement experiments of Haakon Forwald provide interesting examples of scoring declines followed by recovery. Forwald (1897–1978) was an internationally known, Swedish, high-voltage switching engineer who became interested in his own psychic abilities. Figure 2 (McConnell & Forwald, 1968) shows the results of an experiment very similar in format to the experiment we are reporting in this paper. Forwald began each testing session with the magnetic release of six wooden cubes down a slope toward a table top while he wished for those cubes to move laterally. In the analysis the mean lateral (transverse) position of this first release of dice was subtracted from its oppositely-wished-for mate from the second half session. When averaged over 50 sessions, this first-release displacement difference was found to be 9.8 cm [$p = 10^{-30}$]. By the fourth release of cubes, the displacement difference was 2.8 cm [$p = 10^{-3}$], but in the wrong direction. By the fifth release the difference was again positive (0.9 cm, nonsignificant).

These curves suggest a smoothly changing scoring rate. We find it reasonable to suppose that "decline" and "incline" are merely conspicuous aspects of psychokinetic fluctuation.

Forwald obtained results comparable to these throughout his parapsychological career. He spent years testing specific hypotheses about how the physical nature of the cubes might affect his results—largely ignoring the question of psychological contamination by unconscious preconception. He asked, for example, how would the use of metal cladding of different atomic weights affect his success (Forwald, 1969). We treasure his engineering curiosity as an explanation of motivation and an indicator of honesty. No physicist would have wasted so much time or have achieved such astounding results.

Still other variations of the "decline effect" have come to light which suggest that this expression is inadequate. For example, Rhine and Humphrey (1944b) reported an experiment in which small and medium-sized dice were thrown at the same time and a scoring decline on the medium-sized dice accompanied an incline on the small.

What may be the most complex of carefully observed psycho-kinetic patterns in the literature appears in Figure 3 from a retrospective study (McConnell & Clark, 1983) of the die-face experiment of Figure 1. This later study includes a first page of cup-thrown dice, which were omitted from Figure 1.

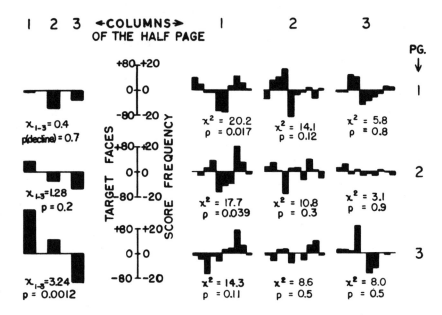

Figure 3. Complex success patterns within the testing sessions of a die-face experiment. These are the data of Figure 1, as examined more closely by McConnell and Clark in 1983. Cup-thrown dice data (constituting "Page 1") were brought into the analysis, and the scores for each of the three data columns between half-page resting periods were tested for goodness-of-fit to the expected binomial distribution ($p = 1/6$, $n = 24$). Shown are the deviations from expectation for scores ranging from 0 to 9+. The overall pattern of probabilities strongly suggests the operation of nonchance factors in this photographically-controlled experiment.

From a close examination of Figure 3, it will be seen that, at the beginning of the experimental session, psychokinesis appeared strongly in the first columns of the first data page as a scattering of low and high scores whose extrachance nature is shown by their badness-of-fit to the expected binomial distribution. This was a $p = .017$ violation of a familiar mathematical model. As the experimental session progressed, a decline effect emerged. On the third, final page, a probability, $p = .0012$, occurred, but this null test was for a decline in scoring—which is a "task-structure effect" anticipated from the psychokinetic literature (McConnell, 1983). Truly, we have come a long way from the total deviation of score that the Rhines set out to find.

The scoring patterns that have been seen over the last fifty years of psychokinetic research have been interpreted as departures from the subject's wished-for pattern. It is now known that psychokinesis does not always start in the session, or in the data block, as the desired effect and then drift away in various patterns. It can first appear in a sense opposite to what is desired. It can wax and wane simultaneously in different parts of the same experiment. It can disappear or, instead, it can progressively organize into a recognizable pattern. This complexity raises interesting questions.

How much have we missed? How much psychokinesis has been unrecognized because its patterns appeared to be of chance origin?

Have we adequately considered the known features of psychokinetic manifestation as they might affect our strategy in seeking understanding and control of this phenomenon?

How powerful is psychokinesis? It can act for or against the subject's wishes, can shift unaccountably from one direction to another, and, while shifting, can pass through zero and disappear altogether. It is believed from poltergeist phenomena, as well as from the gross disturbance of physical systems in equilibrium, that psychokinetic energy can be enormous in comparison to the neural synaptic energies with which it might hypothetically interact (McConnell, 1983). In everyday living it appears that psychokinesis is held on leash by countervailing factors, presumably of a motivational nature. What might we find if we overcome what appears to be mere subconscious inhibition?

APPARATUS

In the present experiment six dice were released as a group by an electromagnetic trigger. They fell by gravity and, after horizontal deflection, came to rest on a rectangular surface marked off in rectangular coordinates. Most of the mechanical apparatus used to release, control, and record these dice is shown in Figure 4.

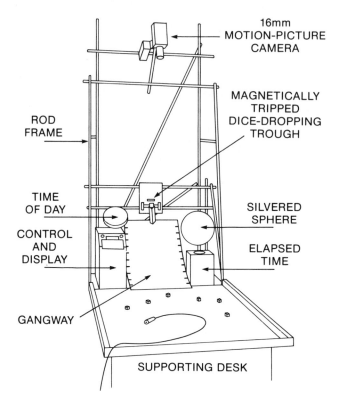

16mm
MOTION-PICTURE
CAMERA

MAGNETICALLY
TRIPPED
DICE-DROPPING
TROUGH

ROD
FRAME

TIME
OF DAY

SILVERED
SPHERE

CONTROL
AND
DISPLAY

ELAPSED
TIME

GANGWAY

SUPPORTING DESK

Figure 4. Apparatus used in this experiment as sketched from a photograph. Not shown are the camera-timing device, ceiling floodlights, and posted, supplementary instructions.

Releasing Machine

Near the center of the figure is an aluminum trough which is shaped to a 90-degree vee and hinged at its distant end about a transverse ball-bearing axis. This trough, illustrated at its 60-degree fallen angle, was released from a horizontal position by a magnet, which, in turn, was activated by a pushbutton, shown with its electrical cord curled on the tabular surface below.

The dice, which had been placed by hand more or less randomly in the horizontal trough before its release, fell with the trough, striking the felt covered, 40-degree-inclined surface shown below the trough, and ended in positions as typically indicated.

The dice-dropping trough turned freely in its bearings without perceptible play. The trough assembly was clamped to a half-inch aluminum-rod frame, rigidly braced and independently mounted on a three-quarter-inch plywood base. The entire apparatus lay snugly upon a heavy, oaken office desk, which rested stably on the concrete floor.

The die-receiving surface was window glass, finely ground on one side to encourage tumbling rather than sliding of the dice. Its thickness was only 0.24 cm to facilitate photographing the rectangular scale beneath.

The glass surface was 80 cm from the floor and extended 100 cm in the X direction of principal motion and 80 cm in the Y, or transverse, direction. Along each side there was a 6-cm fence to contain the dice. The X and Y spaces were numbered from 0 to 99 and from 0 to 79, respectively, with a least count of 1 cm.

The turning axis for the dropping trough was located at $X = -38$ cm and was 44 cm above the glass. Relative to that turning axis, the center of gravity of the six cubes before release was 2.1 cm above, and 7.0 cm in the $+X$ direction.

Dice Specification

The six dice used throughout the experiment were 16 mm on edge, with 3.7 mm, slightly concave, white painted spots and a mass of 2.48 g. They were made to order by the H.C. Edwards dice company from black walnut wood, chosen to provide good photographic contrast.

Because the subject's task in this experiment was to achieve a horizontal separation of tumbling dice according to whether they would show faces 1, 2, or 3, or faces 4, 5, or 6 when they came to rest, we can think of no way in which dice bias toward particular faces could influence our analysis of the outcome. Nevertheless, it may be of interest that the total number of 1, 2, and 3 faces in this experiment was 18,160 where 18,000 was expected. The difference is not statistically significant.

Photography

The operation of the apparatus was photographed from above at a mean distance of 160 cm by a Bell and Howell Autoload, 16-mm motion-picture camera, equipped with an Angenieux 10-mm wide-angle lens, and operated at 12 frames per second. The camera started when the dice-release button was pushed, and ran for 2.2 seconds, by which time the dice had come to rest. The timer is not shown in Figure 4.

The fifty-foot magazines were factory loaded by Eastman Kodak with black-and-white, Tri-X reversal film. The needed 128 magazines were serially numbered by M and commercially developed. A film-magazine log was kept by M, listing subject numbers and shipment dates for chemical development.

The dice were in the field of view of the camera while they were in the trough and until they came to rest on the table beneath. Also recorded by the camera were a time-of-day clock, a Standard Electric Time elapsed-time clock, a 20cm-diameter blown-glass sphere, internally silvered to provide an image of the entire room, and a control and display device, which is separately described below.

The elapsed-time clock recorded time in hours to 1/100 second and operated only while the camera was running. It was internally disabled so that it could not be reset throughout the course of the experiment.

Also not shown in Figure 4 are two, ceiling flood lamps. These operated below rated voltage except when switched to normal brightness while the camera was running.

Control and Display

The control and display device was designed by M for this experiment. Its purpose was to count releases for the subject, to remind him or her of the wishing task (which changed midway in each testing session), and to record essential data on the film. The device was placed as it appears in Figure 4 so as to be visible to both subject and camera.

On the circumference of a ten-inch disk were mounted thirty-six, 2x7-cm card holders. Printed signs, placed in these holders, were exposed through a window, one at a time, to the experimental subject. Rotation to the next sign started with each pushbutton release of dice and completed automatically five seconds later. Stepping relays were used to allow a prechosen number of button pushes (15 in the present experiment), after which the pushbutton was disabled and a signal lamp changed from green to red. Before the next testing session the counters were reset by the experimenter by means of a hidden switch. A fixed frame below the sign window received a 3x5-inch card to display the subject's name and certain prechosen experimental parameters.

The Experimental Room

Subject testing was done in Room 304, on a quiet floor of Clapp Hall at the University of Pittsburgh. The floor space was 8x10 feet, reduced to 6x10 feet by unused furniture. Ceiling height was 11 feet. Walls and ceiling were covered with a near-white, patterned, sound-absorbing material.

A double, west window gave an uninteresting view of parapet, buildings, and sky. Blinds were set six inches open at top and bottom, or as needed to prevent sunlight from affecting photography. One window was left unlatched to allow the subject to adjust ventilation. At all times the door blind was kept down and the door locked against possible intruders.

The equipment shown in Figure 4 was placed with its distant end against the west wall and its right side several inches from the north wall of the room.

EXPERIMENTAL PROCEDURES

History

In November, 1960, Haakon Forwald completed an epic series of experiments with falling cubes whose analysis took several years (McConnell & Forwald, 1967; 1968). In the following month, M began gathering data for the present experiment, for which planning started in 1959. Data-taking for the required 500 subjects was completed in October, 1964. M was assisted in the gathering of data by M. L. Anderson from January, 1961, to February 1962, while she was a graduate student in Education at the University of Pittsburgh.[2]

---

[2] M. L. Anderson is remembered for her series of papers on extrasensory perception in children beginning in 1956. She was awarded the William McDougall Prize for an experimental study published in the *Journal of Psychology* (Anderson & McConnell, 1961) and served as president of the Parapsychological Association in 1962. That same year she received the doctor of philosophy degree for a dissertation on Albert Camus and began a career of research and teaching in education. She retired as Professor of Education at the University of Pittsburgh in May, 1985, and died at age 66 on 12 February 1986, a victim of lung cancer.

Data Format

In the belief that several advantages might be gained by combining "die-face" and "die-placement" experiments as typified by Figures 1 and 2, M chose for the present experiment a psychokinetic testing procedure that followed closely the format of Haakon Forwald but added the requirement that the direction of wishing for lateral movement of each die should depend on the number of spots that would appear on the uppermost face of that die when it came to rest.

Each subject had one 50-minute test session only. Die throwing within that session followed the pattern of Figure 5. In the first half session there were seven releases of six dice. The first was a practice release, of which the subject made no record. In the six formal releases that followed, the subject wished for the dice to fall in such a way that those with faces 1, 2, or 3 would roll to the low-Y-coordinate side of the table (to the left in Figure 4), while the 4, 5, and 6 faces would go to the high-Y side. This wishing pattern is shown in Figure 6.

In the second half session the subject was asked to reverse the direction of wishing. Again, there was a practice release followed by six formal releases.

In an unsuccessful attempt to find an operational distinction between the psychokinetic control of face (given a chance, die location) and the psychokinetic placement of a die (whose face was chance-determined), half of all subjects were instructed with a slightly different protocol (which appeared on the second half of the control-display drum). In this second mode of instruction the subjects were asked to wish only for the placement of faces 1, 2, and 3 and to ignore faces 4, 5, and 6. No further information was given. This variation appears later in this paper as one of eight grouping variables. Because no significant difference was found for these two conditions of instruction, all procedural description is given in terms of faces 1, 2, and 3, versus 4, 5, and 6.

The student subject was given two, blank data sheets, one for each half of the test session. On these, after some initial training, he or she recorded the face and Y-coordinate for each die of each release. This data recording was primarily for the satisfaction of the student. Although these subject-written records were later transcribed, time has not allowed the originally intended study of

TESTING SESSION PROCEDURE

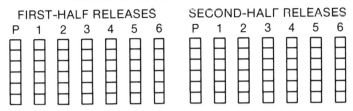

Figure 5. Procedural pattern followed by each subject in his or her experimental session. Six dice were magnetically released by the subject a total of 14 times while wishing for their horizontal displacement. The wishing pattern was reversed at the end of the first half session. Each half session consisted of a practice release followed by six formal releases. Only the formal releases are analyzed in this paper.

FIRST HALF-SESSION WISHING PATTERN

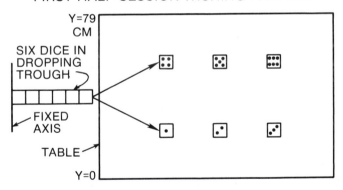

Figure 6. Idealized wishing pattern for the dice falling from the releasing trough on the left to the table on the right. Six gambling dice were placed by hand, more or less randomly, in the horizontal trough. In the first half of each session the trough was magnetically released six times by the subject while wishing the dice with future upturned faces 1, 2, or 3 to move toward the low-Y side and those that would come up 4, 5, or 6 to move toward the high-Y side. Wishing was reversed in the second half session.

student-recording accuracy. All analyses in this report are based on the motion-picture film records.

Solicitation of Subjects

Our 500 subjects were self-selected from a population of 2300 students in 70 lower-level psychology classes and 31 elementary physics classes at the University of Pittsburgh.[3] A form letter was first sent to the class instructor explaining the nature of the experiment and asking permission for M to slip into the classroom exactly three minutes before the ending bell on a day to be arranged and to use the last two minutes to invite the students to participate.

After the classroom announcement a student could either insert his or her name in a vacant cell of a calendar card for the current or following week (and carry away a reminder card) or could telephone later for an appointment.

Data Gathering

The subject was welcomed warmly by the experimenter on duty in an office adjacent to the dice room and was asked to fill in a multiple-choice questionnaire covering:

1. Belief in the possibility of extrasensory perception (one, three-level question).

2. Belief in the possibility of psychokinesis (one, three-level question).

3. The quality and degree of imagery experienced by the subject, both awake and asleep (12 questions).

4. Attitude toward, and success in playing, games of chance (9 questions).

While the student answered these questions, the experimenter

---

[3] When a preliminary version of this paper was presented at a meeting of the Parapsychological Association in August, 1985, the president of that organization, Dr. Robert Morris, reminded the authors that he had been one of the subjects in this experiment while an undergraduate student of psychology at the University of Pittsburgh. In 1985, Dr. Morris was appointed as the first Arthur Koestler Professor of Parapsychology at the University of Edinburgh.

went to the dice room to prepare the equipment. Upon returning, the experimenter sat down with the student, inspected the questionnaire answers for completeness, and entered the student's name, sex, and mailing address on a 3x5-inch camera-display card. The experimenter also entered the date, his own initial, the mode of wishing instruction, and the student's answers to the ESP and psychokinesis belief questions.

The experimenter accompanied the student to the dice room, taking along data sheets and name card but leaving the questionnaire in a locked file. The name card was mounted, and, when the student was ready, an instruction tape-recording was played. Each experimenter used his own pre-recording of the same set of instructions, which came to about 1000 words plus pauses and stops for detailed demonstrations.

At the beginning, the experimenter (via tape) told the subject that he or she could decide after instruction whether the experimenter should remain during the testing session.

After explaining what was to be wished for, the experimenter loaded the dice into the trough and casually tripped it by hand (nonmagnetically and without camera). Using a sample data sheet, the experimenter then showed how to record the fallen dice.

Thereafter, the experimenter allowed the subject to lift and magnetically trip the empty trough once, thus giving experience with trough, pushbutton, camera, and lights. (This was the first of the allowed 15 button pushes described earlier under *Control and Display.*)

Next, the pattern of releases was explained (along with the instructions that would appear on the control-display panel and those posted on a page nearby to aid memory and cover unforeseen contingencies). Finally, the subject decided whether he or she wanted the experimenter to leave or to stay and act as data recorder. The experimenter retired or remained accordingly.

After the session the experimenter chatted with the student, serviced and closed the machine, and placed all records in a locked file.

Documentation

The documents relating to the performance of this experiment were the following:

1. Apparatus maintenance instructions and log.

2. Subject solicitation calendar cards.

3. Film magazine exposure and chemical development log.

4. Questionnaires completed by the students.

5. Dice-data sheets filled during the testing sessions.

6. Name-display cards for identifying subjects on the film.

7. Subject serial-number log for the next-above three items, as maintained by M.

8. Detailed protocols for handling subjects.

9. Audio tapes used for instructing subjects.

10. Motion-picture film of falling dice (6,000 feet).

11. Adding-machine tapes (1,500) used in data reduction.

12. IBM punch cards (7,000 for each of two film readings).

13. Data-reduction protocols and eight reduction-procedure logs.

14. Printouts of the statistical analyses herein reported.

15. The apparatus shown in Figure 4.

All of the above were on hand at the time of the completion of this report.[4]

DATA REDUCTION

Film Reading

The task of transcribing from photofilm the face number and the X- and Y-coordinates of 42,000 dice was not lightly undertaken. Three considerations dictated the procedure that was followed:

– In its final form the record had to be machine-readable and so nearly error-free as to eliminate all doubt as to its representational sufficiency.

---

[4] M formally retired from employment at the University of Pittsburgh at the mandatory age of 70 in June, 1984, and his program will terminate in the near future. For several years he has searched unsuccessfully for an archival institution to which these and similar materials gathered over 40 years might be consigned for evaluation.

- The die positions were to be read to the nearest whole centimeter—within two-tenths of a centimeter. This meant that film-reading uncertainties could not be eliminated but must be held below an acceptable level.

- The work had to be divisible so that it could be shared with assistants but the procedure had to be one in which the responsibility for final accuracy rested with M alone.

These requirements were met by parallel, independent readings of the film in which all correcting was formalized and tightly controlled.

The fifty-foot rolls of exposed and developed 16-mm film were given a preliminary inspection on a motion-picture editor and spliced in pairs to fill 100-foot reels (usually holding eight subjects), each of which was then processed as a unit.

The film reading was done between July, 1962, and November, 1965, under the supervision of M on an Eastman Recordak 310 microfilm viewer. The film readers, who also assisted in other stages of data reduction, were N. J. Axelrod, W. S. Brown, and M. C. Nock. Before starting, each reader was trained on a miniature replica of the die-table grid until he or she could give at a glance the coordinates of any of the 8,000 centimeter squares.[5]

The face number of each die of a release and its coordinates to the nearest centimeter were read onto an adding-machine printed tape from the last or next-to-last motion-picture film frame, as follows. Each tape held the 14 releases of one subject. For each release, the first tape line showed the person reading the film, the subject's serial number, the release number, and minutes from the Figure 4 time-of-day clock. The adding machine was cleared, after which a die face and its two-digit X- and Y-coordinates were entered on one line with a space between each. This entering was done for the six dice, and then the total was printed (as an aid to finding errors later). After 14 releases, the 32-inch tape was torn off, initialed, and dated. Dice were read in the order of increasing

---

[5] N. J. Axelrod, a student at Swarthmore College, later received a PhD in biology at Harvard. She is now a faculty member at the University of Connecticut Medical School. W. S. Brown, an undergraduate in electrical engineering, subsequently received a PhD at M.I.T. He is now on the staff of the Charles Stark Draper Laboratory. Mrs. M. C. Nock, a retired bookkeeper, has since died.

Y-coordinates. Unreadable faces and positions were entered as nines.

The film readers were not told the targeting procedure and could not infer it because the typewritten instructions displayed to the subject were not resolvable on the motion-picture film. Thus, the readers were blind (as well as indifferent) to the subject's wishing task.

Each subject's film record was read twice using different readers. The resulting tapes were designated *A* and *B*. Another set of tapes, labelled *S* was transcribed from the subject's hand-written records. These had only *Y*-coordinates and no practice releases. They played only an ancillary role in the film transcribing.

Adding-machine tapes *A* and *B* were compared visually. Discrepancies fell into several classes, which were processed differently: (a) Missing dice data. (b) Dice transcribed in nonstandard sequence. (c) Die-face reading errors. (d) Coordinate (and clock) reading errors recognized by a discrepancy of two or more centimeters (or minutes). (e) Coordinate reading differences of one centimeter (or one, clock minute) representing borderline cases or careless reading.

Missing dice were simulated by M according to protocol and entered in a "Data Simulation Log." The number of die faces simulated was 58, and the number of dice (face and position) simulated was 42.

Face-reading discrepancies were resolved by a majority vote using the *S* tape or by film rereading. To resolve coordinate discrepancies, the entire release was re-read from the film and the resulting new tape fragment was clipped by M to tape *A* or *B* over the erroneous release and later pasted to it. Corrected adding-machine tapes were formally recompared.

There were 22 steps to the tape-comparing and correcting process. As these were carried out for each film reel of subjects, each step was marked on a "Tape Correction Log" to show the date and the person doing it. All needed re-readings were listed. All crucial steps were done by M.

With 16-mm dice lying on a 10-mm grid, it was possible under ideal conditions to determine at a glance for more than 90% of cases which centimeter cell held the center of gravity of the die. In the data after final processing, the one-centimeter coordinate differences between *A* and *B* readings were less than 15% of all readings. These unbiased errors disappeared in the averaging, adding negligibly to the variance.

Along with the "Tape Correction Log," each reader kept a journal of "Film Reading Notes," giving a list of all noticed film irregularities (such as a student's hand or head visible over the measurement grid).

Some 37 subjects were discarded by M according to formal criteria and were logged in a "Data Log by Serial Number." Reasons for discard: Mechanical failure (19). Subject error (15). Excess subjects (3).

The foregoing process created three sets of 500 adding-machine tapes. In sets *A* and *B*, which had been read from the film, most of the discrepancies had been found and corrected. The rest would be caught in the steps to follow.

Transcription

An IBM 026 card punch was rented and the two sets of adding-machine tapes were punched into two decks, labelled *A* and *B*, each with one card per dice release.

First, however, beginning in May, 1963, the subjects' earlier answers to questions about imagery and luck were scored, verified, and entered by M onto the 3x5-inch camera display cards, along with a symbol showing whether the experimenter had remained or departed during the testing session. This information, together with that entered earlier on this card, determined eight "grouping variables", which were key-punched twice, making two temporary master decks, each of which had one card per subject.

After comparison and correction of matching cards, their information was auto-punched into detail (release) cards while key punching from the adding-machine tapes the release number, release time of day, and the face and *X*- and *Y*-coordinates for six dice.

At this point, W. S. Brown, who was familiar with computers, convinced M that, rather than carry 14,000 cards to a batch station a few hundred at a time and wait a day for turn-around, it would be faster for him to lay one card from deck *A* on top of the corresponding card from deck *B* on a light table and visually detect all die-face differences and all clock and *X*- and *Y*-coordinate differences greater than one. All such discovered differences were logged, the sources of error found, and the errors corrected—by formal re-reading of the photographic film where appropriate.

By January, 1966, the data were safely stored on punchcards in nearly final form. Thereafter, other activities of greater apparent importance forced a delay until advances in digital computing had reduced the task of statistical analysis to an acceptable size and M had received from his son, Tron, many hours of tutoring on the intricacies of computer use.

In 1982, M and C transferred the data from punchcard to magnetic tape and completed the reduction process. All fields of decks *A* and *B* were compared by a program allowing differences of one minute of time and one centimeter in *X*- and *Y*-coordinates. All other differences were corrected, going back, where necessary, to the photographic film. The correction log shows that there were five film-reading errors and eight card-punching errors.

The analysis of the data of this experiment was begun in July, 1984. The only subsequently discovered error was one die face recorded in both card decks as a "9", which meant that an unreadable die face, requiring simulation, had been missed 20 years earlier.

ANALYTICAL METHOD

Statistical Structure

As described earlier, in this experiment, over a period of 46 months, each of 500 subjects had one fifty-minute test session. All subjects used the same wishing pattern in the first half session. This pattern was reversed at the session midpoint. In each half (H) of the session (S) the subject made six releases (R) of six dice (D).

For each die the data recorded were face number and the *X* and *Y* coordinates to the nearest whole centimeter. The *X* coordinates (and the release clock times) were reduced but not used in the analysis. Each subject was classified according to eight grouping variables (G), each of which had two or three levels.

Of the four independent or treatment variables, S, H, R, and D, H and R were fixed, S and D were random, and S, H, and R were crossed. D was nested in cells, and S in G. Ignoring G, all cells of the data contained the same number of *Y*-coordinates. This experimental structure lends itself to univariate, factorial analysis of variance (ANOVA) in which one can calculate main effects and interactions for all independent variables under the assumption of linear additivity.

Our analyses were carried out with BMDP (1982) Statistical Software on a Digital Equipment Corporation 1099 computer. Most of the work was done with BMDP programs 2V and 8V.

Use of Die-Face Information

Because each subject's purpose was to separate faces 1, 2, and 3 from 4, 5, and 6 by sending them to opposite sides of the dice table, some appropriate use of die-face information was required. We chose to create a virtual reversal of the subject's wishing for the 4, 5, and 6 faces by mathematically reflecting them across a center line on the dice table. To do this, after determining the mean Y position for all dice to be 38.9 cm, we transformed all 4, 5, and 6-face Y coordinates by the equation, $Y' = 78 - Y$. In the subsequent analyses, the transformed and nontransformed dice of each release were lumped together without regard to face. In this way, all psychophysical effects involving the wished-for separation of faces were made evident, and all purely physical effects became self-cancelling.

The dice table was laid out transversely in 80, one-centimeter intervals, numbered from 0 to 79. This placed the geometric midline at 39.5 cm. Some of the ANOVAs were repeated with the transformation, $Y' = 79 - Y$, and the results compared with those transformed by $Y' = 78 - Y$ to confirm the insensitivity of the outcome to the line where the data were reflected. (See later.)

Mathematical Requirements

For these analyses of variance to be correct, the values of the dependent variable must be near-normally distributed and (except for treatment effects) must be statistically independent.

It is evident that six dice tumbling together down a gangway tend to spread out by striking one another and cannot be mathematically independent. Hence, their variance cannot be a correct estimator of the error variance associated with the treatment variables in which we are interested. This is all the more true in the present case because approximately half of the die positions were transformed to give a sign reversal about the grand mean of the data.

In the present experiment about six percent of the dice struck the side walls of the dice table, thereby creating a pronounced non-normality in the distribution of the transverse (Y) coordinates.

There is a simple solution to these normality and independence problems. The mean position of all six dice in one release is a truly independent variable under the chance hypothesis. Moreover, since the individual die positions are approximately normal and roughly independent, we would expect from central limit theory that their mean would be almost exactly normally distributed with a standard deviation that is smaller by the factor SQRT(6).

This can be seen in Figures 7 and 8, the first of which shows the distribution of dice across the table from 0 to 79 cm. Notice how the distribution is piled up at its tails by dice bouncing off the walls. Figure 8 shows the distribution of the release means of the same dice. Analysis confirms that this distribution is close to normal.

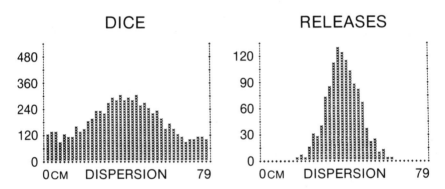

Figure 7 (On the left). Frequency distribution of the dice across the playing table as they fell, i.e., without transformation (the first 100 subjects).

Figure 8 (On the right). Frequency distribution of the averages over the six dice in one release (the same 100 subjects). Before averaging, the positions of die faces 4, 5, and 6 were transformed by the equation $Y' = 78 - Y$. The analyses of this paper are based on such release means.

Idealized ANOVA Effects

To assist interpretation of the ANOVA results, it may be helpful to consider what scoring patterns could give rise to pure H, R, and H x R effects in the present experiment.

Of the three patterns of Figure 9, the topmost shows a uniform response of the dice to the wishing of the subject. Constant deviation to the low-Y side over the first six releases is followed by constant deviation to the high-Y side in the next six. This corresponds to a pure Half-session effect.

In the first half of the middle pattern of the figure, the scoring incline represents a decline in terms of the wished-for effect. This incline repeats in the second half session, yielding an overall Releases effect. A nonchance Releases effect could occur in real data to the extent that the subject failed to reverse his wishing at midsession.

In the bottom pattern there is an incline that reverses in the second half-session in conformity with the subject's wishing. This appears in the analysis as an H x R interaction.

Significant H, R, and H x R effects occurring in real data may reflect these idealized patterns. Figure 2, for example, can be seen by inspection to contain strong H and H x R effects but very little R.

Figure 9. Some pure ANOVA effects illustrated by hypothetical average deviations of resting dice from their expected midline in experimental sessions consisting of six releases of dice while wishing for them to deviate toward the "low" side, followed by six releases wishing for the dice to go "high." (In this illustration die faces are ignored.) The three patterns show, respectively, pure Half-session, pure Releases, and pure Halves-by-Releases effects.

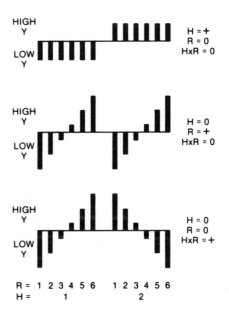

ANALYTICAL FINDINGS

An analysis of variance was applied to the reduced data from the entire experiment to look for data-structure effects involving subjects or sessions (S), half sessions (H), and the six releases (R) within the half session. As previously explained, the reduced-data unit of analysis was the average of the effective transverse positions of the six dice in one release. For die faces 1, 2, and 3, the effective position was the actual Y-coordinate of the die having come to rest. For die faces 4, 5, and 6, however, the effective position, Y', was derived by a mathematical reflection across the grand mean of the experiment, using the equation, $Y' = 78 - Y$. The variation among releases (R main effect) is significant at the level, $p = .0044$. The dependence of releases upon half sessions (H x R interaction) is also significant, with a chance probability of .030. There was no significant half-session (H) effect and no significant subject effects (S, S x H, S x R). These results are shown as Analysis A in Table 1.

Because of our transformation procedure and the care we have taken in handling the data, we believe that these statistically significant effects, if real, must be causally associated with the wishing of the subject or experimenter and not with some obscure, physical artifact. Nevertheless, we thought it would be reassuring to do the same ANOVA without the coordinate transformation for die faces 4, 5, and 6. For this analysis all psychophysical effects associated with the wished-for separation of faces 1, 2, and 3 from 4, 5, and 6 should self-cancel and give chance results. The result is shown as Analysis B in Table 1. Analyses C and D will be discussed later.

Encouraged by these probabilities, we next investigated the eight grouping variables which had been determined for each subject's data at the time of his testing session. The first grouping variable recorded the sex of the subject. The next four variables came from the subject's answers to a self-describing questionnaire. The sixth grouping variable registered two slightly different wordings of the experimental instructions to the subject. The last two grouping variables identified the experimenters, Anderson (A) or McConnell (M), and told whether that experimenter remained in the presence of the subject during the testing session.

Analyses of variance were applied to the data of all 500 sub-

Table 1

Analysis of variance of the experiment as a whole. Five-hundred student subjects were tested, one at a time, in 50-minute sessions in which six, magnetically released dice tumbled in the horizontal X-direction and were wished to move laterally in the horizontal Y-direction. For six releases (R) in the first half (H) of each session, die faces 1, 2, and 3 were wished to move to the side of the table with low-Y coordinates, while 4, 5, and 6 faces were wished to the high-Y side. In the second half session the wished-for directions were reversed. The unit of analysis was the mean Y of the six dice in one release. In Analysis A, all dice with faces 4, 5, and 6 were mathematically transformed across the grand mean of the experiment by the equation $Y' = 78 - Y$. Analysis B uses the same data as A but without the transformation of coordinates necessary to explicate the wishing. Analysis C is an independent replication of Analysis A, starting with data independently re-read from the motion-picture film of the falling dice. In Analysis D, die faces 4, 5, and 6, were transformed about the midline of the playing table by the equation $Y' = 79 - Y$, and gave results close to Analysis A despite the half-centimeter shift of the reflection line.

EFFECTS	d.f.	ERROR TERM	ANALYSIS A (Y'=78–Y) MEAN SQUARE (cm**2)	p	ANALYSIS B (Y'=Y) MEAN SQUARE (cm**2)	p	ANALYSIS C (Y'=78–Y) MEAN SQUARE (cm**2)	p	ANALYSIS D (Y'=79–Y) MEAN SQUARE (cm**2)	p
SUBJECTS	499		64.7		63.3		64.7		65.0	
HALVES OF SESSIONS	1	SxH	79.2	.28	0.3	.94	77.2	.29	73.8	.30
RELEASES OF DICE	5	SxR	225.2	.0044	108.7	.071	226.6	.0042	220.5	.0051
S x H	499		68.6		59.5		68.6		68.4	
S x R	2495		65.8		53.5		65.8		65.9	
H x R	5	SxHxR	167.7	.030	66.7	.31	166.6	.031	168.8	.029
S x H x R	2495		67.5		55.7		67.4		67.6	

jects, using these grouping variables one at a time and thereby adding a fourth independent variable to the previous three (S, H, R). The results were unexpected but clear. No new extra-chance effects were found for any of the first six grouping variables. For the last two variables, which recorded the experimenter's identity (E) and his presence or absence (P), there were significant interactions, H x R x E and R x P, with respective chance probabilities .014 and .030. (See Table 2.)

These interactions suggested that we were dealing with three statistically different groups of data. There were three groups instead of four because experimenter Anderson had only eight subjects who requested that she be present during the test session. This was too few to treat as an independent group, given the small absolute magnitude of our effects.

We divided the remaining 492 subjects into the three groups, McConnell-present, McConnell-absent, and Anderson-absent. We applied ANOVAs to these groups, separately, and in two combinations, McConnell-present vs. McConnell-absent, and McConnell-absent vs. Anderson-absent. Again, we found significant effects as shown in Table 2.

The McConnell-present group, which amounts to less than 20% of the subjects, has an R-effect probability of less than one in one thousand, but nothing of interest for the H x R interaction. The McConnell-absent group reaches $p = .04$ for the R effect and $p = .006$ for H x R. Between these two groups, there is an R x P interaction with $p = .007$. The Anderson-absent group does not reach significance by itself, but has an H x R x E interaction with the McConnell-absent group for which $p = .014$.

Again, we thought it would be interesting to repeat these ANOVAs while neglecting the fact that the subjects were asked to separate faces 1, 2, and 3 from 4, 5, and 6. The resulting probabilities are given in parentheses in Table 2.

From our analyses we tentatively conclude that the presence or absence of the experimenter affected the result of the experiment and that the identity of the experimenters influenced the statistical outcome even when they were not present.

VERIFICATION

Are these results believable? Although we had carried out the overall ANOVA a second time, intentionally omitting the necessary die-face-based transformation, and had seen the previous probability significance disappear, we still wanted to know: Could our extra-chance results have been caused by a mistake in our assumptions or in handling the data?

For this univariate ANOVA to be valid, three conditions must be met: The values of the dependent variable must be mutually independent (under the chance hypothesis) and near-normally distributed, and the variance of the groups being compared must be homogeneous. We have already discussed the first two con-

Table 2

Selected results from twelve ANOVAs showing effects obtained by two different experimenters who were present or absent while their subjects wished for the lateral deflection of falling dice. H: half sessions. R: six releases (of six dice) per half session. E: experimenter. P: presence or absence of the experimenter during the testing session. Chance probabilities are shown only for those effects, R and H x R, that were statistically significant in Analysis A of Table 1. For comparison, beneath each of these probabilities will be found in parentheses the Analysis-B probabilities obtained when the data were processed without acknowledging that the subject was asked to wish oppositely for faces 1, 2, 3, and for 4, 5, 6, i.e., without transformation of coordinates. The comparison provides compelling evidence that the statistically significant effects are psychological rather than physical in origin.

EXPERIMENTER	PRESENT	INTERACTION (P)	ABSENT	TOTAL
M.L.A.	8 SUBJECTS (Too Few)	(Too Few)	108 SUBJECTS p(R) = .22 (.27) p(HxR) = .064 (.89)	116 SUBJECTS p(R) = .23 (.25) p(HxR) = .085 (.88)
INTERACTION (E)	(Too Few)		400 SUBJECTS p(RxE) = .12 (.28) p(HxRxE) = .014 (.99)	500 SUBJECTS p(RxE) = .31 (.42) p(HxRxE) = .014 (.99)
R.A.M.	92 SUBJECTS p(R) = .0008 (.37) p(HxR) = .56 (.40)	384 SUBJECTS p(RxP) = .0070 (.34) p(HxRxP) = .74 (.79)	292 SUBJECTS p(R) = .040 (.11) p(HxR) = .0060 (.86)	384 SUBJECTS p(R) = .0063 (.12) p(HxR) = .0036 (.44)
TOTAL	100 SUBJECTS p(R) = .0011 (.36) p(HxR) = .51 (.23)	500 SUBJECTS p(RxP) = .030 (.53) p(HxRxP) = .53 (.54)	400 SUBJECTS p(R) = .082 (.11) p(HxR) = .032 (.72)	500 SUBJECTS p(R) = .0044 (.071) p(HxR) = .030 (.31)

ditions. To test homogeneity, we compared the standard deviations of the 12 releases of the testing session. These values were found to be: 8.0, 8.2, 8.0, 8.3, 8.3, 8.3, 8.1, 8.0, 8.7, 8.3, 7.6, and 8.0 cm. By Bartlett's test, the chance probability of so great a variation is 0.4.

As described earlier, the data were twice, independently read from the motion picture of the falling dice, yielding two sets of IBM punchcards. The second set of data was now called up from magnetic tape and given an ANOVA similar to that used to obtain the results of Analysis A in Table 1, but with BMDP Program 8V instead of 2V. These two, independent statistical programs accept a different range of problems and give different supplementary outputs, but both were suitable for our present purpose. When we compared the output from these two ANOVAs, each using an independent reading of the original photographic record of the dice, we found that the mean die positions for each of the 12 releases of the experimental session agreed to within 0.01 cm, which is one part in 4000. This is consistent with the several-millimeter uncertainty in reading a die position from the photographic film. The verifying ANOVA is presented in Table 1 as Analysis C.

A more precise agreement could not have been hoped for, but one final doubt remained. These mutually confirming computations took place inside a computer where they could not be watched! To meet the supposition that we might have misused both computer programs in some obscure way, we chose a small part of the raw data as they came from the magnetic tape and carried out an analysis by hand calculator. In this way we could start with statistical equations and watch the results grow in a step-by-step fashion. We chose the McConnell-present group, which has 92 subjects and yields an R-effect probability of .0008. By hand calculator we obtained R and S x R mean-square values that agreed with the computer values to four significant figures and gave, of course, the same probability figure, namely, .0008. We therefore conclude that our ANOVA calculations represent the behavior of the dice to a precision greater than necessary for our statistical purposes.

Although from theoretical considerations we believed that our ANOVAs would be insensitive to the data-reflection line for die faces 4, 5, and 6, we thought it would be worthwhile to confirm this empirically. In Analysis D of Table 1 we present the result of changing the reflection line by 0.5 cm from the grand mean of the data to the geometrical centerline of the dice table.

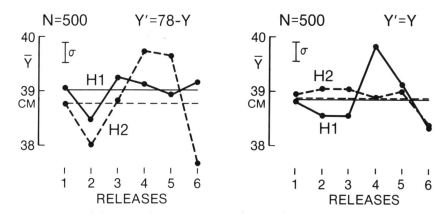

Figure 10 (On the left). Mean transverse *effective* coordinates of the final resting positions of 16-mm wooden dice, magnetically released to the table top in the present experiment. These curves show the data from 500 subjects, each of whom made six formal releases per half session using six dice per release. Thus, each point on the curves represents 3000 die positions. The subjects were asked to wish for the dice to separate laterally according to whether the faces would be in the group 1, 2, and 3, or the group 4, 5, and 6. In the first half session (solid line) subjects wished for 1, 2, and 3 faces to go to the low-Y side and for faces 4, 5, and 6 to go to the high side. In the second half session (dashed line) the direction of wishing was reversed. To cancel physical effects, the Y-coordinates corresponding to the 4, 5, and 6 faces were transformed by the equation $Y' = 78 - Y$ as the first step in data analysis. The points of these curves yield significant ANOVA probabilities for Releases ($p = .0044$) and Halves-by-Releases ($p = .030$) as shown in Analysis A of Table 1. The vertical line is one standard deviation for any plotted point. The locations of the points on this graph were found to be the same within 0.01 cm when the 36,000 dice were independently re-read and processed from the motion-picture film that recorded their fall.

Figure 11 (On the right). Mean, transverse, *actual* coordinates of the final resting positions of dice. These curves are based on the data used in Figure 10, but were analyzed without transforming the coordinates of the dice showing faces 4, 5, and 6. This figure exhibits the basis for Analysis B of Table 1.

DIE-PLACEMENT PATTERNS

Our analyses of variance indicate extrachance variations in the average die positions of the 12 releases of the experimental session. To discover the pattern of those variations, we must go to the data themselves. In Figure 10 we have plotted, for all 500 subjects combined, the average effective die position for each of the six releases (R1 to R6) in the first and second half-sessions (H1 and H2). We have used the format of Figure 2, which showed the Haakon Forwald pattern that we had hoped to obtain.

For comparison, we show in Figure 11 the nonsignificant pattern that results if the data analysis is done without taking into account that the subjects were asked to separate faces 1, 2, and 3 from 4, 5, and 6, that is, without coordinate transformation.

In Figures 12, 13, and 14, we break up the data to show the scoring patterns for the groups McConnell-present, McConnell-absent, and Anderson-absent.

There is no evident relationship between the Forwald pattern of Figure 2 and our patterns, and we are unable to explain our curves in terms of subject wishing.

We have carried out our experiment under rigid controls that exclude ordinary physical causation of the patterns we obtained and that appear to leave only two alternative explanations: Either our patterns were psychophysically caused in the sense intended by the term "psychokinesis," or they are of chance origin.

Is it reasonable to dismiss this experiment as an example of the vagaries of chance? To help answer this question, we might consider the 492 subjects that fall into the three groups, McConnell-present, McConnell-absent, and Anderson-absent and look at their six independent probabilities for the R and H x R effects as shown in Table 2. When combined by Fisher's method, these give a resultant probability of one in 100,000. This is small enough to allow a correction for selection of the analysis and still leave us embarrassed by the supposition that the experimenters were simply lucky when they asked 500 students to spend an hour of their time releasing dice.

In the light of the total history of psychokinetic research, we think it is probable that we have observed a real psychophysical effect, caused by, but not conforming to, the wishing of the agents. By further study we hope to gain some understanding of the data we have recorded in this experiment. We suspect that,

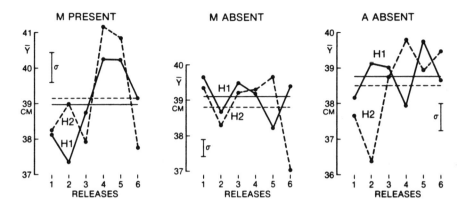

Figure 12 (Left). **Mean die positions of those 92 subjects who asked experimenter M to remain during the testing session. Solid line: First half session. Dashed line: Second half session, with wishing reversed. Probabilities from Table 2: *p*(R) = .0008; *p*(H x R) = .56.**

Figure 13 (Center). **Mean die positions for those 292 subjects who preferred that experimenter M withdraw during the testing session. Solid line: First half session. Dashed line: Second half session, with wishing reversed. Probabilities from Table 2: *p*(R) = .040; *p*(H x R) = .0060. Between Figures 12 and 13, *p*(R x P) = .0070 and *p*(H x R x P) = .74.**

Figure 14 (Right). **Mean die positions for those 108 subjects who preferred that experimenter A withdraw during the testing session. Solid line: First half session. Dashed line: Second half session, with wishing reversed. Probabilities from Table 2: *p*(R) = .22; *p*(H x R) = .064. Between Figures 13 and 14, *p*(R x E) = .12 and *p*(H x R x E) = .014.**

hidden within our erratic patterns, lies the answer to the skeptic's time-worn question: "If psychokinesis is real, why isn't it used successfully in gambling casinos?"

REFERENCES

Anderson, M.L., & McConnell, R.A. (1961). Fantasy testing for ESP in a fourth and fifth grade class. *Journal of Psychology, 52*, 491–503.

Forwald, H. (1969). *Mind, Matter, and Gravitation: A Theoretical and Experimental Study*. New York: Parapsychology Foundation.

McConnell, R.A. (1983). *An Introduction to Parapsychology in the Context of Science*. Pittsburgh, Pennsylvania: Author.

McConnell, R.A., & Clark, T.K. (1983). Progressive organization and ambivalence within the psychokinetic testing session. Chap. 5 in R.A. McConnell (Ed.), *Parapsychology and Self-Deception in Science*. Pittsburgh, Pennsylvania: Editor.

McConnell, R.A., & Forwald, H. (1967). Psychokinetic placement: II. A factorial study of successful and unsuccessful series. *Journal of Parapsychology, 31*(3), 198–213.

McConnell, R.A., & Forwald, H. (1968). Psychokinetic placement: III. Cube-releasing devices. *Journal of Parapsychology, 32*(1), 9–38.

McConnell, R.A., Snowdon, R.J., & Powell, K.F. (1955). Wishing with dice. *Journal of Experimental Psychology, 50*(4), 269–275.

Reeves, M.P. & Rhine, J.B. (1943). The PK effect: II. A study in declines. *Journal of Parapsychology, 7*(2), 76–93.

Rhine, J.B., & Humphrey, B.M. (1944a). The PK effect: Special evidence from hit patterns: I. Quarter-distributions of the (PK) page. *Journal of Parapsychology, 8*(1), 18–63.

Rhine, J.B., & Humphrey, B.M. (1944b). PK tests with six, twelve, and twenty-four dice per throw. *Journal of Parapsychology, 8*(2), 139–157.

Rhine, L.E., & Rhine, J.B. (1943). The psychokinetic effect: I. The first experiment. *Journal of Parapsychology, 7*(1), 20–43.

5

EXCURSIONS FROM THE LABORATORY

RELATIONS WITH THE PUBLIC

Throughout my career in parapsychology I have avoided news-media publicity and the occasions that generate it. In the first years after World War II, I gave perhaps a dozen parapsychological lectures to physicists and psychologists and to community discussion groups with intellectual aspirations. These talks gave me firsthand familiarity with the attitudes of intelligent people who, for the most part, did not believe in psychic phenomena.

Later, I gave no lectures except to scientists assembled for a larger program devoted to parapsychology. Whatever need there might be for popular lectures could be better met, I thought, by other parapsychologists for whom entertaining the public was a more rewarding experience.

My avoidance of contact with the public at large did not mean that I isolated myself from intellectual leaders or from people who experience spontaneous psi.

As to the former, as I have indicated in this and previous books, I have communicated extensively with prominent scientists and laymen. My purpose, as a rule, was not so much to change, as to sample, leadership opinion.

My contacts with psychic people, on the other hand, were usually not of my own arranging. No matter how circumspectly one goes about it, when one does research in parapsychology at an urban university, news of that fact trickles off campus through students, and one begins to receive telephone calls from outsiders who are having problems that they think may involve psychic phenomena.

Eventually, through no initiative on my part, our university telephone operators learned to channel "parapsychological" calls to me. I have also received referrals routinely from our Psychology Department secretaries and, occasionally, from the University's associated psychiatric institute.

I was initially not well prepared for these inquiries from lay people. Training to be a physicist does not leave much time for the soft sciences. When I discovered from the literature that at least some psychic phenomena are real and I decided to make understanding them my life work, I knew that I must study, not only the literature of parapsychology, but also abnormal psychology in depth and the whole of psychology in summary. Since then I have read enough books and spent enough hours unavoidably counseling the mentally unsettled to give me the outlook, if not the qualifications, of a clinical psychologist.

In thirty-nine years, with a willing ear against the telephone, I have heard many tales. Sometimes the conversations lasted more than an hour. Collectively, they represent a substantial expenditure of time of a kind scientists do not usually incur. I listened so that I might learn and also because many of these callers were asking for help.

I was soon able to recognize by various tell-tale signs the obviously psychotic. These I advised as gently as possible to seek help from a psychotherapist.

Many callers gave no evidence of mental illness but needed help in placing their possibly psychic experiences in an acceptable conceptual framework. In the simplest cases I was able to explain that the strange things that had happened were probably physically ordinary events. However, a substantial fraction of those who called seemed to be experiencing genuine spontaneous psi.

Although I kept an address file of persons who might be useful as subjects in later experiments, and in a few cases arranged for an interview in my office, I made no attempt to systematically collect and organize the stories I heard. It was rarely possible to assign a high probability to the factuality of a case.

Nevertheless, over the years, certain patterns and ideas emerged that made sense when measured against what I knew from the scientific literature of parapsychology. I have selected several cases and ideas from my nonlaboratory experience that may be of interest to others.

PSYCHOTHERAPY WITH PSYCHIC PEOPLE

Traditionally, psychic persons are thought of as those who "foretell the future." Some day, this may prove to be one of the less important manifestations of psi. Faith healing, political leadership, salesmanship, and especially teaching may possibly utilize interpersonal psychic relationships. Given what we know about the widespread, although usually trivial, manifestation of psi, it would not be surprising if it occasionally supplemented ordinary human communication in a hidden fashion.

It also seems likely that psychic endowment is sometimes a major determinant of individual personality. For example, through personal observation I have been convinced that there are people who are inherently good. These saintly persons are recognized and respected by their peers. They have a gentling effect upon animals and infants that can be uncanny to watch. I hazard the guess that the influence of such persons is a manifestation of psi and that eventually we shall know in a scientific sense that the nonuniform distribution of goodness is a characteristic of humans. Theologians say that some persons are given more spiritual grace than others, meaning, among other things, a proclivity toward benign and loving behavior. It seems more likely that such grace, or the lack thereof, is, indeed, "given by the Lord"—but in the form of genetic endowment. I say "lack thereof," because it would follow from symmetry as well as from real-life experience, that there are naturally evil persons—persons with a capacity to be so morally bad as to be beyond social redemption.

Those who telephone for parapsychological advice present a variety of problems. One of the more unusual was from a young woman who asked: "What should I believe—what my psychotherapist tells me or my own experience?"

She had been recently divorced for the second time. Because she had been physically abused by both husbands, she went to a psychotherapist to learn whether she was somehow at fault. She had several helpful sessions, but when she revealed that throughout her life she had had disturbing premonitions that later came true, her counselor told her that these were imaginary experiences created to gain attention. Not surprisingly, this accusation caused anxiety and impaired the patient's confidence in the therapist.

I suggested several books that might help her to answer her question about ESP.

The therapist's rejection of this young woman's psychic ability reminded me of the following letter from an adolescent male whose return address was a YMCA "youth shelter." Except for periods and commas added by the editor, and italics substituted for underlines, the letter is reproduced as received.

Dear Dr. R. A. McConnell

I have some things I have to ask you about, and I realy need your *help*. I am 16 years old. Sometimes when I'm upset with someone or I am feeling realy good, I get PK and then some other things happen to me. "Say if someone I know will hurt themself," I can feel it before it every happen, and if I get mad at my mother sometime, I look at things and they *move* or *brake*! Is there any way I could have help *please*! Thank you.

J.T.

This letter required a response; so I did two things. First, I telephoned the youth shelter to learn if the boy lived there. I was referred to his caseworker at the courthouse. She confirmed my surmise that he had an emotional problem, and she added that, in all probability, his letter to me was just one more of his many attempts to manipulate people.

I have no doubt that all delinquent youths strain caseworkers' patience, and it is quite possible that this boy had imagined his psychokinetic ability. All that I could immediately conclude was that this caseworker's attitude would not be helpful to any delinquent or emotionally disturbed adolescent who was, incidentally, psychic.

I asked the social worker whether she thought it would be useful for me to send the boy a gift copy of my book, *Encounters with Parapsychology*, which is a nontechnical collection of essays by people who had encountered parapsychology in their professional careers and had not turned away from it. With her permission, I sent the book. Later correspondence from the boy tended to confirm my impression that he was being honest with me.

The second thing I did in this case was to ask our psychology department chairman whether he knew of any "closet parapsychologists" among his clinical professors. He said he was sure there were none, but he offered to inquire at our university's psychiatric institute and around the city generally. He called back two days later to report failure, but he offered to give the names of several therapists who he knew would be "gentle and accepting of an adolescent's beliefs."

I am not able to report how this case ended, but it did set me thinking. If a person in need of psychological counseling claims to be psychic, he or she needs a therapist who knows the parapsychological literature and can accept the possibility of a psychic factor in a patient's illness.

From these and other experiences I have been convinced that

psychotherapists and social caseworkers have an unmet need for parapsychological information. Conversely, we parapsychologists are missing an opportunity to gain professional support for our field from these potential allies.

THE CLERGY AND THE FAITHFUL

Religion is a natural haven for two groups: mystics and psychics. It is a reasonable assumption that, in one sense or another, the strength of organized religions is intimately dependent upon these groups.

Everyone has some psychic ability, but only a minority experience the more dramatic manifestations of psi. How large is that minority? At one time, parapsychologists thought that "gifted psychics" were rare. Certainly they are rare in the laboratory. I am inclined to believe, however, that perhaps five percent of the general population has psychic experiences of such frequency and force as to demonstrably affect the individual's life style.[1]

Almost all of us experience mystical exaltation at some times in our lives. It may be a singular and overwhelming event, as it was for St. Paul. For most it may be nothing more than occasions of intense, emotional wellbeing, coupled with a sense of competence and harmony. Whether they be rare or frequent, these are perceived as holy events.

Psychic experience, on the other hand, may be an entirely mundane expression of extrasensory perception or psychokinesis. For the individual, it may have practical and philosophic implications, but it is not usually reported as an uplifting occurrence.

It may be that mystical and psychic experiences are, respectively, subjective and objective manifestations of the same psychological domain. Both kinds of experience tend to have occurred together in canonized saints. For most persons, however, they are distinct happenings. When we refer to "psychics" and "mystics", we mean two different groups of people who emphasize one or the other class of phenomena. For either group, if the experiences are sufficiently dramatic or frequent, they must be dealt with by the individuals who have them.

---

[1] For some related figures, see J. Palmer (1979): "A community mail survey of psychic experiences." *Journal of the American Society for Psychical Research.*, *73*, 221–251.

The only place in our culture where such psychological experiences are accepted with more or less approval is in organized religion. I suspect that the core strength of institutional religion lies in those clergy and lay followers who are drawn in, at least initially, by a need to resolve incongruities between private experience and our materialist culture.

A parapsychologist looking for psi should expect clergymen and lay adherents to conventional sects to be reticent about their psychic experiences. For them, everything is already explained. They have tamed and tethered the psychic monster. Why should they look for trouble in an outside world that denies experiences they know to be real and that they may treasure as a gift from God?

This line of reasoning suggests that there may be more, gifted psychics than is commonly believed. I would expect this to be true even among scientists, despite the likelihood that excellence at symbol manipulation correlates negatively with spontaneous psychic experience. When a scientist finds himself to be strongly psychic, he joins a church and compartmentalizes his thinking. Unless he wants to risk investigating parapsychology, what other choice does he have? I have had occasional hints from scientists in unrelated fields that they accept psychic phenomena as a part of their religion.

Perhaps more significant are the implications of these speculations for church leadership. Some unknown fraction of the clergy may have taken to the cloth in an attempt to accommodate emotionally their exceptional psychic powers. Of these, some may have lacked the mystical or humanistic urges that could sustain them in the arduous task of sharing the burdens of others.

Because psychic phenomena are mundane in their expression and not intrinsically rewarding, some clergy whose original "calling" stemmed from psychic ability could become disillusioned and be tempted to use their psychic endowment to control others in an immoral fashion. From stories of psychic abuse that have come to me, I am inclined to believe that a history of psychic experiences is not, by itself, a favorable sign in a candidate for the ministry.

6

UNINTENDED PSYCHOKINESIS

In the parapsychological literature there are cases where the isolated sudden motion or breakage of objects was thought to be of psychokinetic origin even though not associated with the conscious wishing of an agent. There are, of course, many reported poltergeist cases in which the repeated toppling or flying of objects seemed to originate by psychokinesis (PK) from a single agent without his conscious intention.

Laboratory psychokinesis, on the other hand, has ordinarily been defined as the direct response of a physical system in accordance with the expressed wish of an agent. Formerly, it was supposed that, if the desired experimental effect or some simple variant thereof did not happen, psychokinesis had not occurred and the experiment was a failure.

In chapter 4 we present strong experimental evidence that an agent can affect a physical system through a causal chain so complex that the system response may be impossible to recognize as "wished for" and may, instead, be misconstrued as normal physical fluctuation.

We suspect that the concealed results we obtained are typical of the everyday expression of psychokinesis by ordinary persons who have no special psychic gift or training. This should lend interest to our work for skeptics who are puzzled by the variability of psi.

Psychokinesis is probably always acting when people (including scientists) observe physical systems, but usually it is obscured by motivational confusion. Sometimes, however, for reasons unknown it may become temporarily apparent. There are well-documented instances in physics where a new phenomenon was observed for a period of time by one or more scientists and then disappeared. Psychokinesis provides a possible explanation for such occurrences.

Nonrepeatability is expected more often in psychology than in physics. Still, it is surprising that, in psychology, replications of experimental findings by other laboratories are rare,[1] appearing in probably less than one percent of cases (Bozarth & Roberts, 1972; Smith, 1970; Sterling, 1959).[2]

NEAL MILLER'S RATS

If, as sometimes happens, a psychological experiment is widely regarded as having important theoretical implications, replication may be attempted and may fail. An interesting case of this kind involved Professor Neal Miller of Rockefeller University, a member of the National Academy of Sciences and past president of the American Psychological Association.

In the period 1967-1969, Miller, then at Yale University, published with others a series of ten studies in which, by operant conditioning using both reward and punishment, rats paralyzed by curare were taught to control certain autonomic functions (DiCara & Miller, 1968a, 1968b, 1968c, 1968d, 1968e, 1969a, 1969b; Miller & Banuazizi, 1968; Miller & DiCara, 1967, 1968). Most of these studies were significant at the $p = .001$ level, and in all cases the effect could be plainly seen by inspection of the plotted data. In most studies, heart rate was the dependent variable. In one experiment of exceptional interest, rats were taught to blush in one ear relative to the other (DiCara & Miller, 1968b).

Nine of these experiments were carried out by Leo DiCara under Miller. Eventually, DiCara moved on to distinction elsewhere. His successor with Miller, Barry Dworkin, was unable to repeat DiCara's work (Miller & Dworkin, 1974; Dworkin & Miller, 1977).

Operant conditioning of heart-rate control in curarized rats has been independently observed by others under conditions ostensibly comparable to those of DiCara (Banuazizi, 1972; Cabanac & Serres, 1976; Fields, 1970; Hothersall & Brener, 1969; Slaughter, Hahn, & Rinaldi, 1970; Trowill, 1967; Yagi & Hirai, 1975). In some cases, however, after initial success, experimenters found

---

[1] This statement does not apply to parapsychology, where every major experimental discovery is repeated in different laboratories and many times before it is fully accepted. See, for example, Radin, May, and Thomson (1985). The abstract of this paper appears as an appendix to chapter 12.

[2] All references are at the end of the chapter.

they were unable to repeat their results (Brener, Eissenberg, & Middaugh, 1974, p. 264; L. E. Roberts, 1978, pp. 252–267). Moreover, in reviewing DiCara's work, Dworkin found a statistically significant temporal decline over three years to 25 percent of the originally achieved heart-rate change (Miller & Dworkin, 1974, p. 313). Miller reported (1978, p. 376) that DiCara was later unable to produce the effect at all.

DiCara has since died, and it now seems unlikely that we shall ever know with certainty how he obtained his earlier results. Three explanations seem possible:

- Fraud by DiCara.
- Ordinary uncontrolled variables.
- Uncontrolled parapsychological variables.

Although several factors in the case make fraud a highly implausible explanation, it cannot be totally discounted, but must be weighed against other possibilities.

NIGHT IN THE FOREST

Miller and Dworkin searched desperately for uncontrolled variables that might explain the disappearance of the phenomenon. Many changes of procedure were tried and sometimes these seemed temporarily successful, but always, with further testing, the sought-for learning effect disappeared (Miller & Dworkin, 1974, pp. 314–316). In his discussion of this problem, Miller said (p. 317):

> To make a long story short, we began to feel as though we were wandering at midnight through a haunted forest with strange, unknown things rustling past us in the dark.
> If this story of our difficulties seems somewhat longwinded, I can assure you it is greatly abbreviated. We have explored many possibilities.

Miller's abbreviated account continues for five thousand words. The following excerpts give the flavor:

> Faced with this extraordinary dilemma, I even explored the possibility that we were the victims of some mass hallucination in my laboratory. This does not seem probable because of the number of people involved . . . . (p. 318)
> To illustrate how far we were pushed in trying to find an

explanation, I remembered that there had been an epidemic of bedbugs in the Yale animal room, located near my laboratory. Therefore the rooms and cages were heavily sprayed with a Chlordane and pyrethrin mixture. On the extremely long chance that the wearing off of the Chlordane residue could be responsible for the decline in the effects, I had Dworkin try giving the rats minute injections of it. Larger ones made them sick but did not seem to interact with the curare to affect heart rate or to induce learning . . . . (p. 318)

Our chief rat supplier. . . had changed their shipment [method] from rail to air express, adopted a superior canned food during shipping, and changed to a more absorbent bedding material . . . . They had been deriving their foundation stock by Caesarian operation in absolutely sterile environment . . . . It is conceivable that the wide adoption of such procedures by the rat industry is preventing infant rats from being subjected to the kinds of stress that could be necessary for the development of the capacity for visceral learning . . . .

We have tried subjecting our adult rats to the experience and stress of active avoidance learning. So far, we have not met any marked success along these lines . . . . I am currently trying to habituate rats to increasing periods of severe restraint and also to other sources of stress . . . . (p. 319)

The fact that half a dozen different investigators in my laboratory were able to produce such large and consistent changes by visceral learning makes it seem unlikely that the phenomenon required hairline precision adjustment of any specific parameter [and also unlikely that DiCara achieved his success by fraud —R.A.M.] (p. 321).

Miller's commitment to the validity and implications of the DiCara work was most clearly set forth in a major review in *Science* (Miller, 1969).

THE PERFECTABILITY OF MAN

Why did DiCara's work justify so much attention? Aside from the embarrassment of failure, why did Miller and Dworkin pursue the matter so diligently and why did so many others join the fray?

Psychologists recognize several kinds of learning, of which only two concern us here:

- Pavlovian, or classical, conditioning in which a stimulus will acquire the power to evoke a certain response if that stimulus is given with, or just prior to, another stimulus already capable of producing the response. (When Pavlov rang a bell before presenting food to a dog, the dog soon learned to salivate at the sound of the bell alone.)

— Operant conditioning or instrumental learning in which a subject discovers by a chance response how to gain a reward or avoid punishment and thereafter learns to repeat the response to enjoy the "contingent reinforcement." (B. F. Skinner's "Skinner box" teaches operantly by giving an animal a food pellet after it has pushed a lever at the proper time.)

The human body has two nervous systems, the somatic or voluntary, and the autonomic or unconscious. Somatic nerves (both sensory and motor) relate to the voluntary muscles and otherwise to the outside world. Autonomic nerves (motor only) control digestion, heart beat, and other self-regulating processes.

For a long time it was believed that one could train voluntary muscles only by operant conditioning, and involuntary muscles only by classical conditioning. DiCara's work seemed to show that one can operantly teach the control of autonomic function.

Many illnesses involve autonomic malfunction (e.g., stomach ulcers and heart arrhythmias). If autonomic control could be taught, such illnesses might be cured by behavioral training.

The autonomic and somatic nervous systems are closely intertwined so that, for example, one can increase blood pressure by tensing the abdominal muscles with the epiglottis closed. However, the amount of autonomic control achievable in this way is generally thought to be too small and fleeting to be of clinical importance.

DiCara's experiments changed all that. His effects were large (20 percent change of heart rate). To rule out the artifactual control of autonomic function, he paralyzed the skeletal muscles of his rats with curare. It was widely believed that by his experiments DiCara had shown direct operant control of autonomic function to be possible and that all that remained was to find how to do it effectively in humans.

As an illustration of the high hopes raised by DiCara's work, L. E. Roberts (1978, p. 249) quotes from an introductory textbook by Katkin (1971, p. 23):

The theoretical work has largely been done. The groundwork has been laid for an exciting future in which our innermost functions may be subject to modification by appropriate applications of external reward. Between now and 1984 you may well discover that you can voluntarily reduce your blood pressure, set your heart to beat at any rate you desire, and tell your kidneys just how fast to produce urine for your maximum convenience.

To understand the strong feelings engendered by DiCara's work, one must recognize that the question of autonomic control goes beyond curing the sick. A whole philosophy of life is at stake: nature vs. nurture—the question of the perfectability of man by education. It was a great relief to many of us, therefore, when order was restored to the world of learning and it was finally decided that DiCara's experiments could not be replicated.

RETURNING THE GENIE TO ITS BOTTLE

In his eighty-page study of the problem, L. E. Roberts (1978) argued in a scholarly and persuasive manner as follows:

- If operant learning of autonomic responses in the curarized rat were possible, it would have been found in the extensive and thorough but unsuccessful replicational attempts (primarily by himself and Dworkin).

- Since Pavlovian heart-rate conditioning in the curarized rat has since been found to require the tight management of certain experimental conditions not controlled by those claiming operant learning, the latter effect could not reasonably be expected to have occured.

- Hence, all apparently successful operant learning of autonomic function in curarized rats must have involved manipulational mistakes in the conditioning process.

Roberts (1978, p. 294) set aside fraud as an explanation because of the number of investigators who have produced this impossible effect.

As the most likely explanation, he offered these ideas (p. 294):

Briefly stated, [the other] possibility is as follows: . . . The experimenters involved in the original work do not appear to have been dispassionate observers . . . . It was strongly believed that positive results would be obtained. These expectations may have led to a succession of [unspecified] procedural errors that eventuated in the production and misinterpretation of the original findings. [Unspecified] disturbing features of the data that in a more neutral climate might have aroused suspicion were overlooked . . . . Publication of the early successes may have raised expectations in other laboratories and created a general bias toward acceptance and reporting of positive rather than negative results.

By this critical tour-de-force Roberts put the genie of the biofeedback-trained superman back into its bottle. In simpler language, Roberts said: Because Roberts and others could not reproduce an effect, DiCara and others who did so were either dishonest or incompetent. I find this argument very appealing, but I am not sure it is true.

LETTING IT OUT AGAIN

To question Robert's conclusion, there is no better place to begin than with his admission that he, too, had produced evanescent operant learning in curarized rats, and that he could only guess as to why it occurred and then disappeared (1978, pp. 295-296):

> The history of the curare problem has not been one in which a few investigators have consistently obtained positive results while others have failed completely. Rather the case seems to be that most researchers who have developed the problem for themselves have at some time or other obtained a result suggestive of learning. In our case, we obtained evidence compatible with a learning interpretation on three occasions.
> The first of these occasions was in 1971 . . . . We were fortunate in this instance to have been able to identify retrospectively a probable cause of the original misleading outcome . . . .
> [On the second occasion] a reliable difference in the direction of training was obtained . . . . Although these results might mean that the observed changes in heart rate were indeed a product of learning . . . a more disturbing interpretation was that the experimenter inadvertantly applied less stringent punishment criteria to those rats that displayed [learning].
> [On the third occasion] the interpretation . . . . was clouded . . . . We could not rule out the possibility . . . .

Brener, Eissenberg, and Middaugh (1974, p. 264), who

likewise have studied this problem in depth, are more cautious than Roberts:

> In spite of the difficulties experienced in replicating many of the operant cardiovascular phenomena reported in the literature, it must nevertheless be conceded that such phenomena exist . . . . In our laboratory, Hothersall (1968) successfully conditioned either heart-rate increases or decreases in 13 curarized rats. All subjects employed in his experiments displayed the desired effect, although in certain cases it did not emerge until the third or fourth sessions of conditioning . . . . Apart from the Hothersall study, which employed multiple conditioning sessions, we have been unable to obtain results as reliable as those reported by Miller and DiCara. Certain subjects provide convincing evidence, while others do not despite equivalent procedures.

The entire situation can be summed up very briefly. Here is a phenomenon (operant heart-rate conditioning in curarized rats) that is mysteriously erratic in its appearance at the hands of competent physiological psychologists.

As I was reading of the difficulties encountered by Miller and others, again and again it occurred to me that in parapsychology we have similar problems. Was it possible that DiCara was unwittingly performing an experiment in psychokinesis?

I have pulled together several parapsychological propostions that, taken together, seem to me to bear upon that question. I offer them for others to ponder:

- A laboratory demonstration of psychokinesis upon falling objects is admittedly an unpredictable venture. Not many parapsychologists have published a study of this kind. Leaving aside the two dozen or so dice experiments that appeared in the *Journal of Parapsychology* in the five years beginning with 1943 and the work of isolated experimenters since then, I know of no massive replicational series such as we find for ESP (Child, 1985; Dunne, Jahn, & Nelson, 1983; Honorton, 1985) or for micro-psi (Radin, May, & Thomson, 1985). Nevertheless, the evidence for the reality of falling-object psychokinesis is rightly regarded as conclusive by professional parapsychologists.

- The expression of psi in the laboratory is different for different experimenters, and some experimenters succeed in circumstances where others, equally well trained, are found to fail. This proposition is supported directly by various studies (*see* White, 1977), as well as indirectly by the experiment reported in chapter 4 of the present volume.

- Psychokinesis can disperse itself in complex and concealed ways, bearing no apparent relation to the intention of the operator. This is a new idea, shown perhaps for the first time in the experiment of chapter 4.

- The visible, psychokinetically-caused motion of physical objects resting in stable equilibrium has been observed many times by competent parapsychologists under conditions that were believed to have eliminated the possibility of fraud (Honorton, 1974; Keil & Fahler, 1976; Keil, Herbert, Ullman, and Pratt, 1976). In my judgment, this manifestation of psychokinesis must be regarded as established.[3]

- Dr. G. A. Sergeyev at the Ukhtomsky Research Institute of Physiology in Leningrad has reported (personal communication, 1973) that in his laboratory the well known psychic, Nina Kulagina, was able to stop a frog heart that was beating in vitro. Dr. Sergeyev is a neurophysiologist who has favorably impressed Western parapsychologists who have visited his laboratory.

- In my opinion there is compelling evidence that the essence of hypnosis is the psychokinetic control of one brain by another. This is a controversial proposition for which I have elsewhere set down part of the experimental evidence (McConnell, 1983, chap. 15) as well as commentary by E. R Hilgard, T. X. Barber, and referees from several journals (ibid., chap. 16). It is well known that hypnosis can be intentionally invoked without the customary stage and classroom rituals. If hypnosis is accepted as a form of psychokinesis, it requires no extension of principle to suppose that psychokinesis can occur when an experimenter's desire is not "to control an animal by hypnosis" but merely to have a specific behavior appear.

All things considered, it is not unreasonable to speculate that DiCara's rats performed, not by operant conditioning, but by his psychokinetic control of their autonomic systems and that this was facilitated by curarization.

---

[3] For a discussion, see McConnell (1983, pp. 126–129).

On August 23, 1976, Leo DiCara died, apparently by his own hand. Perhaps he could not endure the feeling that his colleagues might be doubting his scientific honesty. I believe that an unfair degree of suspicion would be lifted from the memory of DiCara if psychologists would familiarize themselves with the experimental literature of parapsychology.

REFERENCES

Banuazizi, A. (1972). Discriminative shock-avoidance learning of an autonomic response under curare. *Journal of Comparative and Physiological Psychology, 81*, 336–346.

Bozarth, J.D., & Roberts, R.R., Jr. (1972). Signifying significant significance. *American Psychologist, 27*, 774–775.

Brener, J., Eissenberg, E., & Middaugh, S. (1974). Respiratory and somatomotor factors associated with operant conditioning of cardiovascular responses in curarized rats. Pages 251–275 in P.A. Obrist, A.H. Black, J. Brener, & L.V. DiCara (Eds.), *Cardiovascular Psychophysiology: Current Issues in Response Mechanisms, Biofeedback, and Methodology*. Chicago: Aldine.

Cabanac, M., & Serres, P. (1976). Peripheral heat as a reward for heart rate response in the curarized rat. *Journal of Comparative and Physiological Psychology, 90*, 435–441.

Child, I.L. (1985). Psychology and anomalous observations: The question of ESP in dreams. *American Psychologist, 40*, 1219–1230.

DiCara, L.V., & Miller, N.E. (1968a). Changes in heart rate instrumentally learned by curarized rats as avoidance responses. *Journal of Comparative and Physiological Psychology, 65*, 8–12.

———. (1968b). Instrumental learning of vasomotor responses by rats: Learning to respond differentially in the two ears. *Science, 159*, 1485–1486.

———. (1968c). Instrumental learning of peripheral vasometer responses by the curarized rat. *Communications in Behavioral Biology, Part A, 1*, 209–212.

———. (1968d). Instrumental learning of systolic blood pressure responses in curarized rats: Dissociation of cardiac and vascular changes. *Psychosomatic Medicine, 30*, 489–494.

———. (1968e). Long term retention of instrumentally learned heart-rate changes in the curarized rat. *Communications in Behavioral Biology, Part A, 2*, 19–23.

———. (1969a). Transfer of instrumentally learned heart-rate changes from curarized to noncurarized state: Implications for a mediational hypothesis. *Journal of Comparative and Physiological Psychology, 68*, 159–162.

———. (1969b). Heart-rate learning in the noncurarized state, transfer to the curarized state, and subsequent retraining in the noncurarized state. *Physiology and Behavior, 4*, 621–624.

Dunne, B.J., Jahn, R.G., & Nelson, R.D. (1983). *Precognitive Remote Perception: Technical Note PEAR–83003*. Princeton, New Jersey: Princeton University Engineering Anomalies Research Laboratory.

Dworkin, B.R., & Miller, N.E. (1977). Visceral learning in the curarized rat. Pages 221–242 in G.E. Schwartz & J. Beatty (Eds.), *Biofeedback: Theory and Research*. New York: Academic Press.

Fields, C. (1970). Instrumental conditioning of the rat cardiac control systems. *Proceedings of the National Academy of Sciences, 65*, 293–299.

Honorton, C. (1974). Apparent psychokinesis on static objects by a "gifted" subject. Pages 128–131 in W.G. Roll, R.L. Morris, & J.D. Morris (Eds.), *Research in Parapsychology—1973*. Metuchen, New Jersey: Scarecrow Press.

Honorton, C. (1985). Meta-analysis of psi Ganzfeld research: A response to Hyman. *Journal of Parapsychology, 49*, 51–91.

Hothersall, D., & Brener, J. (1969). Operant conditioning of changes in heart rate in curarized rats. *Journal of Comparative and Physiological Psychology, 68*, 338–342.

Katkin, E.S. (1971). *Instrumental Autonomic Conditioning.* New York: General Learning Press. [As listed in Roberts, 1978.]

Keil, J., & Fahler, J. (1976). Nina Kulagina: A strong case for PK involving directly observable movements of objects. *European Journal of Parapsychology, 1*, 36–44.

Keil, J., Herbert, B., Ullman, M., Pratt, J.G. (1976). Directly observable voluntary PK effects. *Proceedings of the Society for Psychical Research, 56*, 197–235.

McConnell, R.A. (1983). *Introduction to Parapsychology in the Context of Science.* Pittsburgh, Pennsylvania: Author.

Miller, N.E. (1969). Learning of visceral and glandular responses. *Science, 163*, 434–445.

Miller, N.E. (1978). Biofeedback and visceral learning. Pages 373–404 in M.R. Rosenzweig & L.W. Porter (Eds.), *Annual Review of Psychology: 1978, Volume 29.* Palo Alto, California: Annual Reviews, Inc.

Miller, N.E., & Banuazizi, A. (1968). Instrumental learning by curarized rats of a specific visceral response, intestinal or cardiac. *Journal of Comparative and Physiological Psychology, 65*, 1–7.

Miller, N.E., and DiCara, L.V. (1967). Instrumental learning of heart rate changes in curarized rats: Shaping, and specificity to discriminative stimulus. *Journal of Comparative and Physiological Psychology, 63*, 12–19.

_____. (1968). Instrumental Learning of urine formation by rats; changes in renal blood flow. *American Journal of Physiology, 215*, 677–683.

Miller, N.E., & Dworkin, B.R. (1974). Visceral learning: Recent difficulties with curarized rats and significant problems for human research. Pages 312–331 in P. A. Obrist, A.H. Black, J. Brener, & L.V. DiCara (Eds.), *Cardiovascular Psychophysiology: Current Issues in Response Mechanisms, Biofeedback, and Methodology.* Chicago: Aldine.

Radin, D.I., May, E.C., & Thomson, M.J. (1985). Psi experiments with random-number generators: Meta-analysis Part 1. *Proceedings of the Parapsychological Association 28th Annual Convention, Volume 1*, 199–233.

Roberts, L.E. (1978). Operant conditioning of autonomic responses: One perspective on the curare experiments. Pages 241–320 in G.E. Schwartz & D. Shapiro (Eds.), *Consciousness and Self-Regulation: Advances in Research and Theory, Volume 2.* New York: Plenum Press.

Slaughter, J., Hahn, W., & Rinaldi P. (1970). Instrumental conditioning of heart rate in the curarized rat with varied amounts of pretraining. *Journal of Comparative and Physiological Psychology, 72*, 356–359.

Smith, N.C., Jr. (1970). Replication studies: A neglected aspect of psychological research. *American Psychologist, 25*, 970–975.

Sterling, T.D. (1959). Publication decisions and their possible effects on inferences drawn from tests of significance—or vice versa. *Journal of the American Statistical Association, 54*, 30–34.

Trowill, J.A. (1967). Instrumental conditioning of the heart rate in the curarized rat. *Journal of Comparative and Physiological Psychology, 63*, 7–11.

White, R.A. (1977). The influence of experimenter motivation, attitudes, and methods of handling subjects on psi test results. Pages 273–301 in B. B. Wolman (Ed.), *Handbook of Parapsychology.* New York: Van Nostrand Reinhold.

Yagi, F., & Hirai, H. (1975). Effects of feedback mode upon instrumental learning of heart rate changes in curarized rats. *Japanese Journal of Biofeedback Research, 3*, 7–13. [As listed in Miller, 1978.]

7

SELF-PSYCHOKINESIS

EXPERIMENTER EFFECTS IN BIOFEEDBACK RESEARCH

After I had surveyed the literature of operant training of autonomic function in curarized rats as described in the preceding chapter, I scanned the corresponding topic for humans. There, one uses biofeedback, for which the rewards to the experimental subjects may be money or merely the satisfaction of success. I restricted my attention to the control of skin temperature, and I examined only the experimental, as opposed to the clinical, literature.[1]

In skin-temperature research one would like to distinguish between (a) direct control of the autonomic nervous system by volition, and (b) indirect control of autonomic *function* by an interaction with voluntary muscles, which are, in turn, controlled by volition. What I found in the journals that I searched was not satisfying. While there were large temperature effects ostensibly caused by direct autonomic control (A. H. Roberts, Kewman, & MacDonald, 1973; Taub & Emurian, 1976),[2] similar effects could be produced by intentionally trained muscular effort (King & Montgomery, 1981). Thus, there was no easy way to resolve this autonomic control controversy. Moreover, as with curarized rats, some experimenters had great difficulty in producing results (Lynch & Schuri, 1978) that others could produce consistently. In this connection, Taub (1977, p. 276) said:

> The data suggest that there may be a surprisingly large "person factor" between experimenters in training self-regulation of skin temperature. An experimenter who adopted an impersonal attitude toward the subjects and who was not convinced of the feasibility of this type of learning

---

[1] In a typical experiment a tiny electrical thermometer, called a "thermistor," is glued to the skin of the subject and its changing temperature is exhibited to him as the deflection of a meter needle permitting visual detection of differences as small as 0.01 degrees F.

[2] References are at end of chapter.

was able to train only 2 of 22 subjects to regulate skin temperature. Another experimenter employed the same technique but had no doubts as to the feasibility of the task. She was able to communicate this confidence to the subjects; moreover she adopted a friendly, informal approach toward the subjects, making them feel that they were in a collaborative effort with her to achieve self-regulatory temperature control. This experimenter succeeded in training 19 of 21 subjects—an almost complete reversal of the results obtained by the first experimenter.[3]

PSI BETWEEN MIND AND BODY

At this point I contacted Elmer and Alyce Green at the Menninger Foundation in Topeka, Kansas, whom I remembered as interested in biofeedback and in the investigation of yogis claiming conscious control of their autonomic functions.

The Greens sent me their chapter (Green & Green, 1986) from Wolman and Ullman's forthcoming *Handbook of States of Consciousness* as well as their book, *Beyond Biofeedback* (Green & Green, 1977), which is an autobiographical summary of their life work.

Both of these publications enlarged my perspective—the first as to biofeedback, and the second as to parapsychology. From them I became convinced that the Greens will some day be regarded, along with the J. B. Rhines, as one of parapsychology's outstanding married couples. Interestingly enough, the Greens are not members of the Parapsychological Association, and I have no reason to suppose that they have ever referred to themselves as parapsychologists.

While parapsychology has traditionally concerned itself with psi as a relation between mind and the outside world,[4] the Greens, it would seem, have been quietly pursuing psi between mind and body under the concealing rubric "biofeedback facilitation of autogenic training." Their work could be regarded as a delayed bequest to parapsychology from Gardner Murphy; for it was in-

---

[3] If, as I suspect, this training involves psychokinesis, such a "person factor" would be expected.

[4] In my use, "mind" refers to a not-yet-understood emergent property of brain tissue, exhibited directly as consciousness and indirectly in other ways.

itiated in 1964 under his aegis as director of research at Menninger Foundation.

From the Greens' chapter in the *Handbook of States of Consciousness* it is apparent to me that the Biofeedback Society of America should apply for affiliation with the Parapsychological Association—or vice versa.[5] Of course, this is a matter of interpretation, and I do not expect other parapsychologists to agree with me without some delay.

The Greens' presentation is primarily in terms of messages exchanged between mind and body. They also give examples of unsought-for information from outside the body (ESP) and of unexplained external effects (PK)—phenomena which they did not pursue because their research interests lay within the body. They refer to these outside-the-skin phenomena as "extrapersonal" rather than "parapsychological."

Their eliciting technique was the same for both inside and outside phenomena, and, indeed, that technique, in so far as it requires mental dissociation plus a passive volitional attitude, is already known by parapsychologists as conducive to the appearance of psi (McConnell, 1983, pp. 60–68).

There are two basic steps to the Greens' method: (1) Put the body and mind into a certain optimum state of consciousness, and (2) receive the desired information from the body or send it the desired instructions.

The optimum state of consciousness, according to the Greens, is one in which the EEG shows substantial theta-frequency content (4–8 hertz). This is the hypnogogic condition lying between sleep and the state in which alpha frequencies (8–13 hertz) predominate.

---

[5]The Biofeedback Society of America (membership, 2200) was founded in 1969 for persons interested in the "interrelationships of external feedback systems, states of consciousness, and the physiological mechanisms involved." Prior to 1976 it was known as the Biofeedback Research Society. It is distinct from the American Association of Biofeedback Clinicians, which was founded in 1976 (membership, 1200). Between these two organizations there is considerable overlap of membership and interests.

AUTOGENIC BIOFEEDBACK

To reach the theta stage, one must relax physically, emotionally, and intellectually. Toward that end, biofeedback is helpful in three ways. Initially, temperature feedback monitors vascular relaxation, and EMG feedback assists muscular relaxation. In the final stage, EEG feedback guides the brain into theta activity.

How does self-regulation work? Green and Green (1986, p. 566) tell us that

> the answer to the question about the "how" of autonomic self-regulation would seem to be the same as the answer about striate (voluntary muscle) self-regulation. Each kind of control, striate or autonomic, is preceded first by visualization and then by volition. We spent years as children learning to get the striate system under control, aided by exterocepter and interocepter feedback to the cortex. And now, with machine-aided feedback to the cortex, we are learning to use visualization and volition to get autonomic mechanisms under control. The ultimate question, how can *anything* be intentionally controlled by the central nervous system . . . cannot [yet] be answered by science.

Thus, the controlling of autonomic functions of the body by volition is, in principle, the same as controlling voluntary functions, but it is more difficult and the technique one uses is different.[6]

Autonomic training is a two-way, information receiving and sending process. Biofeedback has to do with the information receiving aspect. The objective in biofeedback training is to bring into consciousness certain weak, normally subconscious cues from the body and then to shift to the use of the body's interocepters. All biofeedback training is training in self-awareness and, more specifically, in body awareness. The aim in such training is to dispense with the feedback machine as soon as possible. This is essential for a strong and lasting result.

Relaxation and, later, the receiving of information or the giving of instructions, are achieved by "visualization," which may be pictorial, verbal, emotional, or kinesthetic. Such visualization is

---

[6]What this may imply (see later) is that all volitional motion of the body is psychokinetic. This, of course, is not a new idea. *See* Myers, 1886, p. 172–173; Rhine and Rhine, 1943, p.22; Alvarado, 1981.

the essence of "autogenic training." "*Biofeedback* autogenic training" goes further by emphasizing the individual's responsibility for his change.

Biofeedback aside, the Greens' description of how to train the mind to receive and send body messages (ibid., pp. 570–577) deserves detailed comparison with the prescriptions available from parapsychologists for the purpose of eliciting psi.[7]

Explaining the importance of training, the Greens say (ibid. p. 575):

> Developing deep mental quietness simultaneously with mental alertness is not easy for most people, even with theta brainwave training. Nevertheless, that training is a relatively simple method that Westerners can use without long yogic practice. To be able to enter the theta state at will is an important accomplishment . . . . The same state of deep quietness which is used in *getting* answers from the unconscious can also be used in *programming* the unconscious for physiological and psychological change.

"Autogenic training" is a system of self-hypnosis (Green & Green, 1977, p. 26). The Greens are aware of what they call the "possibility" that hypnosis of one person by another is the psychokinetic control of one brain by another (Green & Green, 1986, p. 578):

> Concerning "trance" as a state of consciousness, it is interesting to consider the possibility that in hypnosis the researcher, or therapist, is "talking directly to the limbic system" of the subject, without the help (except acquiescence) of the subject's cortex. In self-regulation training, on the other hand, the subject's cortex [consciousness] may be said to be talking to its own limbic system.[8]

Biofeedback training, as the Greens emphasize, is primarily

---

[7]The most provocative presentation known to me of techniques for developing psychic ability appears in Chapter 10 of one of the truly important parapsychological books of the present century—a work largely ignored, I suspect, because the authors, Russell Targ and Keith Harary (1984), have courageously placed themselves outside the main stream of laboratory research.

[8]For an elaboration of these ideas, see the appendix to this chapter.

self-training. The trainer is of secondary importance. One of the Greens' clinical objectives is to develop "field independence" in their subjects, i.e., resistance to control from the outside (Green & Green, 1977, p. 178f.).

CAUSES OF BIOFEEDBACK FAILURE

Most academic explorers of biofeedback fail to achieve useful and lasting results. The Greens explain it this way. If the objective is "to publish or perish" and the goal is to confirm the Skinnerian learning paradigm, the following mistakes may be made:

- Too few training periods.
- Training unconsciously rather than consciously.

In an experiment that trains unconsciously, the subject successfully affects the feedback meter but does not learn to recognize consciously the corresponding signals coming directly from the body. By such quick training experiments one can demonstrate "acquisition" and "extinction" (beginning as soon as feedback is stopped) and can prove in the journals that nothing useful can be accomplished by biofeedback. This has been done many times.

In a properly performed experiment, the patient is not merely the subject or even a collaborator. He is in charge, and the experimenter is an adviser.

The Green's discussion of the placebo effect (ibid., p. 564) is similarly enlightening. Placebos work by unconscious self-regulation, but only as long as the patient has confidence and enthusiasm. In other words, placebos work by unwitting self-hypnosis.

The Greens emphasize the principle of physiological and psychological homeostasis, or the tendency of any system to maintain its existing state of operation, be it good or bad. To make well a body or mind, special attention must be given to overcoming physiological or psychological advantages of sickness enjoyed by one's body, one's psyche, or one's family. In many cases, one must first resort to psychotherapy to discover psychological problems.

Parapsychologists cannot fail to profit from the Greens' years of experience in helping patients to control body functions by putting them into the hypnogogic state in which, incidentally, psi phenomena can most readily be produced.

PSYCHICS TURNED SCIENTISTS

Beyond Biofeedback, the Greens' scientific autobiography (Green & Green, 1977) commanded my attention because Elmer Green was an engineering physicist who, before earning his Ph.D. in psychobiology at the University of Chicago in 1962, had been "head of the assessments division [at the Naval Ordnance Test Station at China Lake, California], supervising the work of sixty-five mathematicians, physicists, electronics engineers, and statistics aides in evaluating optical and electronic data obtained in [guided missile] tests" (Green & Green, 1977, p, 13).

In his doctoral dissertation Elmer Green showed that the discrepancy between Fechner's 1860, logarithmic law and S. S. Stevens' 1961, power law for the sensation of brightness as a function of light intensity arose from the fact that Stevens observed light increments for only one second, while Fechner made his observations after adaptation (Green, 1962). Green subsequently derived a general equation for visual brightness, for which Fechner's and Stevens' laws are special cases (Green and Green, 1977, Appendix II). Had Green chosen to remain in academic psychobiology, this achievement alone would have earned him a place in future textbooks of physiological psychology.

Technical competence and scientific common sense shine through in the Greens' handling of clinical data at the Menninger Foundation.[9] Many times in the book, however, I was puzzled by this question: Why did this engineer and his wife dive into the middle of this scientifically difficult field of biofeedback instead of nibbling safely at its outer parapsychological edges?

The answer came in a chapter near the end of their book, where the Greens give their personal life histories. They are both psychically gifted. Separately and together, and particularly in their formative years, they experienced dramatic psychic phenomena. This must have given them a sense of urgency and self-assurance.

As I have described elsewhere (McConnell, 1983, pp. 308–310), I have known directly or through someone close to me only rare and trivial spontaneous psi effects. In the laboratory, I

---

[9]See, for example, their discussion of "auras" (pp. 239–241).

have seen only the pallid derivatives of psi that are elicited by repeated-trial experiments. Thus, the Greens have had an advantage that I never enjoyed.

The Greens' description of their early, spontaneous, psychic experiences and of how they dealt with them was more convincing to me than the same tales told by scientifically uneducated, professional psychics whose good faith and level of intelligence had not been established. I was amused to discover that, even after a professional lifetime in parapsychology, I found it unsettling to have to move my boundaries of "the reasonably possible."

There was still another way in which the Greens' *Beyond Biofeedback* was rewarding to me. In my library there rests a handful of well-recommended books on "Eastern thought" which I have never had time to read. Through the Greens' detailed accounts of their adventures with professional yogis while testing their claimed abilities, both in Topeka and in India, I gained a feeling for the sense and nonsense in the lives of such contemplational experts. The mystery of the East had at last become one with the mystery of psi.

It is perhaps not surprising that, to support their courage and that of their subjects in twenty years of data gathering, the Greens have erected a comprehensive "field-of-mind theory" (ibid., chap. 14) using largely Eastern constructs. I fear that this theory is too ill-defined to guide research and that it may divert the attention of operationally minded readers from the Greens' empirical findings.

The Greens devote their penultimate chapter to the dangers of hypnosis (as opposed to self-hypnosis). Here they write from wide experience, both clinical and historical. I believe this chapter could be read with profit by clinical psychologists.

My judgment at the end of my encounter with the minds of Elmer and Alyce Green was that the Parapsychological Association would do well to offer them honorary memberships—an idea that I doubt will be welcomed by either the Association's council or the Greens themselves.

The Greens' seminal research has drawn together diverse areas: biofeedback, psychosomatic medicine, hypnosis, the dissociative disorders (and, in particular, multiple personality syndrome). Their work reveals parapsychology as the basic science of consciousness, to which all of psychology must some day pay homage.

BEHAVIORAL MEDICINE

After this chapter was completed to this point, I received an informal survey by William Braud of an emerging discipline called psychoneuroimmunology (PNI) in which he said, "There are encouraging reports that immune functioning may be influenced by psychological processes such as biofeedback, hypnosis [including self-hypnosis], relaxation, and visualization (Braud, 1986, p. 2)."

In discussing the possibility of an interface between PNI and psi, Braud said, "similar mechanisms may be involved in the two processes (*ibid.*, p. 3)." From Braud's review of several laboratory reports with striking results, as well as of clinical remissions of cancer and AIDS, it is clear that PNI investigators are using techniques identical with those developed by the Greens at Menninger Foundation.

Braud listed as a clearinghouse for PNI information the Institute for the Advancement of Health which publishes a quarterly journal, *Advances*.[10] Puzzled by the vagueness of these names, I telephoned for their literature. The Institute proved to be a membership organization with a distinguished panel of directors and scientific consultants. It is formally devoted to "furthering the scientific understanding of how mind-body interaction affects health and disease."

Dr. Neal Miller is a vicepresident.[11] Joshua Lederberg, Nobel laureate and President of Rockefeller University, had this to say: The Institute is "a most important step in joining the motives and methodology of 'humanistic medicine' and rigorous laboratory science."

From its publications as well as from its stated objective, it is evident that the Institute for the Advancement of Health does not concern itself solely with psychoneuroimmunology, but seeks to embrace the entire field of experimental and clinical mind-body interaction. For this kind of study the medically preferred name seems to be "behavioral medicine," although some practitioners use the adjective "holistic."

In a review of major programs in behavioral medicine Dreher

---

[10]16 East 53rd Street, New York, N.Y. 10022.

[11]His tantalizing work with rats is described in the chapter preceding this one.

(1986) referred to the program at Harvard University as possibly the oldest and certainly among the most established. This work was started in 1967 and was formalized in 1972 as a section of the Harvard Medical School.

The diseases being helped on an experimental basis at Harvard include migraine headache, high blood pressure, cardiac arrhythmias, angina pectoris, Raynaud's disease, colitis, peptic ulcer, nausea, low back pain, arthritis, diabetes mellitus, and cancer.

Treatments involve nutrition, exercise, psychotherapy, and biofeedback, but the key idea in the program is "relaxation." The word "hypnosis" is not used. In an effort to define the basic physiology of relaxation the program is investigating prayer, meditation, and repetitive exercises and has conducted studies in India and China in non-Western approaches to healing.

It is interesting that, although the Dreher review refers by name to 20 institutions engaged in behavioral medicine, no mention is made of the Greens' program at the Menninger Foundation Biofeedback Clinic. The Menninger program was started three years earlier than the Harvard program, was a pioneer in the biofeedback and relaxation techniques that are used at Harvard, and, in the five years ending with 1985, has treated 1700 patients with an improvement rate of 80% for many of the same medical problems being investigated at Harvard.

From the perspective that I have provided in the first part of this chapter concerning the Greens' work at the Menninger Foundation, I suspect that we are witnessing the beginnings of the long-awaited convergence of parapsychology with orthodox science. Dr. Braud's diffidence regarding the implications of this work for parapsychology matches that of most physicists early in the period between Einstein's 1905 prediction of mass-energy equivalence and Hahn and Strassmann's 1939 discovery of nuclear fission—or so it seems to me.

Chapter Appendix

HYPNOSIS AND MULTIPLE PERSONALITY

Ego-State Therapy

In the introduction to his *Handbook of Innovative Psychotherapies*, R. J. Corsini (1981) listed 241 systems of psychotherapy, most of which may be presumed to do some good for some patients with some therapists. However, in science, when there are many mutually incompatible explanations, it is safe to assume that none is correct.

It is my belief that no theory of personality or of psychotherapy can be converging toward ultimate understanding if it fails to take into account the facts of multiple personality. John and Helen Watkins' (1986) ego-state system of psychotherapy *starts* with those facts. My reason for discussing it here is its possible parapsychological interest.

Extending an idea of Paul Federn, the Watkinses define an "ego state" as "an organized system of behavior and experience whose elements are bound together by some common principle but which is separated from other such states by boundaries that are more or less permeable" (Watkins & Watkins, 1986, p.145).

By this definition clinical multiple personalities are ego states in which the boundaries are relatively impermeable (amnesic) and the shifting between states is spontaneous without hypnosis.

The Watkinses prefer to restrict the term "ego states" to "*covert* personality patterns that seldom come to full conscious awareness spontaneously, but which exist as underlying sources of 'unconscious' influence on the normally overt personality. They can usually . . . be activated through hypnosis" (Watkins & Watkins, 1986, p. 145).

On the basis of their clinical and research experience the Watkinses claim that, in hypnosis, previously covert ego states often spontaneously emerge and that such states may be associated with psychological problems of the waking state. In their system, therapy is directed to the ego states where the problems originate.

They explain this in more detail in earlier papers, from which I shall quote, rather than paraphrase, to avoid inadvertent distortion of meaning:

> Ego-State Therapy holds that perceptions, thoughts, feelings, motor reactions, and experiences are organized into coherent patterns that are relatively more or less discrete from one another. This means that "the ego" is not a unitary phenomenon, but rather is more like a confederation of states . . . .
>
> Each ego state is composed of behavioral and experiential elements organized around some common principle—such as being six years old, [or] dealing with authority figures, protecting the individual from harm, acting as a center of

common scnsc, representing a parental introject, and so forth.

When the boundaries of the ego states are so rigid and impermeable that little or no communication occurs between them, the individual may develop a multiple personality. However, [some?] persons also suffer from clashes between *unconscious* ego states that operate like "covert multiple personalities." Special procedures are required to resolve such conflicts. (Watkins & Watkins, 1981, p. 252)

Ego states may develop normally in childhood through the introjection of parental figures, through traumatic events, or through normal growth and differentiation . . . . The introjected ego state thinks as a child, and the earlier the introjection, the more primitive the thinking (Watkins & Watkins, 1984a, p. 421).

It is not necessary that these sub-identities be fused or destroyed [in therapy]. Once these units are understood and their needs met, uncooperative ego states change and become more cognitively consonant to the goals of the entire individual. (Watkins & Watkins, 1981, p. 269)

When an ego state becomes dominant and emerges overtly, we say that it is now "executive." Most underlying ego states . . . are aware of the thoughts and behaviors of that state which is normally executive. However, they are sometimes not conscious of one another until they have been hypnotically activated. . . .

We make a point never to suggest a name. The ego state itself tells us whether it has a name or not. However, when a new state emerges, often spontaneously, we will ask, "Whom am I talking to?" It is best to be as nondirective as possible to avoid the chance of suggestive creation or influence of an ego state. However, ego states, since they have an individuality of their own, will often contradict us or present surprising and totally unexpected reactions (Watkins & Watkins, 1982. p. 141).

When first approaching a new case in which ego-state therapy might be useful, we are concerned with reports of conflict, inconsistent behavior, or the existence of moments of amnesia. If the patient insists that he is "compelled" to smoke or overeat, we may inquire under hypnosis whether there is "some part" of him that knows more about why he is under this compulsion; and if this is true, he is to let the index finger lift itself. If a positive response is secured, we try to communicate with that "part." ("Part, will you please come out and say, 'I'm here.' ") Frequently, an ego state will emerge which claims "credit" for the problem. Interviewing it under hypnosis then discloses that the state has some grievance, motive, or purpose in compelling the maladaptive behavior or causing the symptom. It may describe to us its conflict with another ego state, and we then become aware of the existence of that other state.

Each ego state that is a party to the problem is interviewed, and attempts are made to work out a resolution or compromise—as might be done in family therapy. We have found it important to avoid making an enemy of any ego state regardless of how malevolent or unconstructive it appears to be in the patient's psychic economy . . . . Unless an ego state is treated with respect and courtesy, strong internal resistance to the treatment may be mobilized (Watkins & Watkins, 1982, p. 143).

Ego states can be influenced by any of the same procedures used by therapists on whole persons: suggestion, ventilation, reflection of feeling, abreaction, reinforcement, desensitization, free association, confrontation, construction, interpretation, and diplomatic negotiation. Any therapeutic technique used by the various theoretical approaches can be utilized in Ego-State Therapy, except that it is applied to ego states rather than to a presumably whole, conscious person (Watkins & Watkins, 1981, p. 259).

Speculative Interpretation

Ego State Therapy seems like a rational and extraordinarily flexible approach to psychotherapy. My interest in it arises from the parapsychological interpretation to which it lends itself when combined with the facts of divided consciousness (as reported, for example, by Hilgard [1977]) and the idea that consciousness can act directly on parts of the brain (Green & Green, 1986) and the possibility that hypnotism is the psychokinetic control of the brain by operator (or by self, in self-hypnosis) as proposed by McConnell (1983, chap. 15 and 16).

According to this speculative interpretation, each of us at any moment is a forever-changing assembly of brain subsystems organized by our consciousness using self-psychokinesis; i.e., consciousness is, to a degree, autonomous. Although some of us are more stable than others, no one is the same person from one hour to the next. We are all subclinical multiple personalities (McConnell, 1983, 41-45, 213-215, 255-256).

Genetically predisposed individuals who suffer severe psychological stress in childhood may develop "clinical" multiple personalities. However, the criterion for distinguishing clinical from subclinical multiple personalities (repeated, spontaneous, amnesia-demarcated shifts of identity) is arbitrary and misleading.

Suppose, for example, that, like most people, I have a "managed memory" for past happenings but no amnesia for on-going events and, hence, no self-evident changes in identity. Suppose, also, that my personality occasionally shifts from benign to monstrous as a result of unconsciously motivated, transient amnesia for gentling moral or affective memories. Is this a clinical situation? And if, as a monster, I occasionally murder for sport or money, would it be fair to punish the innocent co-inhabitant of my body, who will honestly deny every crime when on trial in a court of law? Is this an improbable situation? Not at all. It happens every day in the world at large—often with the help of alcohol.

The Watkinses, of course, confine their attention to what they can deal with as therapists. They have found that there are innumerable (potential?) ego states that can be made overt in hypnosis by psychological "shaping" (as their critics claim) or by psychokinetic control (if that parapsychological conception is acceptable).

This allows the therapist to work selectively on functional subsystems of consciousness. A successful ego-state therapist is one who helps the patient find therapeutically useful clusters of memory. The success of this method depends upon the hypnotic susceptibility of the patient and the psychokinetic power and clinical skill of the therapist.

This speculative interpretation (with its parentheses) is more conservative than the Watkinses' in that it assumes that in some instances their so-called covert ego states have no existence as entities until created by the hypnotic operator. Prior to that, they may be a cluster of memories, whose exact form is indeterminate until evoked and consolidated. This explains how Corsini could say (1981, p. 252), "In my own 35 years as a clinician, I have interviewed in depth some 10,000 people, only one of whom spontaneously stated that he had a multiple personality." The therapist must intend to hypnotize and must vaguely expect ego states or they will not appear. It also explains how the Watkinses could rightly feel that the ego states they observe in therapy are not created (solely) by the imagination of the patient under the therapist's guidance but are, in fact, particular expressions of existing constellations of memories.

On the other hand, this interpretation is more radical than the Watkinses' in that it suggests that psychokinesis is the defining element of hypnosis, and that the therapist, like a surgeon, is using it to gain access to the brain of the patient and to assemble and bring forth partial persons on which repair work can be done. The day may come when this kind of psychic surgery is the method of choice for treating functional mental illness.

Regardless of how one interprets hypnosis, the Watkinses' clinical success suggests that, by calling forth suitable ego states by hypnosis, parapsychologists might systematically search for personality trait clusters that are favorable to the production of psi phenomena.[12]

It may also be true that successful hypnotists and parapsychologists must, themselves, have psychic power if they are to elicit psychic effects from their subjects (with or without formal hypnotic induction). I suspect that every good therapist uses psi pervasively.

REFERENCES

Alvarado, C.S. (1981). PK and body movements: A brief historical—and semantic—note (letter to the editor). *Journal of the Society for Psychical Research, 51* (No. 788), 116–117.

Braud, W.G. (1986). Psi and PNI: Exploring the interface between parapsychology and psychoneuroimmunology. *Parapsychology Review, 17*(4), 1–5.

Corsini, R.J., (Ed.). (1981). *Handbook of Innovative Psychotherapies.* New York: John Wiley & Sons.

Dreher, H. (1986). The perspectives and programs of behavioral medicine. *Advances, 3*(1), 8–21.

Green, E.E. (1962). Correspondence between Stevens' terminal brightness function and the discriminability law. *Science, 138*, 1174–1175.

---

[12]Hypnotizing holds unexpected hazards for the operator, and especially when used to evoke secondary personalities. "One or more of such personalities may be definitely paranoid . . . . A violent or murderous attack [is] possible." (Watkins & Watkins, 1984b, p. 114). "As normal controls are dissociated off, a seductive secondary state may proceed directly to the business of sabotaging the treatment of a therapist whom it perceive as attacking its independent identity." (*ibid.*, p.117).

Green, Elmer, & Green, Alyce. (1977). *Beyond Feedback.* New York: Delacorte.

Green, E.E., & Green, A.M. (1986). Biofeedback and states of consciousness. Pages 553–589 in B.B. Wolman & M Ullman (Eds.), *Handbook of States of Consciousness.* New York: Van Nostrand Reinhold.

Hilgard, E.R. (1977). *Divided Consciousness: Multiple Controls in Human Thought and Action.* New York: John Wiley & Sons.

King, N.J., and Montgomery, R.B. (1981). The self-control of human peripheral (finger) temperature: An exploration of somatic maneuvers as aids to biofeedback training. *Behavior Therapy, 12,* 263–273.

Lynch, W.C., & Schuri, U. (1978). Acquired control of peripheral vascular responses. Pages 321–358 in G.E. Schwartz and D. Shapiro (Eds.), *Consciousness and Self-Regulation: Advances in Research and Theory, Volume 2.* New York: Plenum Press.

McConnell, R.A. (1983). *An Introduction to Parapsychology in the Context of Science.* Pittsburgh, Pennsylvania: Author.

Myers, F.W.H. (1886). On telepathic hypnotism and its relation to other forms of hypnotic suggestion. *Proceedings of the Society for Psychical Research, 4,* 127–188.

Rhine, L.E., & Rhine, J.B. (1943). The psychokinetic effect: I. The first experiment. *Journal of Parapsychology, 7,* 20-43.

Roberts, A.H., Kewman, D.G., & MacDonald, H. (1973). Voluntary control of skin temperature: Unilateral changes using hypnosis and feedback. *Journal of Abnormal Psychology, 82,* 163–168.

Targ, R., & Harary, K. (1984). *Mind Race: Understanding and Using Psychic Abilities.* New York: Villard Books.

Taub, E. (1977). Self-regulation of human tissue temperature. Pages 265–300 in G. E. Schwartz and J. Beatty (Eds.), *Biofeedback: Theory and Research.* New York: Academic Press.

Taub, E., & Emurian, C.S. (1976). Feedback-aided self-regulation of skin temperature with a single feedback locus. *Biofeedback and Self-Regulation, 1,* 147–168.

Watkins, J.G., & Watkins, H.H. (1981). Ego-state therapy. pp. 252–270 in R.J. Corsini (Ed.). *Handbook of Innovative Psychotherapies.* New York: John Wiley & Sons.

Watkins, J.G., & Watkins, H.H. (1982). Ego-state therapy. Pages 136–155 in L.E. Abt and I.R. Stuart (Eds.), *The Newer Therapies: A Source Book.* New York: Van Nostrand Reinhold.

Watkins, J.G., & Watkins, H.H. (1984a). Ego-state theory and therapy. Pages 420–421, in vol. I of R.J. Corsini (Ed.), *Encyclopedia of Psychology.* New York: John Wiley & Sons.

Watkins, J.G., & Watkins, H.H. (1984b). Hazards to the therapist in the treatment of multiple personalities. *Psychiatric Clinics of North America,* 7(1), 111–119.

Watkins, J.G., & Watkins, H.H. (1986). Hypnosis, multiple personality, and ego states as altered states of consciousness. Pages 133–158 in B.B. Wolman & M. Ullman (Eds.), *Handbook of States of Consciousness.* New York: Van Nostrand Reinhold.

PARAPSYCHOLOGY
IN
RETROSPECT

Part II: SHADOW

All of us live with the question of good and evil. We want to know in a cosmological sense why this polarity exists and what to do about it.

I have had to live with another question of a similarly all-encompassing nature. For more than forty years I have known that human consciousness can reach directly beyond the body, both to receive information and to exert force. This violates the culture into which I was born. It is not easy knowledge to live with.

The question that has disturbed me, however, is not posed by the existence of psychic phenomena but by their denial by Western civilization. Gradually I have come to realize that this is not a question about parapsychology but about human nature.

We live in a world of pretense. We are surrounded by relevant reality that we distort or ignore. In the second half of this book I shall present what I perceive to be occasions of irrationality in people with whom I have been professionally associated. For most of these people I have respect and, for some, affection. I include this exposition because it is only through my personal experience that I can convincingly explain what I believe to be the self-destructive bent of all of us.

In this book I try to do two things: (1) convey my understanding of parapsychology as an infant science in an irrational world, and (2) display in various ways what may be the most general and over-arching principle of human behavior, namely, that we are all mentally ill.

For the near future, the recognition and acceptance of this fact is, I believe, more important than the advancement of parapsychology. Unless, by an effort of the will, we attain sanity in this historical instant, there will be no future for any of us. My reasons for this belief are illuminated in my final chapter.

We are all ill in that, both individually and collectively, we systematically engage in behavior that is maladaptive for our survival. Our present mode of circumscribed thinking may have been appropriate for each in his own ecological niche, but the cultural eco-system is crumbling. For survival, we must acquire a constant peripheral awareness of our everyday self-deceptions and must unceasingly re-examine our articles of faith.

We are in evolutionary transition from unconscious to conscious beings. This is a crucial interval while we have gained the power to destroy ourselves but do not yet understand our spiritual nature. Can we change soon enough from a reality-avoiding to a reality-seeking species? That is the challenge.

8

EDITORIAL LOGIC

CREDO

Gardner Murphy once said to me, "I am no longer sure of anything." The conversation was casual and one of the few I ever had with that eminent psychologist, but from the context I understood him to be saying: "There is no such thing as certain knowledge." I could not agree with him then, and I still cannot, but now I am more sympathetic to his position.

To begin the second half of this book, I must state my epistemological beliefs. The first step is easy: Cogito, ergo sum.

I believe also that there is a totally real outer world that we share with one another, and concerning which we can learn a little with great difficulty. This second assumption is part of my cultural heritage. Without it I cannot be a scientist. Concerning the difficulty of knowing that outer world, others have written eloquently. For my students it was summarized in my previous book (McConnell, 1983, pp. 47f.)

My third postulate is that we each enjoy some degree of free will. The consciousness of each of us has autonomous power to affect the future. Here again, as a working scientist, I can make no other assumption.

My fourth postulate is the subject of this discourse, and cannot be adequately expressed in a few words. Over simplified, it is this: I believe that we are all, in a certain sense, mentally ill.

Such a proposition cannot be proved by logic, but perhaps it can be explained by example. In the next several chapters I shall relate events from my own experience that may show, in part, why progress in parapsychology is slow and that, at the same time, will illustrate the nature of universal human irrationality.

INDEX LIBRORUM PROHIBITORUM

The present chapter will tell how I decided to publish this book because the journals of parapsychology are closed to the ideas that I wish to express. In parapsychology, as in every field, editors and referees are constrained by fashion, so that it is difficult to display a new idea for consideration.

All scientists have papers rejected, and often for very good reasons. To allow readers to judge my papers for themselves, I have privately published them in the form in which they were rejected, and I have provided information in each case as to the circumstances of the rejection.

Four chapters of my earlier book, *Parapsychology and Self-Deception in Science*, were refused by the serial publications in which they belonged. Explanations will be found in chapters 2 and 3 of that book and in the final chapter of the present book. In my *Introduction to Parapsychology in the Context of Science*, chapters 15, 20, and 23 were rejected by the *Journal of the American Society for Psychical Research* and / or the *Journal of Parapsychology*. The present volume was undertaken after the rejection of its chapter 1 by these journals.

Since 1980, I have placed for publication only two articles. One was a book review solicited by the editor. The other was my report on the free distribution of 4,800 books, which is reprinted as chapter 2 of this volume. Even so, one referee, who was characterized by the editor as a "member of what most would probably consider the top echelon of parapsychology today," kept the latter manuscript more than three months and then recommended rejection in a thousand-word commentary, which I have shortened as follows:

> I do not feel that this paper in its present form either serves Dr. McConnell's personal purposes or advances the field . . . . Perhaps [his three] books are badly flawed as vehicles of communication in some way, such that RAM's distribution of them actually does the field more harm than good . . . . I suggest that, to constitute a contribution to the literature, this article should be expanded . . . . This may well involve collecting new data, contacting [book] recipients via questionnaire, and so on. Perhaps . . . collaboration is called for between RAM and a social scientist colleague who could aid in the design and conductance of a proper evaluation of the impact of RAM's mailings . . . . Without such improvement, this article is little more than a mix of raw data and conjecture.

This referee had apparently not read my six purposes for making a distribution of books. These appeared in numbered paragraphs near the beginning of the paper (chapter 2 of the present volume). My reasons did not include any intention to study the acceptability of parapsychology or my books. I got little verbal feedback from my respondents because I planned it that way. I felt that persons of the kind I was approaching would be offended by any attempt to include them in a poll or to pry into their thoughts. I would not expect Fellows of the Royal Society to respond if I had sent a personal, psychological questionnaire.

As to chapter 1 of the present book, there is no reason why a mixed-purpose journal of science, such as *JASPR*, should consider accepting an autobiography unless it has a policy explicitly favoring such articles. In the present instance, the editor, in discussing proposed changes in editorial policy, had stated in an interview published in the *ASPR Newsletter* (July, 1984): "I believe there is a need in our field for more methodological, historical, biographical / autobiographical, and theoretical papers, as well as literature reviews."

Beyond that, there is no reason why an editor should accept any particular autobiography. But if an editor decides on rejection and offers reasons, those reasons should bear logical scrutiny.

I have known this editor for more than thirty years. Like her predecessor in this journal, she is a wonderful friend—generous, helpful, forthright, diligent to the point of self-destruction, totally devoted to parapsychology, has an encyclopedic memory, and is faultless as a managing editor. What more could anyone hope for?

As editor-in-chief, she does an excellent job in rejecting nonsensical papers. She would be the first to admit that her training as a professional librarian has not equipped her to discriminate among scientific papers. But that is irrelevant in the present instance; for my autobiography is not a "scientific paper."

The reader can decide whether chapter 1 is a worthwhile document to have available in the literature for skeptical scientists or for young students who have never known a parapsychologist. I am sure there is room for a difference of opinion on this point.

What I shall discuss, is not the merit of my autobiography, but the editor's train of thought in dealing with it. In rejecting this paper, she suggested that I enliven it by giving historical accounts of my personal interactions with parapsychologists I have known. I replied that I preferred not to publicly discuss relationships I have had with my friends. I shall make an exception in the present chapter, not only because this friend would wish it so, but also because her communications with me in her public role as editor, unlike my personal associations with collaborators, do not wear the cloak of confidentiality. In an open society no editor expects privacy concerning the reasons given to an author for rejecting a paper.

INDEX EXPURGATORIUS

At the August, 1984, meeting of the Parapsychological Association, I learned from the editor of the *Journal of the American Society for Psychical Research* that, without my knowledge, a friend had mentioned my "retirement lecture" as being of exceptional interest. I subsequently sent it to the editor for her consideration. She responded on August 31 as follows:

> . . . I am not sure *JASPR* is the proper vehicle. [Your retirement talk] is really directed to *non*parapsychologists . . . .
>
> To be publishable in *JASPR*, I think you would have to add an appendix or addendum or supplement in which you seriously consider in depth the two points [on mental dissociation and on hypnosis as psychokinesis] raised in the last two paragraphs of the speech. You can't just leave it at that as far as parapsychologists are concerned. I realize you have gone into considerable depth [on these topics] in your third book (of your recent series). How about revising some of that material . . . as a summing up . . . of what *you* consider to be most important in parapsychology as a result of your long experience? Then I would be happy to consider publishing the two as companion pieces.

I replied on September 12 as follows:

> It is always pleasant to be asked by an editor to write a survey . . . . I have to say, however, that I am opposed, in principle, to republishing what I have already presented (as well as I can) in another, readily accessible publication . . . . Are you objecting to the ideas in the last two paragraphs of the paper (which, I agree, are not autobiographical)? The only explanation you offer is that, "You can't just leave it at that as far as parapsychologists are concerned." . . . I suggest we delete my last three paragraphs. If the paper is not then acceptable for *JASPR* as an autobiography, please explain.

Without acknowledging my suggestion that the paragraphs containing the offensive ideas be deleted, the editor replied on 5 October by shifting emphasis to the general unsuitability of the paper:

> If two referees [hypothetically] turned your autobiography down, I would more or less agree with them. As it is, it is mainly on physics and on Pitt [the University of Pittsburgh]. . . . I am not sure in my mind what educational value it has . . . . I *am* interested in autobiography and biography. For *JASPR* I think it would be important to revise the talk as if it were being addressed to parapsychologists . . . . I really don't think you or I, as editor, can get away with dropping that bomb about hypnosis with no further substantiation. It is too important to be presented that way. It's sort of like publishing in the popular press before submitting an idea or research to one's peers.

I replied on 15 October in part as follows:

> After puzzling for several days about how to interpret your reference to a ''bomb'' and about what you meant by comparing your journal to the popular press, I finally decided that you probably intended merely this: (a) You do not regard the full discussion of the hypnosis idea in my book (after its earlier rejection by your predecessor) as ''submitting [it] to one's peers,'' and, therefore, (b) presenting that idea in your journal in the manner proposed would be improperly sensational.
>
> If I understand you correctly, we are in partial agreement. If I accepted your premise, I would reach your conclusion.
>
> Why is the publication of my idea on hypnosis in my book, *An Introduction to Parapsychology in the Context of Science*, not ''submitting it to one's peers''? The book was professional in format. In its *Preface* I said: ''Although written at an undergraduate technical level, the material is intended to pass scrutiny by the leaders of natural science.'' The book is readily available at a reasonable price, by mail from the University of Pittsburgh Book Center, and wholesale from a commercial distributor. Gratis copies were widely distributed to psychologists and parapsychologists. I understand that it is now being used as a textbook. What is your reason for discounting the legitimacy of this book as a mechanism for the submission of my ideas to my peers? Have you thought about this?
>
> Over the years, I have taught my students that the rule of ''first professional publication'' means that scientific ideas

must be made available to one's peers before those ideas are offered to the public at large, but not that all mention of such ideas in the professional literature should be suppressed until they have been accepted by those who currently dominate the field. In the light of the treatment of parapsychology by other fields of science, parapsychologists should find it easy to understand this distinction.

My purpose in mentioning hypnosis at the end of my paper was to encourage discussion of an important idea that everyone seems to want to avoid. A bit of stirring-up is often needed to make progress in science.

I don't think your suggestion that I submit for your referees a restatement of what I said in my book is realistic—considering the rejection which that material has already received by anonymous referees [for your journal]. What they uncompromisingly rejected was the basic proposition. No revision of my words will make it acceptable. . . .

The arguments favoring the hypnosis idea have been fully given in my book. Having publicly affirmed an admittedly important scientific proposition, I feel an obligation to encourage its critical discussion. I believe you should have allowed me to do so in this case in view of my reputation as a competent parapsychologist and your published disclaimer that "Responsibility for any articles appearing in the *Journal* rests entirely with the contributor and not with the ASPR.". . .

[I have no] idea what you thought I might add that could make my autobiography more interesting to parapsychologists—unless perhaps I were to tell tales of the Arabian nights at some of the parapsychological conventions I have attended. Or I could describe professional quarrels I have had with well known parapsychologists. That would be both dreary and libelous. I am sure you would be displeased.

In this autobiography I have deliberately chosen not to discuss my organizational and scientific contributions . . . . To do so would necessarily involve evaluation of my work, which I regard as inappropriate for me to attempt.

ABSOLUTION WITH PENANCE

On 22 October the editor replied:

> . . . Bob, you are the first president of the Parapsycholog-
> ical Association. There is no mention of that. No mention
> of the work you have done in parapsychology. How about
> Schmeidler / McConnell? Your work with Forwald? With
> Marg? I don't mean you have to go into detail, but some
> paragraphs of basic philosophy, methodology, approach, and
> vignettes of projects and people. More about your course on
> parapsychology; your interchanges with various people in
> and out of print over the years.
> Let me try once more to say what I intended about
> hypnosis / PK . . . . I don't consider publication of your
> paper as a chapter in a book edited by you and published by
> you qualifies as presenting information in a peer-review pub-
> lication . . . .
> I misled you if you think I was displeased with what you
> *did* write. I found it very interesting. I would like to publish
> it *plus* additional details of your interesting and unusual life.
> So how about it? If you like, I'd put the whole thing on my
> computer and you can tell me to insert new things wherever
> you wish.

I replied on 2 November as follows:

> Thank you for your letter of 22 October, replying to mine
> of 15 October regarding the publication of my autobiography
> in *JASPR*. I regret it has taken so long for me to understand
> your point of view. I now realize that this has been partly
> because we do not share the same professional values . . . .
> In my 15 October letter I said: "Why is the publication of
> my idea on hypnosis in my book . . . not 'submitting [it] to
> one's peers'?" Notice that the phrasing within the single
> quotes is yours, from your 5 October letter.
> In your 22 October letter, you reply, not by answering my
> question, but by the statement, "I don't consider publication
> of your paper as a chapter in a book edited by you and
> published by you qualifies as presenting information in a
> peer-review publication." This is a change in your reason-
> ing. Your original idea, "to one's peers," has become "in a
> peer-review publication."
> The word "peer" appears in both expressions, so that, if
> one were merely free-associating, they might seem alike. In
> the first expression (in your context as fully quoted on page 1

of my 15 October letter), "peer" is the receiver of submitted scientific information, while, in the second expression (from your 22 October letter) "peer" is the authorizer of the submission. These are entirely different conceptions. I had assumed that your 5 October words were chosen carefully because they were written in response to my request for an explanation of what you meant in your 31 August letter, where your only justification in condemning my hypnosis statement was, "You can't just leave it at that as far as parapsychologists are concerned."

. . . Yours seems to be an authoritarian view of science. Do you believe that peer review is needed to endorse or to censor what a scientist wishes to present to other scientists? It is my understanding that the purpose of peer review is only to save journal space and the time of journal readers by eliminating improbable propositions, obscure writing, errors of logic, poor or mistaken mathematical analysis, oversights of earlier literature that deserve credit or that controvert an interpretation, etc.

If my view is correct, then the mention in a science journal of an ignored but admittedly important idea that has been adequately presented in book form should be encouraged rather than prevented. The journal space required is negligible, and the readers are implicitly warned that they risk their time if they choose to pursue the offered reference
. . . .

You want me to include in my autobiography "at least brief vignettes" from "all of [my] parapsychological activities," . . .

How can I be sufficiently blunt to get your attention? I would regard it as in poor taste to talk about my accomplishments or my [private] tribulations or to tell newsy little stories about public or private personages. Much of the material you are requesting might be entertaining, but it would not be inspirational. [To publish] a truthful autobiography covering the material you prescribe would unavoidably show lack of concern for the sensibilities of the reader, the tattled-about, or both. Collaborative interaction between aggressively intellectual people (including creative scientists) is not generally peaceful. The autobiography you want would have to be either piously dishonest or the parapsychological equivalent of what sells [the USA's best-known, scandal-mongering, tabloid newspaper]. It would belong to the promiscuous, prying, exhibitionist temper of our time, but it would not exemplify the intellectual tradition of science.

Nor would I presume to write as an elder statesman to my junior colleagues about "basic philosophy, methodology, approach." What I have to say on these topics has already been presented elsewhere in a reasoned, rather than authoritative, context.

In my 2 November letter I asked the editor to complete the consideration of my manuscript by sending it to two "referees" as she had offered. (How does one "referee" an autobiography?) I declined a 19 November request that I restore for her adviser's consideration the three deleted paragraphs on dissociation and hypnosis. I likewise declined her request for a list of ten possible persons from which she said she might or might not choose two anonymous referees. I asked that her advisers receive with my manuscript my letters of 15 October and 2 November, but the editor failed to grant this request.

By a letter dated 1 January 1985, I received from the editor the comments of her two referees. The first referee, Dr. Montague Ullman, allowed his identity to be revealed to the author. His comment, in full was:

My only criticism is that it is too short. It would have been entirely appropriate to have included at least some of his own work—especially his sustained effort to get scientists to face the facts of parapsychology.

The second referee preferred anonymity and checked two evaluative options: "manuscript is of sufficient quality, but not appropriate for the *JASPR*" and "manuscript is appropriate but requires substantial revision." He went on to criticize style and to suggest material for possible deletion. This referee felt that most of the first half of the paper, covering my childhood and my experience as a physicist prior to reading about Dr. Rhine in 1943, was "hardly relevant to the author's decision to go into parapsychology." How does one answer a referee who thinks it permissible to tell a colleague how to write his autobiography?

In her accompanying letter, the editor offered to publish my manuscript, but only if I expanded it along the lines she had previously requested. This condition I reluctantly declined to accept.

My above-described experience illustrates the proposition that many people—including those who are singularly successful in life—make little use of linear logic. Their judgments are reached intuitively, against the subconscious background of their experience. They use words in the belief that they are reasoning, when, in fact, they are speaking poetry. They live in a reality whose conformity to the consensual world, at least in certain areas, is somewhat a matter of chance. As a consequence they are not easily reached by reasoned discourse.

9

BOOKS IN REVIEW

A DECEIVING SPECIES

To understand the rejection of parapsychology by scientists, one must understand the thinking of Homo sapiens. We are a deceiving species. Self- and mutual deception are interwoven as warp and woof. We affirm the truth of what we believe, and most of us believe whatever we wish.

We are dimly aware of this state of affairs as it pertains to religion. Roman Catholic and Southern Baptist, for example, feel no obligation to sit down together to compare their doctrinal tenets, one by one, for reasonableness and compatibility, so that they may discover the truth and publish a joint paper in *The Journal of Ecumenical Religion*. Rather, each person thinks to himself, "I treasure my religious beliefs for my emotional satisfaction. I do not wish to examine them objectively. To do so would make me uncomfortable."

Only fringe religions proselytize among their neighbors, but it is considered admirable to send missionaries to stone-age savages whose psychological defenses we can easily overwhelm. Few educated adults will publicly engage in rational defense of their spiritual beliefs. On the contrary, we are obligated by custom to pretend respect for the other person's religion no matter how internally self-contradictory his beliefs may seem to be. If we criticize another's religion impersonally, we are ignored. If we ridicule to force a response, we are called an intolerant bigot, even though we are not intolerant of belief but only of unexamined belief.

What is not so well known is that flight from reality is practiced, not only in religion, philosophy, and everyday living, but also in the social sciences and, to a surprising degree, in the biological sciences as well. Whenever truth is not yet known—and often when it is—we fill in to please ourselves, while ignoring opinions differing from our own. In the "soft" sciences, as in religion and life generally, the dominant purpose of most communication is to protect self-esteem. Beginning in childhood, we are taught to reason defectively and to avoid social analysis (McConnell, 1983, chap. 23).

Parapsychology is more than just another soft science. In some subtle and not yet understood way, its phenomena challenge conventional religious and ethical beliefs and thus offend the spectrum of scientists. For this reason, among others, parapsychological evidence has not received a competent examination by scientists.

The foregoing paragraphs present the implicit message of my recent writing. It is not surprising that this message has proved unacceptable to critics and supporters of parapsychology alike—even as it is unacceptable to me. It blasphemes man as self-deity. It mocks the Existential excuse that life has no meaning. It is an unthinkable absurdity. Nevertheless, it is true—or so I believe. We are all mentally ill in that we deny reality in areas of importance while pretending not to do so.

I also believe that the circumspectual study and eventual acceptance of this proposition of universal self-deception is our sole hope. It is self-deception, stemming from lack of self-awareness, that keeps us headed down the road to extinction.

REFUSING TO ABIDE

Because my purpose in this chapter is not to evaluate books or reviews but to exemplify reality avoidance, I shall contrast pairs of reviews dealing, in the first instance, with my *Introduction to Parapsychology in the Context of Science*.

The *Journal of the American Society for Psychical Research* (*78*, 372-378) published a 2500-word review of my *IPCS* by a well known parapsychologist whose background is in English literature. Her opinion of my book is conveyed by the following excerpt from her review:

> McConnell in this book refuses or fails to abide by the basic principles of science . . . . he shows himself to be as intransigently rigid in his opinions as those he attacks . . . . McConnell's paper [on hypnosis] barely qualifies as a statement of opinion, much less a paper of any theoretical importance . . . . he has failed to defend it with even the slightest bit of supporting evidence . . . . he consistently . . . refuses to engage in any meaningful dialogue with colleagues . . . . his response, to bypass the normal channels of communication while still professing faith in the scientific method, seems akin to taking the law into one's own hands while still

professing faith in the legal-judicial system. If other scientists followed his lead and communicated their ideas in this manner [i.e., directly, by self-publication], science would quickly collapse in anarchy.[1]

The following quite different review of the same book appeared under the classification "Psychology" in *Choice* for February, 1984. *Choice* is the review journal of the Association of College and Research Libraries, a division of the American Library Association. Reviews in this journal are written anonymously by knowledgable scholars.

A splendid introduction to parapsychology for readers with a background in science. The work is neither highly technical nor otherwise difficult, but it will have special appeal to readers sharing the scientific tradition of respect for observational fact. McConnell presents some of the data that seem to provide strong evidence for the reality of psi phenomena, and he raises the question of why a number of scientists depart from this tradition in actively opposing dissemination or further development of this knowledge. At several points, McConnell enlivens his treatment by drawing upon his own very pertinent experiences. He is a physicist long active in parapsychological research, who has been an interested observer also of the social conflicts involved in controversies about parapsychology. He is remarkably conversant with relevant developments in psychology, including the study of hypnosis, and the book includes a clear statement of original theoretical ideas that deserve to be widely

---

[1] This reviewer is concerned with the question of whether the remote hypnotic control of sleep represents ESP or PK—the latter possibility being abhorrent to many parapsychologists. The following excerpt from my reply to this review may be helpful to the readers of this book: "[The reviewer may] not understand what is meant by an 'operational definition' . . . . When person *A*, through psi mediation, causes person *B* to do some observable act (such as waken from sleep), and person *B* does not consciously consider doing that act, then *B* is controlled by *A*, and the operationally correct term is 'psychokinesis' rather than 'extrasensory perception.' " (*JASPR, 80*, 344)

known. Level: upper-division undergraduate and above.[2]

Like the Southern Baptist and the Roman Catholic, the above reviewers cannot both be right. Together, these reviews illustrate the following aphorism: *Unless one personally knows the reviewer, the only dependable information one can gain from a book review are the facts of publication.*

THOUGHTS WORTH READING

Another pair of disparate reviews, this time of my *Parapsychology and Self-Deception in Science*, provides a second illustration of disagreement between scholarly book reviewers.

The first review is by John Palmer, a past president of the Parapsychological Association, and appeared in the *Journal of the American Society for Psychical Research* (*78*, 70–75, January 1984). Dr. Palmer correctly understood and reported many complex points that I had hoped to convey in my book. In his 2500 words I found no errors of fact. While there was far from an unqualified endorsement of my ideas, the review was both fair and sympathetic, as can be inferred from its final paragraph:

> This book is provocative and controversial. McConnell holds extreme views and he is not afraid to express them, yet he does so in a manner remarkably free from personal vindictiveness. At times I get a sense of resignation or fatalism in his writing, yet he has also presented us with a challenge to action if we choose to accept it as such. In any event, he makes us think and expand our vision. He deserves to be taken seriously even by those who disagree with him.

The contrasting mate to the Palmer review appeared in the *Journal of Parapsychology* (*48*, 236–237, September 1984). Because in Chapter 3 of *PSDS* I published my correspondence with the *Journal of Parapsychology* concerning their earlier rejection of the experimental papers appearing as Chapters 4 and 5 of that book, I was curious to know whether my book would be reviewed

---

[2] Not all reviews of this book outside of parapsychology were so favorable. I have added as an appendix to this chapter the correspondence that followed a review by a leader of the "Committee for the Scientific Investigation of Claims of the Paranormal," which appeared in the American Psychological Association's book-review journal.

at all. Two copies of *PSDS* were sent to the *Journal* in March, 1983. When I learned by inquiries to the *Journal* staff that no review was in preparation and that review decisions were made personally by the editor, I twice contacted him, asking his intention in this matter. Because the editor of the *Journal* is also the Director of the Foundation for Research on the Nature of Man and of the Institute for Parapsychology, I thought his response would be of special significance.

The "review" when it finally appeared in September, 1984, was a 16-line comment under "Books in Brief," prepared by a member of the research staff. Concerning the previously rejected papers, this reviewer said:

> Two chapters are spent on some of [McConnell's] own work with PK on dice. There is an in-depth discussion of patterns within the data and possible psychological reasons for the patterning. These two chapters are worth reading. [The others are not.]

This review and that of Dr. Palmer provide differing perceptions of the book in relation to parapsychology.

STICKING THE COBBLER TO HIS LAST

It is never quite proper to compare reviews between journals. If a particular journal gives less space to a book, one needs to know the editorial objectives of that journal and what other claims there were for page space. Unlike the *JASPR*, the *Journal of Parapsychology* is not a quasi-popular publication. It was founded by J. B. Rhine in 1937 for the purpose of reporting experimental (as opposed to spontaneous or clinical) evidence for psi.

Some information as to the reviewing policy of the *Journal* can be gained from its December, 1984, issue (which followed the one just referred to). For that issue the editor, himself, provided a 1000-word review (pp. 356-358) of a book telling how to test for ESP using cards.

Before proceeding with my example of seeming irrationality, I wish to explain that the editor is a highly respected investigator who has twice served as president of the Parapsychological Association. I believe he has contributed significantly to the advancement of the field.

The review in question is not of a book but of a booklet having four pages of text, a scoring table, a filled-in sample scoring sheet, 12 blank record sheets, and eight sheets of detachable cards. Its selling price is $3.50, and it is obviously intended as a money-making how-to booklet.

At this point one might wonder whether this was perhaps an exceptionally good tool for educating the public about "how to make a careful test for your own ESP." It is, in fact, a very bad guide for the layman, containing numerous procedural errors of the most obvious and inexcusable kind. In his review, the editor patiently pointed out these flaws and concluded with a summary:

> In the past I enjoyed reading some of [this author's] writings. But in these few pages I found too many places where I am not sure what he is really saying . . . . After all [the author is] not a parapsychologist. [If he] really means what he writes, "The search for the truth about claims of ESP is an important one," he should save his energies for doing things he is best able to do and leave psi testing to those who are better prepared for doing it.

Who is this author that deserves two pages of technical criticism followed by a friendly, collegial scolding in the world's most scientific journal of parapsychology? I was once invited to attend a lecture given by him. Afterwards, I sent a letter to my host, which I reproduce below in slightly shortened form:

23 July 1984

Dr. _____
Physics Colloquium Chairman
Westinghouse Research and
    Development Center.
Pittsburgh, Pennsylvania

Dear Dr. _____

Thank you for allowing me to attend your Interdepartmental Physics Colloquium on Friday to hear a lecture by Mr. F.A., a professional magician who makes his living by lecturing on parapsychology.

It was with considerable surprise that I heard his performance before your group of scientists and engineers. His hilariously vituperative condemnation of parapsychology, consisting of an unending string of "one-liners," evoked several laughs per minute. His audience was with him from start to finish. Whatever else, it was successful entertainment.

From his introduction by you I learned that he lectures regularly to industrial scientists. For that purpose he has spiked his talk with "scientific" jokes. I remember best the one where he said approximately as follows:

> Old Man McDonnell did not want to die until he knew where he was going; so he gave half a million dollars to parapsychological research at Washington University at St. Louis, where Professor Peter Phillips somehow convinced him that "spoon bending" would tell something about survival after death. McDonnell is the man who gave us both psychic metal bending and the DC-10.

The DC-10 is well known to engineers to have crashed after engine-mount failure. The audience roared its approval. This double-barrelled association of metal failure and death was clever showmanship, but was it honest?

Since that lecture, by consulting with people who would know, I have confirmed what I had suspected from my own personal contacts with James S. McDonnell, Jr. The association of (1) the $500,000 given to Washington University for parapsychological research with (2) a personal interest by James McDonnell in either "postmortem survival" or "psychic metal bending" is totally false.

On the basis of my knowledge of parapsychology I would describe F.A.'s talk as a sequence of lies and distortions, of which the most egregious was his statement (approximate quotation): "What I have described to you is the best research in parapsychology. Think what the worst must be like."

When someone asked about research at Princeton University, F.A. referred flippantly to Robert Jahn, Dean of the School of Engineering and Applied Science, as the "latest glamour boy of parapsychology." Had F.A. wanted to inform his engineering audience, he could have mentioned that Dean Jahn is the co-author of a recent report of 300 trials[3] replicating the Puthoff and Targ "remote perception" experi-

---

[3] An abstract of this report appears as appendix *D* to the chapter titled "Forces of Darkness."

ments that appeared in the *Proceedings of the Institute of Electrical and Electronics Engineers* of March, 1976.

In his talk at Westinghouse, F.A. bragged about the good living his lecturing provides. I am sure it would not be possible for him to tell the complex, often disheartening, but sometimes inspiring, truth about parapsychology and to be paid for it as a magician-lecturer. His audience wanted a hyperbolic circus, and that is what he delivered.

You may ask: What's wrong with a little Friday afternoon relaxation? Must we always be serious?

Mr. F.A. gives his lectures to closed meetings of industrial scientists and engineers with no opportunity for a rebuttal. His evident attitude is that of a good-natured, self-satisfied bearer of truth. Because of the way the world is arranged, his activity tends to prevent responsible, governmental and private agencies from funding parapsychological research, regardless of its intrinsic merit.

The objective of parapsychology is to investigate by scientific methods the role of human consciousness in the universe, a subject that has hitherto been the exclusive province of revealed religion. Whatever you may think of the evidence for extrasensory perception, I am sure you will agree that parapsychologists have a worthy objective—and one conceivably of great importance in an age that is seeking new values or the validation of old.

Sincerely yours,

R. A. McConnell

Except for parapsychology, I know of no field of science that would respond within its professional journals to a showman who is scientifically illiterate and whose sole purpose in associating himself with the field seems to be to make money by misrepresenting that field to the public and to scientists.

Two conclusions seem warranted. (1) Somewhere there has been a misperception of reality in dealing with this magician as though he were a scholar. He is a founder, and is currently a member of the Executive Council of the Committee for the Scientific Investigation of Claims of the Paranormal.[4] (2) There

---

[4] This committee is described in the chapter titled "Forces of Darkness," where it is explained that F.A., F.B., etc., are persons publicly listed as "Fellows" of the Committee.

was no lack of page space in the *Journal of Parapsychology* in the fall of 1984.

Chapter Appendix
ADMIRATION FOR A DAMNING REVIEW

The following correspondence is from *Contemporary Psychology, (30*[1985], 743-744), the book review journal of the American Psychological Association.

Parapsychological Protagonists

I have considerable admiration for F.B.'s damning review of my book *An Introduction to Parapsychology in the Context of Science (CP*, 1985, *30*, 25-26), but I think he could have done better. It is hard to believe that there is nothing worthwhile in a seriously intended book on parapsychology written by a physicist after thirty-five years of intensive study of the subject in a university setting.

A leading theme of my book is that authority in science rests upon consensus among experts and, hence, that in controversial fields there can be no "authorities"—merely self-selected protagonists, such as F.B. and myself. Anyone, scientist or not, who wants to evaluate such a field must go to the original research papers.

One of F.B.'s criticisms concerns my introduction of controversial material extraneous to parapsychology. He did not mention my reason for including this material, which was to show by examples from other fields that generally prevailing opinion is not to be trusted. To make this point, I drew upon diverse controversial areas to which, for one reason or another, I had given personal attention and about which I could speak with confidence.

F.B. fails to mention that the three "noteworthy examples" that he cites as themes out of keeping with the book's title came from appendixes to my book and not from the text, and he otherwise distorts their presentation. For example, from a discussion of the relation of intelligence[5] to inherited biological structure, F.B.

---

[5] The readers of this book can find a brief and lucid but rigorous description of intelligence in A. R. Jensen (1986).

quotes an intentionally provocative statement, which begins, "Legislation that attempts education beyond what is biologically feasible wastes money, alienates the intended beneficiaries . . . ." (p.306). F.B. would have conveyed a different flavor if he had told his readers that this passage appeared under the subheading "Propositions Deserving Public Examination."

I am pleased that F.B. recognized as a central theme of my book the idea that mental dissociation is helpful for the production of parapsychological phenomena, but he did not get it straight. He says, "McConnell argues that dissociation occurs in hypnosis, and he advances the thesis that the essential element in bringing this dissociation about is the psychokinetic influence of the hypnotist" (p. 25).

That is nonsense, but it is not my nonsense. On page 162, I said,

> It is generally accepted that no physiological variable has been discovered whose values can identify exclusively the hypnotic state. This [failure] might be expected if dissociation (achievable by various means) is a physiological condition and psychokinesis is a superimposed process that defines the resulting behavior as "hypnotic."

My book was intended as a discriminating introduction to parapsychology from the perspective of science as a whole. The experimental literature is sampled in Chapter 10, Chapter 12, and Chapter 14. Out of 275 references appearing at the end of the book, 30 experimental papers are marked as "having unusual evidential interest regarding the reality of parapsychological phenomena." This is the kind of information that would have been helpful in a review intended to encourage psychologists to go to the literature rather than to believe protagonists.

R. A. M.
Biological Sciences Department
University of Pittsburgh

Response to McConnell

McConnell complains of being taken out of context regarding statements about education and about the relationship between psychokinesis and hypnosis. As for education, regardless of his subheading, one wonders why the discussion of biology and intelligence appears in a book about parapsychology. If it was intended only to stimulate thought, why does McConnell, without examining arguments that counter this [*sic*] dangerous proposition, state, "Perhaps it is time that we openly decide what kind of selective breeding we favor" (p. 306)?

Regarding hypnosis, he denies ownership of the "nonsense" he describes. Why then, in discussing his correspondence with T. X. Barber, did he write, "Although I did not say so, I believe that the interpretations I have provided of hypnosis as a psychokinetic phenomenon will resolve the Hilgard-Barber controversy" (p. 167)?

He states that his discussions of education and medicine were intended to show that "generally prevailing opinion is not to be trusted." If this was his intention, the best one can say is that he showed poor judgment in the examples he chose. His discussions of them are gratuitous attacks against apparently favorite whipping boys, and they fail to illuminate the reasons that parapsychological ideas have not won favor within the scientific community. Unfortunately for him, this book, if taken seriously, will only contribute to the difficulties parapsychologists have in gaining recognition within conventional science.

F. B.
York University

Something Much More Unacceptable

Once again, F.B. misleads by omitting what preceded, namely, "If hereditarians are right . . . legislation that raises the [relative] birthrate of the poor . . . is selective breeding" (p. 306).

Concerning hypnosis, the nonsense that I disclaimed was F.B.'s notion that psychokinesis is essential for the production of mental dissociation. What I propose is much more unacceptable and probably true, namely, that hypnosis *is* psychokinesis.

I am deeply touched by F.B.'s concern for the difficulties of parapsychologists as expressed here and in his other antiparapsychological writings. His long and close association with the so-called Committee for the Scientific Investigation of Claims of the Paranormal confirms the obfuscatory nature of his interest.[6]

R. A. M.
University of Pittsburgh

REFERENCES

Jensen, A.R. (1986). Intelligence: "Definition," Measurement, and Future Research. Pages 109–112 in R.J. Sternberg and D.K. Detterman (eds.), *What is intelligence?* Norwood, New Jersey: Ablex Publishing.

McConnell, R.A. (1983). *An Introduction to Parapsychology in the Context of Science.* Pittsburgh, Pennsylvania: Author.

---

[6] F.B. is a member of the Executive Council of that organization. See chapter titled "Forces of Darkness."

10

ON THE ACADEMIC CUSTODY
OF RESEARCH MONEY

IN THE FOOTHILLS OF THE INTELLECT

If reality denial is universal, how does the world's work get done? Our insanity emerges as we try to capture reality in words. The failure of expression in a particular instance depends upon the topic of conversation, the limitations of the language, and the skill and emotional involvement of the speaker. Not all reality is equally elusive. One can describe a "dinner plate" more easily than "jealous love." In the river plains of elementary thought, all are sane save those who need asylum.

Scientists, lawyers, administrators, and other specialists of above-average intelligence develop unusual skill with words. In the foothills of the intellect, where lesser mortals can be confused, they tread their way with ease. Because stupidity can serve as a convenient cover for intentional deception, it is not uncommon for those in the professional and governing elites to misrepresent reality while appearing to be clumsy with words. Often, when this is done, one cannot tell where stupidity ends and dishonesty begins.

There are many techniques by which the administrator can control those under him. Unless he is being cross-examined in a court of law, it is rarely necessary for him to tell an outright lie. If asked an embarrassing question, he may, for example, give a "perpendicular answer." To his secretarial staff and to the outside world that answer will seem sufficient. The first privilege of power is to be nonresponsive to inquiry while appearing superficially to be answering in good faith.

Over the years, I have been obstructed by a wide variety of manipulative techniques and have had frequent occasions to sympathize with friends who were similarly treated. The following recent, firsthand experience illustrates an evasion of responsibility pertaining to parapsychology.

ANDREW MELLON TRUST SUPPORT

The A. W. Mellon Educational and Charitable Trust has provided the principal financial support for my research in "psychological physics" since 1952.

This trust is best known for its gift to our nation of the National Gallery of Art in Washington, D.C. The Trust and its trustees were good friends of the University of Pittsburgh. Since 1930, the Trust had given $44 million to the University, including $16 million for the founding of its Graduate School of Public Health. In its later years, after expending most of its assets, the Trust adopted a policy of supporting only the fine arts in the Pittsburgh community. The Trustees nevertheless continued to fund my work because they were convinced of the potential importance of extrasensory perception and psychokinesis if, in fact, those phenomena occur.

With the dissolution of the Trust in 1980 after fifty years of service to Pittsburgh and its cultural institutions, the trustees made final gifts to the University totalling $3.06 million. Among these was a grant of $360,000 to cover the remainder of my career.

The terms of the grant were negotiated between the secretary of the Trust and the dean of the Faculty of the Arts and Sciences, who had conducted similar negotiations in the past. So far as can be determined from the record, no other University officer was involved.

In his initial offer of 2 May 1979, the secretary of the Trust wrote:

> We would hope that the funds would be segregated and that any interest accruing while they are not in use for the program would be added to the balance, thereby modestly increasing the support of Dr. McConnell's research.

In his accepting letter of 10 May 1979 the dean wrote:

> Upon receipt of the major portion of this grant, I will request the Investment Committee of the University Board of Trustees to allow for segregation of these funds so that the interest earned would be designated specifically for the program of psychological physics.

These were the words of agreement between two old friends with a common interest in the fine arts. Although the phrasing was not that of a business contract, the meaning seemed clear and precise. There is no other correspondence of record. This must have been one of the final official acts of the secretary of the Trust; for he was ill at the time and died two months later.

The following year a bank draft for $360,000, dated 31 March 1980, came from the Trust in its process of dissolution. The check was received by the dean of the Faculty of the Arts and Sciences, who forwarded it to the treasurer of the University by letter of 14 April 1980 in which he said:

> Were the A. W. Mellon Educational and Charitable Trust not being liquidated, they would be sending us annual payments as they have done in the past. In view of the fact that they are making a liquidation grant to extend over this entire period, they made the reasonable request that the funds be invested so that the derived interest would be added to the principal for the use of the program in psychological physics . . . . I am specifically requesting that an endowment income account be established into which these funds may be deposited.

MISSING INTEREST

When six months had passed and no interest income had appeared on the monthly posting sheets for my account, I made an inquiry. I was told that this was an oversight that would be rectified.

It was February of 1981 before I could determine from the accounting sheets that interest on the Mellon grant was being paid to my account at a rate of less than 5 percent. At that time, three-month U.S. Treasury Bills were earning 15 percent.

By late March, I obtained an interview with an assistant to the treasurer, who admitted that the grant money had not been segregated for investment but had been pooled with the University's operating funds and was earning interest at short-term loan rates, i.e., at close to 18 percent.

I wrote to the treasurer on 30 March 1981, summarizing the situation as I understood it and asking that the conditions of the grant be adhered to.

The treasurer wrote that he had spoken personally to the secretary of the Trust shortly before his death and had obtained his approval for interest on the grant to be paid at the current savings-bank passbook deposit rate, less one-half percent for administrative costs, which was in conformity with University practice in handling other private-grant research funds.

In my reply of 20 April, I asked whether there was any correspondence supporting this modification of the terms of the grant, and I requested that the entire matter be submitted to the University's legal counsel for an opinion. An informational copy of my memorandum went to the president of the University.

Despite repeated requests in the following years, I have never received an answer to my question about the existence of supporting correspondence. The claim of a conversation between the treasurer and the Trust's secretary was never again mentioned by any University officer. Because of the terminal illness of the secretary, it is doubtful that there was an opportunity for such a conversation.

After letters of inquiry were sent by me on 20 July and on 11 December via registered mail to the president of the University, I received on 7 January 1982 a three-page letter from the University's in-house legal counsel, which began:

> [The treasurer] has requested that this office prepare a legal opinion as to the manner in which the University has managed the research funds from the A. W. Mellon Educational and Charitable Trust that were provided for a project under your supervision. We have completed a detailed review of the history and administration of this grant and are of the opinion that the University's handling of the funds is in conformity with accepted fiscal policy and practice and does not violate the terms and conditions of the donor.
>
> To understand the basis of this opinion, it is necessary to be fully informed as to the precise legal meaning and practice of various terms and accounting procedures which have been used by the University and accepted by various independent auditors through the years. In addition, the terms and conditions placed on the grant by the donor at the time of the conveyance must be carefully considered. The remainder of this opinion consists of the operative facts and analysis used to formulate our opinion.
>
> The generic terms "Endowment Funds" and "General Funds" are often used by persons unfamiliar with the precise legal meaning, accounting practices, and the actual application of these terms to the fiscal management of a complex institution. Within the category of funds termed "Endowment Funds" at the University of Pittsburgh there are, in fact, three (3) categories of Endowment Funds. Each of these subcategories is narrowly defined in accordance with policies adopted by the Investment Committee of the Board of

Trustees. Additions to any of these subcategory accounts must satisfy the operative criteria before they can be administered as Endowment Funds. The rate and nature of expenditures stipulated in the grant with which you are concerned preclude the incorporation of these funds within any of the Endowment Fund subcategories.

There was no useful information here. Two pages later, I found the promised "operative analysis." Referring to the previously quoted sentence from the Trust asking that the funds be segregated and interest added, the counsel said:

It is our opinion that the University has managed this fund in full conformity with the request of the grantor. Initially, it should be noted that the language used to introduce the sentence is, "We would hope . . .". This can only be construed as an aspiration or a request, but certainly not as a requirement. Nonetheless, the University has treated this language most seriously and has taken the previously noted steps to honor the request.

I replied on 13 January 1982, saying:

I would suppose that what we are discussing is a question of contract between the University and the donor trust. In my letter of 30 March 1981, I quoted three relevant statements by the parties to this contract. The first was a sentence from the proposal made by the donor trust (2 May 1979). The second was a responding sentence (10 May 1979) by [the dean] who represented the University in the negotiation of this contract. The third was three sentences in a letter from [the dean] to the treasurer of the University (14 April 1980) showing his understanding of the contract that he had negotiated with the Trust.

Your letter of 7 January 1982 purporting to give a legal opinion in this matter, deals only with the first of these three statements, i.e., with evidence concerning the proposal made by the donor trust. Nowhere have you mentioned, much less discussed, what the University agreed to in accepting the funds in question. By its nature, a contract requires a meeting of minds—in this case between the donor trust and the University. It is not clear how one can prepare an opinion about the nature of a contract by examining only what was said in the preliminary statement by one of the parties thereto. Would you be good enough to write again, explaining how University or other documents subsequent to the donor's proposal of 2 May 1979 justify your interpretation of the contract between the University and the donor trust?

May I call your attention to the time gap between the making of the contract between the University and the Mellon Trust (10 May 1979) and [the dean's] discussion of that contract upon receiving the bulk of the money involved (14 April 1980). I think it must be presumed that [the dean's] request for University action, made eleven months after the contract was concluded, reflected his understanding of the agreement he had negotiated.

I sent an informational copy of the above letter to the president of the University with a same-date letter summarizing the situation as I understood it.

The counsel did not reply. Instead, on 29 January 1982 his secretary telephoned to ask me to attend a meeting of several officers of the University. I demurred on the ground that the agenda was unspecified and that the specific questions in my last letter should be answered first. I sent a letter to the president explaining my refusal.

UNIVERSITY INTEREST

On 23 February 1982 I received a call from an assistant to the president of the University saying that the president wanted me to attend a meeting with his officers, who would explain the University's investment policy. I said I could not understand the need for such a meeting because I had never questioned the University's investment policy, which had already been fully explained to me in writing. I wanted to know the University's legal stance on the use of the income from the funds. In view of the University's contractual obligation, it was not clear to me that the existing investment policy could be applied in this case without modification.

The assistant said that it was not a legal matter and that the University stood by its counsel's opinion. I said that I thought the matter should be referred to the University's outside legal consultant for an independent opinion. I sent a letter to the president summarizing this conversation.

The president wrote briefly on 15 March 1982 saying that he had reviewed the entire correspondence, that his officers were qualified to discuss the University's investment policy, and that if I chose not to confer with them, the matter was closed.

Two things seemed clear: (1) The University wished to hold a meeting for which no clear record might exist, but which could be used to show that the University had tried in good faith to respond to an employee's questions. I decided that I could not attend such a meeting unaccompanied by an attorney. (2) The University did not intend to allow me to engage in what lawyers call a "discovery process" regarding the University's position on this matter.

I anticipated that the University's position would be:

1. That the administration had no choice but to follow the investment policies set by its Board of Trustees.

2. That the administration's actions regarding this grant had been legally correct.

3. That the handling of funds was an administrative matter which I had no standing to question.

My position was that all three propositions were doubtful and deserved an outside legal opinion.

I wrote again to the president, thanking him for his personal concern. I summarized my position and what I presumed to be his. I said that I regarded his intention to consider the matter closed as an invitation for me to take the matter to the Board of Trustees of the University.

I contacted the Pittsburgh banker who was the chairman of the Investment Committee of the Board of Trustees of the University. He agreed to submit the matter to his committee and to pass it along to the chairman of the Board of Trustees if his committee decided it was not within their jurisdiction. By registered mail on 6 May 1982, I sent the committee chairman six copies of the fifteen letters between the administration and myself that constituted the record of the case, and sent a copy of my transmitting letter to the president of the University.

Having received no response, on 8 July 1982, I sent by registered mail a reminding letter to the committee chairman with a copy to the chairman of the Board of Trustees. I have never received a response from the Board of Trustees or from its committee.

In June 1983, I had occasion to express to the dean of the Faculty of the Arts and Sciences my disappointment at the failure of the University to answer my questions about the handling of these funds. He offered to ask for a review of the matter by the University's newly appointed in-house counsel.

The new counsel's response, dated 3 January 1984, dealt only with a question that I had never raised and that was never mentioned in the correspondence, namely, whether the University was within its rights in investing the Mellon money as it saw fit. It did not deal with the use of the investment income.

To further confuse the matter, the second counsel's opinion implied that the funds in question had been yielding interest to the University at only the savings-bank passbook rate, and that this was my reason for complaining.

Although the first counsel had written that the Mellon grant had been placed in current funds for investment purposes, the administration had repeatedly refused to say in writing how these funds were invested. That they were invested in short-term loans conformed to what I had been told informally in March 1981, as well as to common sense and to newspaper accounts of the University's financial dealings.

For proper appreciation, the second counsel's legal opinion must be sampled as he wrote it:

> I reviewed the entire file of both the University counsel's office and [the dean]. In addition I reviewed applicable Pennsylvania and Federal Regulations relating to the fiduciary and trust obligations of universities and others administering endowment and trust funds. A further source was the fourth edition of *College and University Business Administration,* an accounting publication of the National Association of College and University Business Officers, which is the most commonly used guide for accounting and investment of university and college funds . . . .
>
> It is not the function of a university counsel (or outside counsel) to comment upon the wisdom of an investment policy so long as it conforms with applicable rules, regulations, and statutes pertaining to the handling of funds held in trust by a fiduciary. Irrespective of whether the investment of the Mellon funds was wise or whether they could perhaps have produced a greater income, they were invested in a lawful manner. Further, the funds were handled within the guidelines established by the National Association of College and University Business Officers.
>
> For each and all of the reasons set forth above, it is my opinion that the handling of the funds received by the

University for the support of Dr. McConnell's program was proper when viewed in the context of the University's fiduciary obligations. It is not within the scope of this memo to discuss whether a different investment policy might have been preferable. However, it should be noted that had the funds been invested in a manner calculated to produce a greater return but at a greater risk, it may very well be that the handling of the funds would have imposed liability on the University had the investment gone sour. It is universally accepted that investment in bank deposits is a method of investing funds held in trust satisfying a fiduciary obligation and that the imposition of a small handling or administrative fee (such as one-half of one percent) is not unreasonable in this circumstance. [No question had been raised regarding the one-half percent management fee.]

* * * * *

There the matter has rested because I could not devote more time to it and because the amount of money in dispute (about $100,000) would not support independent legal action, particularly in view of the complexity of the legal questions that could be raised.

There is nothing unusual about this story. It illustrates several ways by which people can be manipulated from a position of power. Adults should find it boring. Our children need to know as early as possible how the world works—or it will never be changed. They need to know the complexity of life so that they do not dissipate their idealism tilting with windmills.

Parapsychologists need to know that these same tactics are used against any threat to leadership. The protection of the status quo is to be expected from every group that holds power, be it in business, education, politics, or science.

Why did the administrative officers of this university violate their contractual commitment in this case? My guess is that: (1) Like all universities today, ours is desperately pressed for money. (2) The administrators did not wish to alter their accounting system and to set a precedent by which future donors could expect to deprive the University of a hidden source of income (interest on working capital).

Because people are mainly unreasoning, it can be argued that one cannot govern a corporation (or a country) without deception—just as one must routinely deceive small children.

The only question may be: How much will be self-deception and how much the conscious deception of others? Less damage may be done by conscious deception; for this allows weighing the good and evil consequences of various degrees of candor. If conscious deception is essential in the operation of our daily affairs, I believe we must acknowledge and deal with the moral dilemma this presents—or there can be no hope for a sustainable future. Self-deception with regard to our deceiving others is a destructive luxury we can no longer afford.

11

A FESTIVAL OF SELF-DECEPTION

J. B. RHINE, THE FOUNDING FATHER

The Parapsychological Association was founded in 1957 upon the initiative of J. B. Rhine to be a worldwide professional organization with the following objectives: To advance parapsychology as a science, to disseminate knowledge of the field, and to integrate the findings with those of other branches of science. I was privileged to be its first president and to help resolve the factional disputes of its infancy.

Now, as then, among our members there are many with limited scientific training who by their enthusiasm and service have contributed greatly to our growing strength and who are a treasured part of our organization.

However, given the heterogeneity of the membership, it is not surprising that questions of disciplinary action for violation of professional ethics could arise apart from any consideration of a member's educational background. It is with such a question that this chapter deals.

The material presented herein should have historical interest, but my immediate purpose is to illustrate still another facet of reality avoidance—this time by an Association member of some prominence and by the governing Council of the Association in dealing with the challenge presented by that member.

One of the tragedies of J. B. Rhine's life was his betrayal by an employee to whom he had entrusted the management of his research laboratory. In June 1974, W. J. Levy was discovered by his co-workers to be falsifying data to show ESP in rats in an automated shock-avoidance experiment. Confronted with evidence gathered by electronic surveillance, Levy confessed his guilt, submitted his resignation, and left Rhine's laboratory on the day following the disclosure of his fraud to J. B. Rhine.

The world of science was promptly notified that all of Levy's research, extending over a period of several years, must be assumed to be without scientific validity.

J. B. Rhine died 20 February 1980. Before her death (17 March 1983, at age 91) Louisa Rhine completed a biography of herself and her husband under the title, *Something Hidden.*[1] Although I never had a close relationship with the Rhines, I was deeply moved by this intimate account of the lives of this pioneering couple.

SOMETHING HIDDEN

Subsequently, a professional writer (S), who was also a member of the Parapsychological Association, wrote a review of *Something Hidden* for a mass-market magazine, *Fate*, devoted to occult superstition. S had long been a contributor to *Fate* and was listed on its masthead as a consulting editor.

S took the opportunity afforded by his review to charge that Dr. J. B. Rhine:

> was forced to fire [W. J.] Levy almost against his will, that he tried to cover up the full extent of [Levy's] fraud, and that he attempted to hide the fact that subsequent research was failing to replicate Levy's findings (*Fate*, May 1984, p. 100).

The September, 1984, issue of *Fate*, carried a formal denial of S's charges signed by the Director of the Institute for Parapsychology, which is the operating arm of J. B. Rhine's Foundation for Research on the Nature of Man (FRNM). In that same issue of *Fate*, S renewed and expanded his attack, saying (pp. 111–113):

> It would be nice to believe that Dr. Rhine acted nobly and incisively when he learned that his protégé Levy was faking research—but that is not what happened . . . . [J. B. Rhine] did not immediately fire Levy even when the young researcher openly confessed.
>
> J.B.'s original plan was to give Levy a leave of absence, explain his fraud as the result of a "breakdown," and then rehire him. The plan was not put into effect because other prominent parapsychologists discovered it and persuaded J.B. that he would embarrass himself and the field unless he fired Levy on the spot. In the face of pressure from such prominent researchers as the late J. Gaither Pratt and Dr. R. A. McConnell, Rhine finally acquiesced.

---

[1] Jefferson, North Carolina: McFarland & Co., 1983.
The title is from a poem by Rudyard Kipling.

> Rhine's lapse in judgment in the Levy affair is forgivable
> . . . . But what happened afterward is nothing less than in-
> sidious . . . . I know the whole sordid story firsthand . . . .
> Rhine was trying to interfere with research that was bound to
> place Levy in a poor light . . . . J.B. didn't want news of
> any failures of the Levy replication attempts leaking out until
> a great number of such attempts had been completed and
> could be reported jointly.

Dr. J. G. Pratt had died on 3 November 1979. Since I was available to give testimony, I was asked by FRNM what light I could throw on S's charges. I responded that, in so far as S's charges involved me, I knew them to be false.

On 4 September 1984 I sent a letter to the governing Council of the Parapsychological Association telling what I knew about S's accusations and requesting that the Council investigate the matter to decide whether, in accordance with the bylaws, S should be "dismissed from the Association for conduct injurious to the objects of the Association." That letter appears in full as appendix *A* to this chapter.

The Council had already begun an inquiry into S's public attack on J. B. Rhine. As a result, in late November, I received unsolicited from S a 43-page "report" purporting to explain and defend his actions in this matter. On 2 December, I sent to the Council a letter analyzing in detail S's defense. In summary, I said:

> On page after page, S uses the gimmicks of the literary con
> artist, including repetition ad nauseum, unstated assumptions,
> concealed misstatements, logical non sequiturs, failure to dis-
> tinguish between hearsay and firsthand evidence, padding by
> irrelevancies which are falsely implied to support his case,
> progressive shifting of the meaning of words, verbal distinc-
> tions that are implied to be important but that are never
> defined, pretending to logical precision and fairmindedness
> by making points and then generously conceding that they
> are trivial or irrelevant. Some examples have been given in
> the preceding pages. Others will be found throughout S's
> report.
>
> In the absence of any evidence that outside pressure was
> brought to bear to stop Rhine's supposed plan to give Levy a
> leave of absence, S's case simply falls apart . . . . The
> central charges made by S in *Fate* must be judged as scandal
> mongering by a professional popularizer . . . . In my judg-

ment, S's document, which he wrote to defend himself, serves instead to convict him.

My 2 December letter to Council appears as appendix *B* to this chapter, complete except for its introduction and conclusion.

ACCUSATION AND RETRACTION

S had charged Rhine with planning and attempting to deceive the scientific world. S based his case primarily upon his conversation three months after the events in question with someone who was not present in the city where and when the events occurred, and who does not now remember the conversation. While it was clear from my analysis that S had no proof of the truth of his allegations, I did not expect that, after ten years, it would be possible for anyone to disprove them except as to peripheral details.

Up to December, 1984, according to information given me by members of Council and by employees of the Institute for Parapsychology, S was refusing to publish a satisfactory retraction and the lawyers for both sides were prepared to take the case to court.

Meanwhile, Dr. Richard S. Broughton in his position as Acting Director of Research at the Institute for Parapsychology had been devoting his time to this matter for several months. Digging in the J. B. Rhine archives at Duke University, he struck an informational lode. Rhine or his secretary, either by accident or prescience, had saved the rough drafts of Rhine's letter announcing the Levy fraud. These and other drafts found in a personal file showed by pencilled notations the joint development by staff members of the final letter which went out a week after Levy's exposure. The drafts, together with some two-dozen other documents (including statements gathered from five persons having firsthand knowledge of the affair), proved the falsity of S's charges.

On 6 December 1984 Dr. Broughton submitted a report of his findings to the Council of the Parapsychological Association (which saw itself acting as an intermediary between S and FRNM), together with photocopies of the original documents destroying S's charges.

I have a copy of the report and have seen photocopies of the letter drafts to which it refers. Broughton did a superb job. I was satisfied that all of the important facts in this case had been firmly established. S apparently thought so, too; for a retraction by him, acceptable to FRNM, appeared in *Fate* for April, 1985 (pp. 113-114).

As I learned later, S was given a first hearing by the governing Council of the Parapsychological Association at Dallas, Texas, in August, 1984, three months after his first published attack upon Dr. Rhine. He submitted his defense to Council in writing on 16 November, 1984, as described above. Informational statements by me (appendixes *A* and *B* hereto) were submitted to Council on 4 September and 2 December 1984. Dr. Broughton submitted his analysis of the matter on 6 December 1984. By the end of December, seven months after S's first attack, Council had again formally addressed the problem of S's false accusations of Dr. Rhine, and the evidential aspect of the case was closed.

Under "Articles of Note" the magazine *Skeptical Inquirer* (q.v.) for Winter, 1985, (*9*, 182-183) called attention to S's second article in *Fate* (September, 1984, 111-113). As a follow-up in "From Our Readers," *Skeptical Inquirer*, for Summer, 1985, (*9*, 396-397) printed a letter from S, which said in part:

> The summary you published is extremely inaccurate and misleading. You say: "S reveals that Rhine failed to listen to colleagues' suspicions that something was amiss and that later, when the fraud was apparent, made a series of attempts to keep it from becoming known." I said no such thing.

The *Skeptical Inquirer* followed with: "We maintain that our two-sentence note was an accurate summary of S's letter to *Fate*, and we could excerpt quotes to demonstrate that." *Skeptical Inquirer* went on to say that Dr. Richard Broughton of FRNM had written to them and "stated that the evidence S cited was nonexistent and [that] S was publishing a retraction in *Fate*'s April [1985] issue."

S wrote another letter to *Skeptical Inquirer* (*ibid.*), saying in part:

> I have been sent a copy of the letter that Dr. Broughton sent to you . . . . I feel a reply is necessary.
>
> In no sense is my [April] letter to *Fate* a "retraction of my claims." It is a letter of clarification in which I threw added light on the Rhine / Levy matter . . . .
>
> [The Rhine / Levy / S] matter was brought before the Parapsychological Association Council in December [1984] . . . .

> Despite a request from FRNM, the Council would not act on their urging that I be officially censured for what I wrote.

I have since been privately informed that FRNM made no request (and offered no advice) to the officers of the Parapsychological Association as to what action, if any, that organization should take on its own behalf. S's above-quoted sentence becomes correct if it is shortened to, "Council would not act."[2]

In an explanatory letter dated 23 September 1986, the President of the Parapsychological Association wrote to me:

> [W]e have decided that an organization of our limited resources cannot afford the time nor expense of adjudicating grievances . . . . Over the past two years the P.A. first spent quite a bit of time to develop a procedure for placing and adjudicating grievances and then, as new information came into play and we began to consider the wisdom of an adjudicatory system, we spent quite a bit of time considering alternatives and coming to our policy.

The relevance of this post hoc policy is not apparent. Council had already evaluated the grievance of FRNM against S and had arranged a public retraction satisfactory to FRNM. My request to Council was not for redress of grievance but for a consideration of action under the bylaws for the protection of the organization against a member's conduct "injurious to the objects of the Association."

To avoid misunderstanding on this point, I had written in the introduction to my letter to Council which is reproduced as appendix *B*:

> If you will reread my letter to Council dated 4 September, you will discover that I did not ask Council to be my agent vis-a-vis S. Moreover, Council has not consulted with me in this matter. My letter merely gave information, along with a request that Council take action as the facts may dictate.

After two years it would appear that the Council members have

---

[2] The constitution and bylaws of the Parapsychological Association have never contained a provision for the censuring of a member, and such an action would have been legally inappropriate. Had S been dismissed from the Association, his dismissal would necessarily have been carried out in the customary manner of professional societies, i.e., without a public announcement.

decided that the repeated slandering of the scientific reputation of the deceased founder of the Parapsychological Association by a popular-science writer is not sufficient grounds for his dismissal from membership in the Association. We have already seen in chapter 3 how a neuroscientist Fellow of the Royal Society believes that Rhine's research has been "discredited" — presumably by attacks from outside the field. In view of the reputational difficulties under which the young science of parapsychology labors, it is hard to imagine why the Parapsychological Association would officially ignore the slandering of Dr. Rhine by one of its own members. After reading appendixes *A* and *B*, the reader may wish to consider whether this behavior by the governing body of this thirty-year-old organization does not define it as a social, rather than a professional, society, thereby violating the expectation of the founder, J. B. Rhine, and the high hopes of the charter members.

S's offense and his subsequent defense thereof are puzzling in that they raise a question about the nature of his thought processes. Was his self-defending brief composed out of cynical bravado or pathetic confusion? After examining appendix *B*, the reader's first reaction, like mine, may be that S was knowingly deceptive. To me it now seems more probable that, like many people, S lives in a well-ordered world of his own that connects only loosely with the consensus world of the rest of us. His skill lies in tying his world to ours by verbal strings that have for him a satisfying flavor of logic. Nevertheless, according to *Parapsychology Review* (July–August, 1986, p. 5), which is published by the Parapsychology Foundation, S "currently serves on the graduate faculty of the John F. Kennedy University [and] he is the author of over twenty books on the paranormal."

Chapter Appendix A

CONCERN

4 September 1984

This letter brings to the attention of the Council of the Parapsychological Association what I believe to be "conduct injurious to the objects of the Association" by one of our members, Mr. S. I request that Council consider this matter under Section IV, Paragraph 8, of the Fourth Edition (1978) of the Bylaws of the Association and that it decide after proper investigation whether Mr. S should be dismissed from membership in the Association.

In his review of Dr. Louisa Rhine's *Something Hidden*, which appeared on pages 96–102 in *Fate* magazine of May, 1984, S charged (p. 100) that Dr. J. B. Rhine "was forced to fire [W. J.] Levy almost against his will, that he tried to cover up the full extent of [Levy's] fraud, and that he attempted to hide the fact that subsequent research was failing to replicate Levy's findings."

These accusations were denied by K. R. Rao, Director of the Institute for Parapsychology at Durham, North Carolina, in the "Report from the Readers" section on page 111 of *Fate* magazine of September, 1984. In the same issue of *Fate*, on pages 111–113, S rejected Rao's denial in these words:

> I am dismayed by Dr. Rao's reaction to my review . . . .
> Perhaps Dr. Rao is simply unaware of the true story, a story
> that has never been fully told. It would be nice to believe
> that Dr. Rhine acted nobly and incisively when he learned
> that his protégé Levy, was faking research—but that is not
> what happened.

S then resumed his attack up J. B. Rhine, claiming that, when presented with the evidence of fraud, Rhine "did not immediately fire Levy even when the young researcher openly confessed." S expanded this accusation as follows:

> J.B.'s [Rhine's] original plan was to give Levy a leave of
> absence, explain his fraud as the result of a "breakdown,"
> and then rehire him. The plan was not put into effect be-
> cause other prominent parapsychologists discovered it and
> persuaded J.B. that he would embarrass himself and the field
> unless he fired Levy on the spot. In the face of pressure
> from such prominent researchers as the late J. Gaither Pratt
> and Dr. R. A. McConnell, Rhine finally acquiesced.

This is a serious charge. It is also an inherently improbable charge, as I shall presently show. Moreover, from my own knowledge, it is a false charge in so far as my purported role is concerned. S continued his accusations as follows:

> Rhine's lapse in judgment in the Levy affair is forgivable
> . . . . But what happened afterward is nothing less than
> insidious.[3]

---

[3] The context suggests that the writer may have meant "invidious."

Rhine invited J, a young researcher who had previously worked with Levy, to come [back] to Durham and replicate their much-heralded experiments on precognition in small rodents. If J were successful, Levy would be vindicated. But it just didn't work out. (At the time, J was working primarily as a research assistant at Maimonides Medical Center's division of parapsychology [in New York City] where I was also visiting regularly. We communicated frequently so I know the whole sordid story firsthand.)

In this statement S also accused Rhine of "trying to interfere with research that was bound to place Levy in a poor light" and of then trying to pressure the 1975 Parapsychological Association Research Briefs Chairman "into keeping the J research off the program." The nature of the "insidious" and "sordid" behavior with which S charged Rhine was not explained by S, who said merely that:

J.B. didn't want news of any failures of the Levy replication attempts leaking out until a great number of such attempts had been completed and could be reported jointly.

S's commentary is followed on pages 113–115 in *Fate* by a statement from J in which he says that he spent three weeks at Rhine's laboratory in May, 1975, a year after the Levy exposure, attempting unsuccessfully to replicate his earlier work with Levy and that, later, despite a previous understanding to the contrary, Rhine refused to allow the presentation at the August, 1975, Parapsychological Association meeting of any research reflecting on Levy's work.

Neither S nor J mentions that this work by J was, in fact, presented by J at that 1975 meeting under the title "Levy Replications: Continuation of the Rodent Precognition Experiments" and appears on pages 11–14 in *Research in Parapsychology—1975.* Instead, S seems deliberately to imply otherwise by saying that the paper was first rejected and then withdrawn (p. 113).

Taken as a whole, S's and J's statements would support the idea that, having publicly announced in June, 1974, that Levy had engaged in fraudulent research and having explicitly said that all of Levy's research findings were in doubt, Rhine preferred to proceed in a deliberate and conservative manner in publishing later findings bearing upon the extent of Levy's fraud. His purpose could have been to minimize publicity which, by its nature, would in the public mind necessarily tend to generalize adversely to the field as a whole. Contrariwise, S and J seem to have believed that maximum exposure should have been given to the Levy affair by stringing out the reports of replication failures, beginning a year after the original announcement of fraud.

The J statement is followed on pages 115–116 by a statement by R of

Los Angeles who bears witness to the fact that S had heard rumors of fraud in Levy's spectacularly successful experiments as early as 1972 and that ten months before Levy's final exposure, which occurred in June, 1974, S believed that "accusations of fraud on Levy's part were being commonly spread," and that "unsuccessful attempts had been made to bring these accusations to Rhine's attention."

The foregoing would be consistent with the idea that, while Rhine may have heard rumors of Levy's dishonesty, he refused to act until the case had ripened and strong evidence had been obtained—a procedure that would be followed by any cautious and fair-minded administrator.

In judging S's activities in this matter, Council will need to consider the nature of the magazine in which he published his charges and also his ongoing relation to that magazine.

Fate is a five-by-seven-inch monthly serial devoted to occult and related interests. According to the 1984 *Ayer Directory of Publications*, its claimed circulation is 135,000. The September, 1984, issue of *Fate* had 130 pages. Thirty-four percent of the page space was devoted to 278 advertisements. This issue included articles on unidentified flying objects, a poltergeist (by S), and handwriting (subhead: "Can poor penmanship habits turn you into a criminal?").

Advertisements in this issue of *Fate* had titles or subtitles such as these: "*Winning with Witchcraft*", "The Gold Cross of Lourdes" ($10 each), "Pocket numerology calculator", "Jackie's horoscope says . . . ." (full page with a picture of Jacqueline Onassis, the widow of the late President John F. Kennedy), "*The Practice of Magical Evocation*" ($19.95), "Ball-bearing Planchettes", "I got rid of my cancer", "Complete correspondence course in Voodoo", "Jesus never existed", "Age Old Chant" ($6.00). From the foregoing it seems safe to infer that *Fate* is not a scholarly journal.

S has had a long association with *Fate* magazine. He is listed on its masthead as a consulting editor. His picture and by-line regularly appear as part of the heading of the "Books, News, and Reviews" section. From time to time, he does full-length articles. However else he may describe himself, S is also a professional journalist.

According to its 1982 *Directory of Members*, S is a Full Member of the Parapsychological Association with specific interests in spontaneous phenomena and altered states of consciousness. In 1972 he received a Bachelor of Arts degree in music at California State University at Northridge. He lists himself as having expertise in the history and literature of parapsychology.

As described above, S has publicly written that I put pressure on Rhine to convince him that he should discharge W. J. Levy instead of giving him a leave of absence. Although it is generally impossible to prove that one did not communicate a particular idea to a now-deceased person on some unspecified date ten years ago, I can say in this instance that I have no memory of any communication with Rhine on the matter of *discharging* W. J. Levy and that I have considerable circumstantial evidence showing that no such communication ever took place.

It is my custom to save copies of all professional letters and to make and save notes concerning significant visits or telephone conversations with people of importance who are outside my daily acquaintanceship. Hence, if the alleged persuading contact with J. B. Rhine had actually taken place, I would expect to find a record of it in my files. Despite a diligent search, I have found nothing relating to the employment or discharge of Levy.

What my records show is that on 13 June 1974, I was telephoned on her own initiative by Dorothy H. Pope, then co-editor of the *Journal of Parapsychology*. She told me she had just learned that Levy had been caught faking data by several members of the laboratory and she felt it important for the field that anyone who might be professionally relying upon his data should be informed as quickly as possible.

Thereafter, on the same day, I telephoned the news to Robert Morris, President of the Parapsychological Association, and to Charles Honorton, a member of the Association's governing council.

The next day, in the belief that I needed an official confirmation in case I was questioned by a news reporter, I telephoned Rhine. My notes show that he confirmed the bare fact of the discovery of Levy's dishonesty but refused to elaborate or even to tell me the names of those involved in the discovery. Instead, he wanted to know whether I had heard about it from his own people or elsewhere. He said that a statement to the Board of Directors of the Foundation for Research on the Nature of Man was in preparation and that I and others would receive a copy—which I did within a week. That statement gave a brief description of how the fraud was discovered and said that Levy had "resigned from all his official connections with the Foundation."

(Upon reading the present letter in draft form, Dr. T. K. Clark, who shares my office and is a member of the Parapsychological Association, confirmed from her memory that, after I learned of Levy's fraud, I made a telephone call to J. B. Rhine, seeking confirmation and offering sympathy but nothing more.)

A longer account of the Levy uncovering was published on pages 215–225 of the *Journal of Parapsychology* for June, 1974, in which Rhine (p. 217) said that "all of Levy's experimental reports, published or unpublished, authored by him alone or jointly with others, were to be considered unacceptable, even though there was only one acknowledged instance of falsification."

The most concise account of the Levy affair known to me is that by

James Davis (one of the three persons who collaborated in uncovering Levy's dishonesty). It was presented orally at the August, 1974, convention of the Parapsychological Association (two months after the proof of fraud) and appears on pages 11 and 12 of *Research in Parapsychology—1974*. Davis states that:

> . . . I witnessed Dr. Levy going in and manipulating the apparatus in such a way as to produce the effects that we saw on the [secretly taken] independent record. The following day we spoke, first with Louisa Rhine, and then with J. B. Rhine, and that afternoon J. B. Rhine confronted Dr. Levy with the evidence, at which point he admitted he had manipulated the data in the manner described, and promptly submitted his resignation . . . . It is, of course, necessary for all of Dr. Levy's work to be held suspect . . . .

I remember congratulating Davis for the clarity and forthrightness of his presentation.

Even aside from my failure to find objective records that would support S's position, my lack of any memory of a communication on this matter is by itself all but conclusive evidence that no such communication occurred. I had visited Dr. Rhine's laboratory several times beginning in 1947, but our relationship was never a close one and I had only infrequent contacts with him after 1963. Hence, any telephone conversation with him in 1974 about the firing of an employee would not soon have been forgotten.

Moreover, a proposal to condone an experimenter's dishonesty by giving him a leave of absence as ascribed to Rhine by S is in conflict with my sense of scientific propriety. Therefore, I would expect it to remain in my memory if it came from the leading scientist of parapsychology. Nevertheless, I had no memory of that idea prior to reading S's statement prepared for the September, 1984, issue of *Fate*.

Over the years, young people associated with Rhine have complained to me that he was heartless in discharging employees whom he judged no longer useful in his laboratory. For this reason, too, I would have perceived the soft-hearted action ascribed to Rhine by S to be out of keeping with Rhine's reputation and therefore noteworthy.

For a further reason, which I shall now explain, in my judgment S's charge is so inherently improbable that it would have been laid aside by any responsible journalist unless incontrovertible proof of its truth were forthcoming. S says that, although Levy had confessed to falsifying his experimental data, Rhine nevertheless planned to rehire him after he recovered from his breakdown (meaning, I suppose, after the furor over his dishonesty had died down).

The one passion of Rhine's life was to advance parapsychology as a science. The major difficulty of research in this field is to produce the phenomena. It is well known that to do so requires a tranquil and dedicated laboratory environment. Moreover, the question of the sanity of both subjects and experimenters has always been an open one in the minds of many critics of the field. In view of Rhine's sensitivity to the psychological factors in his research, I find it difficult to suppose that he would have considered bringing back into his laboratory a former director who had been forced out because he was either dishonest by nature or had suffered a mental breakdown.

Rather, the question comes to mind as to what motivation could have led a professional journalist, who was also a member of the Parapsychological Association, to publicly embrace this supposition? How could he justify to himself an attack in this unsupported fashion upon the memory of the man who, in the opinion of most parapsychologists, had done more than anyone else to advance parapsychology as a science? The only clue I could find to S's thinking is his final paragraph (p. 113):

> Now that Rhine is dead, there is no reason to cover up either his handling of the Levy affair or its aftermath. If he ultimately acted honorably, it was only because outside pressure was brought to bear.

By his research, Rhine gained serious attention for the field worldwide; even while, through his books, he made ESP a household word. To the best of my knowledge, his scientific integrity has never before been publicly questioned. Unless some appropriate counteraction is taken beyond mere retraction, I fear that this unsubstantiated accusation against Rhine will do irreparable damage to the field.

Leaving to Council the consideration of these larger issues, I can only say, in summary, that I have no recollection or record of receiving, at the time, the idea that Levy might not be, or had not been, promptly discharged after the discovery of his dishonesty. Had any such idea been given to me, I would expect to have saved it on paper and to have it in my memory. Thus, so far as I can determine, Mr. S's statement regarding me is false. I shall now present evidence to show that this statement was carelessly or maliciously published by Mr. S.

On 17 May 1984, I received from S an unsolicited letter dated 15 May (copy attached hereto as Enclosure *A*) in which he disclosed his plan to publish in an unspecified forthcoming issue of *Fate* a statement by K. R. Rao, along with one by himself, concerning his earlier criticism of J. B. Rhine in the May, 1984, issue of the same magazine. S invited me to submit any comment I wished for publication as part of some future roundup of reader opinion. He enclosed copies of (1) his original review of Louisa Rhine's *Something Hidden*, (2) K. R. Rao's response thereto, and (3) his proposed statement rejecting Rao's defense of Rhine. (A copy of the last is attached as Enclosure *B*.)

Mr. S did not, at any time prior to writing his review of *Something Hidden* or prior to sending me the above-described letter of 15 May, contact me to ask if it were true that I had knowledge of a plan by Rhine to grant Levy a leave of absence and, if I did, whether I had objected to Rhine about it. Since receiving his 15 May letter, I have had no further word from Mr. S.

A comparison will show that there are some changes between S's statement as sent to me privately and that which he later published in the September, 1984, *Fate*. These changes (presumably made by S or by the editor of *Fate*) are mainly deletions of words or ideas (1) that suggest a strong emotional involvement by S in this affair, or (2) that, by their removal, make S's accusations more vague and therefore more difficult to disprove. For example, as can be seen in the enclosed copy of what was privately sent to me, S said:

> [Rhine] did not immediately fire Levy, even when the young researcher openly confessed . . . . J.B.'s original plan was to give Levy a leave of absence, explain his fraud as the result of a "breakdown," and then rehire him. The plan was not put into effect *only* [emphasized in the original] because other prominent parapsychologists discovered it and started phoning J.B., reasoning with him that he would embarrass himself and the field unless he fired Levy on the spot. The most pressure came from the late J. Gaither Pratt and Dr. R. A. McConnell, two prominent researchers. Rhine finally acquiesced.

In the published version (which I quoted near the beginning of this letter) the word "only" was deleted, the words "started phoning" became "persuaded," and the phrasing "The most pressure came from" was changed to "In the face of pressure from."

S's letter of transmittal to me (Enclosure *A*) was not a request for confirmation or denial of the action he ascribed to me, but was simply (1) an announcement of his plan to publish a statement dealing, in part, with my supposed activity, plus (2) an invitation to me to discuss any aspect of the matter I might choose. S said in his transmitting letter:

> After much deliberation, we at *Fate* . . . have decided to run Dr. Rao's letter along with my response. We are asking other researchers knowledgable about this matter to comment . . . . We would like you to respond either to the review, to Dr. Rao's letter, or to my own comments. These will be published in an upcoming issue of *Fate* in which the entire correspondence column will be given over to this controversy.

In this letter there was no promise to publish, uncut, whatever I might send. Nor was it clear whether the invited comments would appear in the same issue with, or in an issue following, the Rao statement cum S reply. (The antecedent of "These" is vague.) Post hoc, it is apparent that S already had plans to publish statements by J and R in the same issue as his own and that he hoped for a supporting statement from me.

I regard this letter from S as a news-journalist's attempt to expand an ongoing controversy of his own creation by publishing an unproved and, in fact, false statement about an outside party while offering that party a chance to deny the statement at some time.

I did not reply to S's letter. My reasons included the following. Despite his clear expression of intent to publish his statement about me, I believed it possible that he was merely applying pressure upon me to confirm or to deny his statement and that he would not be so foolish as to publish it without telephoning me for confirmation. Contrariwise, if S did publish his false statement about me, that fact could be significant in the later public assessment of any evidence for his charge that Rhine had to be dissuaded from giving Levy a leave of absence. Thus, his subsequent actions with regard to naming me could serve as a litmus test of his journalistic integrity. As it turned out, such a test is un-necesary because S has published no evidence whatsoever to support this charge.

I assume that Council will decide to investigate this matter. Please call upon me if I can provide further information and inform me as to the final action of Council.

Chapter Appendix B
CONDEMNATION

2 December 1984

[I have received] a 43-page legal-looking document signed by S on 16 November 1984. It is identified on its title page as a report to Council [of the Parapsychological Association], and claims under *Introductory Remarks* to be "interim only" because Mr. S hopes in the future to gain support for his defense by corresponding with W. J. Levy and L.

Since this document came to me from Mr. S, unsolicited and without restrictions (but with a demand that I retract an allegation I had not made), I feel free to use it as I choose. At this time, I offer the following comments to Council, for which I am sure they will be grateful.

For ease of reference, I have numbered the pages of the body of my copy of this report from 1 to 31, starting with the page following the table of contents. If I received all pages, this numbering should agree with a similar numbering of the copy you must have received.

The S affair can be approached from various points of view, two of which I shall briefly describe.

1. J. B. Rhine is dead and therefore fair game for historians and scandal mongers. The Parapsychological Association Council's task is to decide into which category S falls. For Council, the truth or falsity of S's charges against Rhine is important only as it bears upon the classification of S's behavior. If his allegations were presented without qualification (and they were so presented), and if they cannot be proved to be true, Council has a prima facie case against him and the burden of proof that he acted in a professionally proper manner shifts to him.

2. The Foundation for Research on the nature of Man, founded by J. B. Rhine—and perhaps parapsychologists generally—have a different task. They would like to show that S's charges are false and thus protect the memory of Rhine as a scientist of integrity. Because it is usually impossible to prove a negative contention of this kind, the best FRNM can hope to do is to show that there is no reasonable basis for supposing S's charges are true. This is a more difficult task than that of Council. [I was wrong in this prediction. As already described in the text of this chapter, FRNM was able to disprove completely S's charges. —RAM]

There is a curious feature of S's report which raises a question as to his motivation and which I bring to Council's attention at the outset of my commentary, namely: S attempts to show only that his charges against Rhine might reasonably be supposed to be true. Typically, he says "This probability is certainly substantiated by L's remarks." (p. 3) He does not try to defend himself against the charge of unprofessional behavior by proving that his charges are undeniably true, but is satisfied to weaken FRNM's contention that they are false. In my judgment, he fails to reach even this more limited objective.

The foregoing and other bizarre features of S's report make sense in my mind only as attempts to confuse the thinking of the reader. The entire report can be briefly characterized as pitched at the level of the readers of *Fate* magazine and insulting to the members of the Council of the Parapsychological Association.

S's Main Charges

There are three related central elements to S's public attack upon J. B. Rhine, which I shall discuss separately.

1. Rhine "did not immediately fire Levy even when the young researcher openly confessed" to experimental fraud. [*Fate, 37*(9), p. 111]

2. "J.B.'s original plan was to give Levy a leave of absence . . . and then rehire him." [*Fate, 37*(9), p. 111]

3. Rhine "was forced to fire Levy almost against his will."
[*Fate, 37*(5) p. 100]

I shall not cover S's subsidiary charges that there was widespread suspicion of Levy prior to his exposure and that, afterward, there were delays in publishing failed replications of Levy's work. These topics were discussed in my 4 September letter to Council.

Charge 1: Rhine Did Not Immediately Fire Levy

S has not questioned FRNM's statement that within a day after Rhine learned of his dishonesty, Levy had left the laboratory, leaving behind a signed letter of resignation, and that seven days after the discovery of the dishonesty, Rhine mailed an announcement of the events to his Foundation Board of Directors as well as to senior parapsychologists, including myself.

One would think this settled the question of a delay in the termination of Levy's employment. Nevertheless, S argues that, in some obscure way, even though Rhine had received Levy's resignation, he did not "accept" it. S continues to defend his statement in *Fate* that Rhine "did not immediately fire Levy even when the young researcher openly confessed" his guilt.

S bases his defense on a letter from Mr. L., dated 5 October 1984, written in response to an inquiry from Mr. S. With regard to a delay in accepting Levy's resignation, L wrote the following paragraph. (Mr. L is one of the three experimenters who, acting jointly, produced evidence of Levy's fraudulent manipulation of data. I understand that the other two have already stated their support of Rhine against Mr. S's accusations.)

> However, you state that "right after the scandal broke, Rhine had initially stalled accepting Levy's resignation, and only accepted it when outside pressure was brought to bear on him." This is not my interpretation of the events. It is not my impression that Rhine was stalling, but that he was simply living through a crisis which he knew in his heart to be a severe blow to his own reputation and to the reputation of parapsychology as science. I think it understandable that it took Rhine a few days to admit to himself that the man he had put all of his faith and trust in, as the next leader of parapsychology, had betrayed him. I do not view this as stalling [S's "Report", p. 36].

Although S had asked about "accepting Levy's resignation," L does not use that expression. It is obvious that L is talking about an emotional acceptance of Levy's dishonesty and not about the acceptance of

Levy's resignation. Since emotional acceptance is usually known only by inference, one may wonder as to the observational basis of L's comment.

Possibly, after several days, Rhine decided that it was time to get his laboratory back into production. Possibly because he had heard a rumor that he planned to give Levy a leave of absence, Rhine may have said to some or all of his staff, "Levy has given me a letter of resignation. He will not return. It is time we get on with the business of research."

This is my speculation. L's letter gives no clue whether any observed event occurred to mark off the emotional adjustment to Levy's dishonesty.

S sees a sinister meaning in this L description, and he further argues that the seven-day delay in mailing a news announcement is incriminating because Rhine had the final draft of his letter ready to go within two days except for minor word changes.

The question of a few days delay in the handling of the consequential details of the Levy termination is legally frivolous. The obvious truth, despite S's five-page litany of argument and counter-argument, is that such a delay cannot imply reprehensible activity. It would lie within the range of normal behavior for any conservative administrator, and it cannot justify S's public accusation that Rhine "did not immediately fire Levy."

Charge 2: Rhine Had a Plan to Give Levy a Leave of Absence and Later Rehire Him

The second main element in S's attack is his charge that Rhine planned to give Levy a leave of absence and later to rehire him. In his letter of inquiry to L, S wrote:

> Right after the scandal broke, I heard a story that Rhine had initially stalled accepting Levy's resignation, and only accepted it when outside pressure was brought to bear on him. His plan was to actually give Levy a leave of absence and then rehire him, explaining his "lapse" as a breakdown. Can you verify the accuracy or not of this story [*ibid.*, p. 35]?

The following paragraph from L's letter responds to this inquiry:

> From my point of view, your picture of Rhine's reactions to Levy's exposure is only partially true. In the 72 hours or so just after Rhine was confronted with Levy's fraud he quite naturally sought ways to clear his protégé of the charges. Eventually [This could only have been no later than the day following his exposure. —RAM], Levy offered the excuse to

> J.B. that his behavior was due to self-imposed pressure to produce consistently positive results "for the good of the field of parapsychology." Rhine or Levy or both did come up with the plan you mention: to give Levy a leave of absence, explaining his behavior as a temporary breakdown [*ibid.*, p. 36].

You will notice that the above paragraph does not say that the leave-of-absence plan is known to have come from Rhine or that Rhine accepted it even tentatively. Yet, on page 3, S translates "Rhine or Levy or both" into "At long last, Mr L states unequivocally that Rhine *and* Levy (either together or *independently*) did come up with the 'plot' to give Levy a leave of absence and explain his fraud as due to a temporary breakdown." (Italics added by RAM.) At this point, S should be thrown out of court for trying to make fools of his judges.

How might one interpret L's discussion of a leave-of-absence plan? For the reasons outlined on page 6 of my 4 September letter to Council, I do not think Rhine could have been senile enough to have seriously considered such a plan. But if Rhine's brain had deteriorated so as to impair his judgment on such matters, I think it highly likely that his wife, with whom he worked as a colleague throughout his career, would have pointed out the inevitable and overwhelming consequences of such a plan. She was an intelligent woman, and no one has suggested that she was senile in 1974.

On the other hand, it is conceivable that, if he were offered a leave-of-absence plan by Levy, Rhine might have mentioned it to a staff member—not as an indication of acceptance, but to touch base with reality by getting third-party reactions to the catastrophe. Every intelligent person does this kind of reality testing when he knows he must make decisions under emotional pressure.

More probably, however, the Rhine-is-thinking-of-a-leave-of-absence idea was merely a rumor conceived as speculation in some staff member's mind, which subsequently spread until everyone had heard it and therefore was certain it must be true. This sort of thing is commonplace in times of sudden crisis. That such a rumor would be bitterly cynical was likely in the present case because of the dislike and jealousy that Levy had engendered by his sudden rise to prominence.

The foregoing seems to me the most reasonable interpretation of L's letter as it relates to a leave of absence for Levy. S sees it differently.

On page 3 of his report, S says: "Mr. L's letter fully supports the information I received from B in 1974, but which he now does not recall telling me."

We have just seen that L's letter does *not* fully support S's claim that Rhine's "original plan was to give Levy a leave of absence," but merely suggests it as a possibility. But wait, more was slipped in while our attention was elsewhere. On page 15 of his report, S says:

[In its preliminary response] FRNM goes on to state that "S goes on to fabricate a scenario in which Rhine was supposed to have made a plan to keep Levy after a leave of absence *but was pressured by other parapsychologists* to fire Levy." [Italics added by RAM.] Calling this information a fabrication is not only ridiculous, but also defamatory. I have made it quite clear to FRNM and to the P.A. Council that my original source of information was B, who gave it to me in September, 1974, while visiting my home . . . . [It may be helpful to remember that B was not at Rhine's laboratory during the Levy exposure, and that his meeting with S was three months later. S's point is that he did not "fabricate" the scenario, but heard it from someone. —RAM]

Thus, according to S, the idea of outside pressure (discussed below) is a part of the information that S claims (on p. 3) to have received from B in 1974. But L's letter admits to no knowledge of outside pressure. How then can L's letter be said to "fully support" the information S claims to have received from B? Nevertheless, S goes on, in italics: *"The fact that this story has come to me from two independent sources should be sufficient to convince FRNM of the accuracy of the scenario I published and which has caused so much hard feelings."* (p. 3)

So now, S's scenario, which included two elements (leave of absence and outside pressure), is said to be accurate because it is supported by two independent sources—one of which denies any memory of talking to S about either element, while the other offers nothing about outside pressure and says only that the leave-of-absence idea did have a life of its own at Dr. Rhine's laboratory and may have come from Rhine himself.

Having laid the groundwork by linguistic legerdemain on page 3, S continues his modification of reality on page 7 while arguing the significance of Rhine's five-day delay in mailing an announcement of the Levy fraud:

It is my contention—and it has been all along—that *it was* during these [five extra] days *that* [Rhine] was trying to work out a plan to explain Dr. Levy's fraud as a temporary breakdown, give him a leave of absence, and then bring him back to FRNM at some later time . . . . The scenario I published has now been fully confirmed by Mr. L.

S's scenario, which was said to be "fully supported" on page 3, now becomes "fully confirmed" without the addition of substantive fact. The confirmation rests largely in the use of the three words I have italicized. If the quotation is read with and without them, it is evident that these three words presume that it has already been shown that Rhine "worked [on] a plan" and that the only remaining question is *when*; whereas, in fact, S has produced no evidence that Rhine seriously considered such a plan. S might call this creative writing.

At this point, apparently recognizing that he has not yet discussed the bring-him-back-to-FRNM angle, S refers to information he received from H.

In 1974, H was evidently both an employee at Dr. Rhine's laboratory and a member of the P.A. Council. On a recent letter of inquiry from S, which is photographically reproduced in S's report appendix, H replied by marking as correct a statement by S that Dr. Rhine "asked" H "to lobby with the Council so that they would not ask Levy for his resignation" from the P.A.

I would interpret this as a request by Rhine to minimize unnecessary adverse publicity. Levy's guilt was already established by those who had the primary policing responsibility. If the P.A. were to beat a dead horse by formally expelling Levy, the fact that he had been detected in fraud and dealt with by the laboratory where he worked would tend to be obscured, while the myth that all successful parapsychologists are either dishonest or experimentally incompetent would be strengthened by the unnecessary, added publicity.

S has a different idea. On page 7, and again on page 16 of his report, he changes the H-approved expression "Rhine asked" to "Rhine instructed" and then, by adding together the ideas of "leave of absence" and "don't expel Levy from the P.A.," S concludes (p. 16): "So it is obvious that Dr. Rhine wanted to keep Levy in the field and—considering the circumstances—FRNM would have been the only place he could have found work at a later date." Ergo, Rhine hoped to rehire Levy.

Charge 3: Outside Pressure Was Brought to Bear to Stop the Leave-of-Absence Plan

In *Fate* magazine for September, 1984, S wrote:

> J.B.'s original plan was to give Levy a leave of absence, explain his fraud as the result of a "breakdown," and then rehire him. The plan was not put into effect because other prominent parapsychologists discovered it and persuaded J.B. that he would embarrass himself and the field unless he fired Levy on the spot. In the face of pressure from such prominent researchers as the late J. Gaither Pratt and Dr. R. A. McConnell, Rhine finally acquiesced. (*Fate,* *37*[9], p. 111-112)

My 4 September letter to Council explains how I know this statement about me to be false. I understand that Council now has information from Dr. Ian Stevenson explaining why he regards as extremely improbable that the late Dr. Pratt communicated in any way at all with Rhine on the Levy matter. S now concedes that he has no defensible evidence for his published statement that a leave-of-absence plan was abandoned because of outside pressure. He says (p. 17): "In the light of Mr. L's comments, however, I am perfectly willing to retract my statement about Rhine bowing to outside pressure."

To excuse his false allegation, S says with regard to my supposed involvement (p. 16):

> I tried to check out this information by querying Dr. McConnell directly, although he deliberately refused to answer my letter to him. (It will be up to the P.A. Council to determine whether Dr. McConnell acted ethically in refusing to provide data requested by a fellow P.A. member.)

As his letter (a photocopy of which is now in Council's hands) shows, S wrote to me, not to inquire about anything, but to tell me what he planned to publish and to invite me to comment in a letter-to-the-editor of *Fate*. Notice in the above quotation how S's misrepresentation is given credibility by a pious appeal to ethics.

Summary

In the letter that he now proposes to publish in *Fate* as a "clarification" of his earlier writings, S says, in part (p. 29):

> There is evidence that Dr. Rhine was ambivalent about what steps to take . . . . According to a recent communication . . . from Mr. L . . . Dr. Rhine did attempt to work out a plan whereby Dr. Levy would take a leave of absence only. His fraud would be explained as a temporary breakdown, and Dr. Rhine further planned to keep him in the Parapsychological Association. Dr. Rhine eventually thought better of this course of action and did not implement it, although Mr. L and others with whom I have spoken do not feel that he bowed to any outside pressure to terminate Levy. Dr. R. A. McConnell has specifically denied that he exerted any such pressure. (Dr. McConnell refused to answer a query from us on this issue when we were preparing to publish my original material.)

This proposed letter by S would publicly reinforce and expand his previous charges against Rhine by misrepresenting information he has received from L and H and what he wrote to me. It makes a fitting climax to S's legalistic tour-de-force.

S's is a devilishly clever document, built upon the idea that, if you have an empty case, make your brief heavy, long, and tedious, so that it seems important when it is first picked up but is too complex to be analyzed by busy people. He apparently believes that no one will carefully read his report, or, if one or two do, most others will simply refuse to believe how bad it is.

On page after page, S uses the gimmicks of the literary con artist, including repetition ad nauseum, unstated assumptions, concealed misstatements, logical non sequiturs, failure to distinguish between hearsay and firsthand evidence, padding by irrelevancies which are falsely implied to support his case, progressive shifting of the meaning of words, verbal distinctions that are implied to be important but that are never defined, pretending to logical precision and fairmindedness by making points and then generously conceding that they are trivial or irrelevant. Some examples have been given in the preceding pages. Others will be found throughout S's report.

12

FORCES OF DARKNESS

PSYCHIC POLICEMEN

Parapsychology has had its dedicated opponents ever since J. B. Rhine published his card-guessing experiments half a century ago. In 1976, the professional skeptics banded together in an organization called "The Committee for the Scientific Investigation of Claims of the Paranormal" (mnemonic: "Psi Cop"). No account of the current scientific status of parapsychology would be complete without a description of the methods of CSICOP, Inc.

The chairman of CSICOP since its founding has been a philosophy professor at New York State University at Buffalo. Control of the organization rests with a small, self-perpetuating Executive Council, under the leadership of this philosopher. Legally, CSICOP is a New York state, not-for-profit corporation.

The leaders of CSICOP express their individual views about parapsychology by writing and lecturing, and by reviewing books written by parapsychologists. A lecture by a professional magician, F.A., who is one of the founders and an Executive Council member of CSICOP,[1] was described earlier in the chapter "Books in Review." The reader will recall that that lecture was given as a physics colloquium at the Westinghouse Research and Development Center at Pittsburgh, Pennsylvania. To that same chapter I have appended the correspondence that resulted when another member of the Executive Council of CSICOP, F.B., reviewed my *Introduction to Parapsychology* in the American Psychological Association's journal, *Contemporary Psychology*. Examples of book writing by CSICOP adherents are given below.

CSICOP publishes a popular magazine, *The Skeptical Inquirer* (*SI*) dealing with parapsychology and other topics. Its policy is presumably represented by the signed comment of the chairman of CSICOP and of the editor, who is also a member of the Executive Council. The thrust of this magazine will be illustrated by excerpts given below.

---

[1] *Skeptical Inquirer, 10*(3), 201.

As of 1985, *SI* had attained a mail subscription circulation of 23,000[2]. *SI* is published four times a year. Each issue has 100, six-by-nine-inch pages on unfinished paper, saddle-stapled to a glossy cover. Without advertising, a plain-text magazine of this size and circulation should yield a profit if sold at two dollars per copy. The annual subscription price of *SI* is $4.50 per issue. The difference [23,000($4.50 − $2.00)4 = $230,000 per year] suggests that CSICOP is a highly successful operation.

CSICOP has stated (*SI, 10*[1], 12) that it has only five full-time employees, all of whom "could make more money elsewhere." In 1985, it launched a Tenth-Anniversary "capital fund-raising campaign," asking for tax-deductible contributions "to guarantee our future."

According to a 1985 Annual Franchise Tax Report to the state of Delaware, the chairman of CSICOP is also the president and treasurer of Prometheus Books, a Delaware corporation located in Buffalo, New York. A woman with the same surname serves as secretary of the corporation. These two constitute the Board of Directors. The number of issued shares of stock is 640. Gross assets are listed as $672,000.

Prometheus Books lists 125 titles, of which twenty are in "paranormal science." Other topics range from sado-masochism to Albert Schweitzer on the messiahship of Jesus. Subscribers to *SI* receive book advertising mail from Prometheus Books.

CSICOP enjoys the endorsement of more than 40 "Fellows," whose names appear on its letterhead, in its promotional advertising, and in *SI*. I have designated four of the more active of these as F.A., F.B., F.C., and F.D. (F.A. and F.B. were mentioned above.)

CSICOP has loosely affiliated "Committees" in nine foreign countries, as well as 15 local groups "with aims similar to CSICOP's" scattered over the USA and listed in *SI*. My experience at the University of Pittsburgh with a member of such a group will be described below.

---

[2] The *Journal of Parapsychology*, by comparison, has 900 subscribers, and the *Journal of the American Society for Psychical Research*, 1900.

UNSCHOLARLY BROKERS

In November, 1985, there occurred an event of singular importance for parapsychology. The American Psychological Association, through its flag journal, *The American Psychologist*, allowed the documentation of the misrepresentation and neglect that
some of the best of parapsychological research has received at the
hands of a few psychologists who for years have been widely
regarded as honest brokers of parapsychological information to
the Psychological Establishment.

These are critics of parapsychology whose books are cited
repeatedly in elementary psychology texts to convince the student
that there is a basis for doubt as to the reality of psi phenomena.

The author of this exposé is Professor Irvin L. Child of the Yale
Psychology Department.   Under the title, "Psychology and
Anomalous Observations: The Question of ESP in Dreams,"
Professor Child (1985)[3] first reviewed the experimental investiga-
tions of ESP in dreams carried out at the Maimonides Medical
Center at New York City and published between 1966 and 1973.
Next, he examined the treatment this research has received in five
books by psychologists purporting to offer critical reviews of
research in parapsychology.

Here is the *Abstract* of Professor Child's paper:

Books by psychologists purporting to offer critical reviews
of research in parapsychology do not use the scientific standards of discourse prevalent in psychology. Experiments at
Maimonides Medical Center on possible extrasensory perception (ESP) in dreams are used to illustrate this point. The experiments have received little or no mention in some reviews
to which they are clearly pertinent. In others, they have been
so severely distorted as to give an entirely erroneous impression of how they were conducted. In so far as psychologists
are guided by these reviews, they are prevented from gaining
accurate information about research that, as surveys show,
would be of wide interest to psychologists as well as to
others.

Dr. Child says, "Some of these books engage in nearly incredible falsification of the facts about the experiments; others
simply neglect them." (p. 1228)

---

[3] Formal references are at the end of this chapter.

Four of the seven authors involved in this scholarly malfeasance and nonfeasance are Fellows of CSICOP. Of the four, I have cited F.B. and F.C. elsewhere in this book for other scholarly failings. (See *Index.*)

AFFILIATED FORCES

Most scientists, if they have an opinion about parapsychology, have taken it from the popular press and television or from a colleague who enthusiastically subscribes to the views of CSICOP. When there are several such enthusiasts in an area, they may form an organization for which the *Skeptical Inquirer* constitutes a source of information and encouragement.

I have such a colleague at the University of Pittsburgh, who in January, 1983, was one of the founding members of The Paranormal Investigating Committee of Pittsburgh. This organization is visible through the news media, from which it is difficult to infer much except that its several active members enjoy giving lectures and interviews in which parapsychology is condemned as pseudoscience.

The motivations of these individuals are doubtless diverse. I shall confine myself to statements concerning one member, Dr. D, whom I came to know personally. Dr. D is a tenured member of the faculty of the Psychology Department at the University of Pittsburgh. His area of experimental research is the measurement of taste and smell.

Dr. D has a longtime interest in parapsychology. A clipping in my file shows that in October, 1976, he published a letter in *Psychology Today* (p. 4) defending a book by F.A., the magician leader of CSICOP to whom I have already referred. In April, 1980, he published a letter in the American Psychological Association's newspaper, *Monitor*, (p. 34) in which, without documentation, he said: "Likely explanations for the apparent evidence for psi in all previous experiments are: sloppy conditions, missing controls, faulty logic, fraud, and/or luck."

Dr. D has continued to give public lectures and interviews condemning parapsychology over the years. At the time of this writing, his most recent appearance was on 12 January 1986 at the First Unitarian Church of Pittsburgh. In a lecture there, he rejected all evidence for psychic phenomena as experimentally flawed.

In the discussion period that followed, he was asked the following question by a member of the congregation who knew him personally: "You have told me on another occasion that as a Christian you accept the miracles of Christ and the doctrine that Christ was born of a virgin. As you know, most Unitarians do not hold these customary Christian beliefs. I think your audience would be interested in your explanation of your acceptance of these beliefs in view of your extreme skepticism for extrasensory perception and psychokinesis."

The psychologist's response, as remembered, was: I am not a theologian. I cannot explain the miracles of Christ. Science does not provide a full description of everything.

The strength of Dr. D's interest in religion is suggested by the fact that in June, 1985, he received a distinguished service award from Geneva College for his contributions to the Reformed Presbyterian Church of North America as a trustee of its national Synod (*Beaver County Times*, 10 June 1985, p. A3).

My personal contacts with Dr. D have been of a professional nature. After I had given a course in parapsychology for two years at the University of Pittsburgh, the Psychology Department instituted a competing course in 1975 under Dr. D. I urged my students to take both courses if possible. (Mine was for only one hour per week; D's was for three.)

Several of my students who took Dr. D's course reported to me their experience with it. In 1976, I gave an invited lecture in his course.[4] I also listened to one lecture, in which Dr. D discussed parapsychological experiments. (Other lectures covered a variety of topics, including stage magic and a telepathic horse.) A colleague listened to the final lecture of the course and provided me with detailed notes. In these ways I became familiar with Dr. D's treatment of parapsychology.

In the lecture I attended, Dr. D's criticism of certain research was inapplicable. I asked him later whether he had actually studied the original papers on which he was lecturing. Dr. D said that this was not necessary because he had studied the published criticisms of these papers by competent psychologists.

After reviewing my notes, I decided that the fairest way to

---

[4] What does a parapsychologist say when speaking in the classroom of an avowed skeptic? The question seems of sufficient interest that I have added my lecture as Appendix *A* to this chapter.

characterize Dr. D's course would be to quote from his published writings. In an article describing his course (D, 1976, p. 66) he said: "After all my reading I found [F.C.'s *ESP: A Scientific Evaluation*] to be the best introductory book on the subject." This is one of the books criticized by Professor Child for its mistreatment of the Maimonides Medical Center research. It is also a book to which I have taken public exception for its misrepresentation of the psychokinetic research of Haakon Forwald (McConnell, 1968).

On page 67 of the same paper Professor D said:

> We did a number of ESP tests in class, including several that were easily biased in such a way as to provide apparent evidence for ESP. For example, when people are asked to choose a color, a number between 1 and 5, and a number between 6 and 10, they tend to pick red or blue, 3, and 7. These tendencies are very strong; nearly half the class picked 7.

This may be a psychological test of some interest, but to call it an "ESP test" with the implication that it is representative of ESP tests appearing in the literature of parapsychology would be keeping the truth about parapsychological research from students who had entered the course with an expectation of being honestly informed.

Dr. D's attitude toward parapsychology might be summed up by this sentence (D, 1983, p. 32): "Parapsychology [is] the most respectable of the pseudopsychologies."

A possible clue to Dr. D.'s thinking in this area is the motivation he ascribes to parapsychologists—as it has come to me orally from him, as well as indirectly from two colleagues.

The colleague, who attended Dr. D's final classroom lecture gave me this approximate transcription of his closing comment:

> Is [parapsychology] a fruitful area? If there is anything worth investigating, it would be "Why does anyone believe in it?" [Following student laughter, the instructor said he was serious about this.] People get into the field because it gives them a feeling of power. It serves as a substitute for religion. If you have a need for this sort of thing, I feel sorry for you.

Another colleague reported that in private conversation Dr. D expressed the opinion that most parapsychological students are motivated by a wish to develop a naturalistic religion. This unsupported opinion suggests to me a fear of conflict between parapsychology and religious belief.

How much weight does Dr. D carry with his colleagues on the subject of parapsychology? One of his fellow psychologists, whom I recently asked to examine the paper, "Anomalous Fall of Dice,"[5] and who is, himself, an excellent scientist by my standards, disappointed me by advising me to seek the criticism of Dr. D, whom he recommended as having "taught a course in parapsychology."

THE ANVIL OF IGNORANCE

To understand the success of CSICOP's leaders in misrepresenting parapsychology, one must know the anvil of ignorance upon which they pound to gain attention. There seems to be no limit to popular belief in pseudoscience.

McConnell (1973) reported (1) the endorsement by the President of the New York City Board of Public Education of the study of astrological birth signs as a possible key to the misbehavior of school children and the subsequent public defense of this astrological nonsense by the Executive Director of the National Association of Adult Educators, (2) the teaching of so-called ESP by nonprofessional personnel in money-making "continuing education" courses at American institutions of higher learning, (3) the international, multimillion dollar commercialization of training in hypnosis and ESP as a way to happiness and success, (4) the promotion of a fraudulent electronic device for the diagnosis and cure of illness by a director of an "Academy of Parapsychology and Medicine," and (5) the use of handwriting analysis by the physician-president of the same organization to detect personality traits, e.g., lesbian hostility toward men.

Targ and Harary (1984) devote a major part of their book, *Mind Race*, to the ways in which the public is misled about parapsychology. They examine mental enslavement by quasi-religious cults, which is achieved:

- By intimidation based on the claimed psychic powers of the leader.

- By providing an emotional haven for gifted psychics seeking refuge from an incredulous society.

---

[5] Chapter 4 of this book.

- By promising power and wealth through psychic training.

Harary investigated the little-known roles played by alleged occult powers in the 1978 mass suicide and murder at Jonestown, Guyana, and, currently, in the success of Sun Myung Moon's Unification Church.

In another place these authors analyze the role of organized religion in discouraging parapsychological research as an infringement on spiritual territory.

Targ and Harary show by specific examples how the entertainment industry has created monstrous psychic stereotypes for the titillation of the public and how the news media, partly out of ignorance and partly to make a saleable story, grossly distort news of spontaneous psychic occurrences.

In the light of the gullibility of the less educated, it is understandable that those with more training should feel a revulsion toward "the occult." CSICOP promotes the generalization of this revulsion to include the scientific study of psychic phenomena.

GOOD FELLOWS, ALL

The Fellows of CSICOP divide roughly into its active leaders (including F.A., F.B., F.C., and F.D.) and those who merely lend the prestige of their names. Among the name-lending Fellows of CSICOP are:

- F. H. C. Crick, (b. 1916). 1962 winner of the Nobel Prize in Physiology as co-discoverer of the double helix of DNA.

- Murray Gell-Mann, (b. 1929). 1969 Winner of the Nobel Prize in Physics for his theory of the quark.

- Sidney Hook, (b. 1902). Conservative political philosopher with a reputation for intellectual integrity.

- Carl Sagan, (b. 1934). Astronomer-showman, to whom the world owes thanks for his lending his name to the publicizing of nuclear winter.

- B. F. Skinner, (b. 1904). Archbehaviorist. Known to psychologists as the inventor of the "Skinner Box" and to the rest of us as the author of the behaviorist utopia, *Walden II*. Professor Skinner served as Honorary Chairman of CSICOP's Tenth Anniversary Fund.

In my previous book (McConnell, 1983, p. 240f) I described the formation of CSICOP and told how the evolution of its policies and its handling of data unfavorable to its position, led to the well-publicized resignation of two members of its Executive Council, Marcello Truzzi and Dennis Rawlins.

Since that description was written, the names of other Fellows have quietly disappeared from the CSICOP letterhead and it has become public knowledge that the leader of its New Zealand Section, the University of Otago psychologist Richard Kammann, resigned after a scathing denunciation of the leaders of CSICOP, in which he related in detail how he had attempted without success to salvage the scientific integrity of that organization:

> After seven months of research I have come to the . . . conclusion [that] CSICOP has no good defense . . . and has progressively trapped itself, degree by irreversible degree, into an anti-Rawlins propaganda campaign, into suppression of his evidence, and into stonewalling against other critics [Kammann, 1982, p. 60].

The resignation of these three Fellows of CSICOP had nothing to do with parapsychology. Its relevance is that it demonstrates the lack of objectivity of those who did not resign.

PARAPSYCHOLOGY VERSUS BIG FOOT

The Skeptical Inquirer (*SI*) engages principally in criticism of organized, supposedly irrational activities. Each of the activities it criticizes might be rated as more or less scientific according to the following criteria:

- The nature of the formal education of an activity's practitioners—ranging from a PhD degree in a recognized area of science to scientific illiteracy.

- The extent to which the special beliefs associated with an activity violate well-established scientific theories. (Parapsychology's findings violate no theories. They violate only experimental expectations. Creationism, on the other hand, violates the theory that man evolved from lower species.)

- The claimed basis for the jointly held beliefs of the practitioners—ranging from divine revelation to controlled experiments conducted and reported in the tradition of Western science.

- Emphasis on the gaining of new knowledge as opposed to the application of existing knowledge.

- Organizational behavior of the proponents of an activity—ranging from exchanging of laboratory findings to attempting to gain for their beliefs the force of law (as in the case of Creationists).

None of these and similar criteria are absolute. Taken together, they reveal a sharp dichotomy between parapsychology and the rest of the topics with which *SI* deals. Parapsychology is a clearly scientific activity. The rest are clearly nonscientific or pseudoscientific, as the case may be.

If we categorize SI-censured activities according to their apparent social value, we find a spectrum reaching from bad to good. Creationism, for example, seeks to substitute religious belief in place of science in our public schools and has partially succeeded because textbook publishing is a profit-oriented business.

Most of the topics dealt with by *SI* are harmless or even quaint: fairies, extraterrestrial beings, astrology, fortunetelling, deception by legerdemain, Big Foot, the Loch Ness Monster, Pyramid Power, the Bermuda Triangle. *SI* uses these topics as comic relief to entertain its readers, few of whom, it seems safe to say, regard such topics as of substantial importance to society.

Parapsychology stands by itself among *SI*'s interests as a subject of great potential value to mankind. Its central proposition is that human consciousness has a direct, physical reach beyond the body. If true, this proposition will have philosophic and scientific importance beyond present conception. On the other hand, parapsychologists offer no threat to science. They present their findings in the forum of science and seek the criticism and approval of the Scientific Establishment. Parapsychology's fringe adherents, of whom there are many, are more a threat to parapsychology than to society.

If we evaluate the effectiveness of *SI* in curtailing the activities of which it disapproves, again we find a dichotomy.

Creationism is being opposed by the professional societies and journals of science without significant help from *SI*.

No one can eradicate the foolish, but mostly harmless, occult beliefs of the general population. For example, *SI* ridicules popular astrology but never reaches the people who practice it.

Presumably, ridicule provides emotional satisfaction for the sub-scribers to *SI*, who most certainly are not believers in astrology.

Only in hampering parapsychology has CSICOP been effective. In this it has been successful primarily by nurturing fanatical skeptics on university campuses. These, in turn, have assumed the role of authorities and have misled their academic colleagues who are too busy to look at the parapsychological evidence them-selves and who want to know what to believe about this strange topic. Secondly, CSICOP has misled scientists directly by news-media misinformation generated in its own name and by its small core of active Fellows.

Working parapsychologists are simply too few, too isolated, too poor, and too busy to be able to answer CSICOP effectively. USA full members of the Parapsychological Association number 85. Of these, perhaps a dozen have a full-time commitment to experimental research in parapsychology.

In summary, parapsychology stands alone among the activities that *SI* condemns in that it is the only scientific and potentially beneficial activity and the only activity that *SI* has effectively in-fluenced.

TACTICS FOR SURVIVAL

If the phenomena of parapsychology were accepted as real by the majority of scientists, *SI* and CSICOP would wither away. Foreboding is the animus of *SI*'s success. Psi strikes fear into my heart and into the heart of every scientist who has been sensitized to its intimations. I believe it will destroy the prevailing worldview, and I cannot envision what will follow.[6]

The men who control CSICOP are not fools. They know which of their activities are emotionally charged and which are merely amusing—which are effective in attracting money and which are decorative. At one level or another of consciousness they know that parapsychology is the reason for CSICOP's existence. If I accept the claim that they receive no economic gain from their ef-forts, and if I ignore the editorial protestations of neutrality

---

[6] For those who are not sleeping, an even deeper fear must be struck by the present convergence of seemingly unsolvable world problems as scanned in the next chapter. It appears certain that the civilization we now enjoy cannot en-dure through, and perhaps not even into, the twentyfirst century.

toward parapsychology by *SI* and consider only what it publishes, then I cannot escape the conviction that those who control CSICOP are primarily bent upon the vilification of parapsychology and parapsychologists. My conviction is based on what I find in *SI*.

In preparing this paper, I examined the first ten years of *SI* for content and style. Perhaps ten percent of the magazine concerns topics that parapsychologists would regard as parapsychological. At least fifty percent relates to topics that are commonly regarded by the public as a part of parapsychology. *SI* intermixes items on pseudoscientific topics, popular parapsychological beliefs, and parapsychological research of all kinds, thereby creating the impression that scientific parapsychology is part of a mélange of ignorance. Aside from topics extensively treated, the pages of *SI* are laced with the parapsychological terms, such as *ESP, PK, psychic*, and *psi*, which are used indiscriminately among words having only a pseudoscientific meaning.

SI publishes intemperate attacks on the field of parapsychology as a whole, while disassociating its editorial policy from such attacks. In *3*(3), 12–13, *SI* devoted a boxed, two-page spread to excerpts from National Academy of Sciences physicist John A. Wheeler's diatribe against the Parapsychological Association at the 8 January 1979 meeting of the American Association for the Advancement of Science at Houston, Texas, in which Wheeler called for the expulsion of the Parapsychological Association from affiliation with the AAAS. One sentence by Wheeler as quoted by *SI* suffices to give the flavor: "Where there is meat, there are flies."[7]

SI attacks individual parapsychologists without justification despite its editorial claim of neutrality toward the research. Here is one example: More than anyone else, J. B. Rhine was the founder of modern parapsychology. The whole trend toward laboratory research in this field gained its major impetus under him at Duke University. Despite his vulnerability as the leader, no charge of scientific fraud has ever been sustained against him. Under these circumstances, a fair-minded editor would refrain from blackening his memory with second-hand innuendo.

Nevertheless, *SI* (*4*[3], 11–12) published a letter from a reader

---

[7] For the sequel to this occasion, see *Science* (*205*, 144).

eulogizing a recently deceased U.K. section chairman of CSICOP with these words:

> [Nineteen years earlier, after failing to produce psychokinesis at the Duke University Parapsychology Laboratory,] he quickly saw through Rhine and understood the blend of showmanship and token scholarship that the laboratory was purveying under the banner of the new science of parapsychology. From that date until his death he devoted a good part of his energy to countering the impact of the salesmen of superstition in Britain.

The editors of *SI* have defective intellectual principles. They will share their pages with anyone if he writes plausibly against parapsychology. The following excerpts are from an article (*4*[2], 73-80) titled "Science, Intuition, and ESP" by the Dean of Instruction at a small Canadian college.

> Believers in paranormality frequently draw an analogy between ESP skeptics and Galileo's inquisitors . . . . But psychic proponents are, in fact, much more like the inquisitors and the skeptics like Galileo. [Having straightened that out, the author goes on to defend the inquisitors.] The inquisitors' position was not a foolish one . . . . Plato had warned about capitulation to empiricism, which he understood would destroy the mythic, moral vision of the world that was attainable only through pure thought. He had warned against replacing the mythic world with simple facts about nature, obtained merely by experiment . . . . Our complete acceptance of rational objectivity as a mode of thought makes it difficult for us to understand Plato's and the inquisitors' legitimate concerns about empiricism. They were trying to protect a beautiful and morally superior and long-standing mythic vision of the world . . . . [pp. 74–75]
>
> Pseudoscience, particularly in the guise of parapsychology, detracts and distracts from the search for richer visions of experience. It substitutes titillating and shallow speculations, and spuriously rational ones, for intuitive vision. It is in poetry and aesthetics and in the complexities of human feelings and intellect that we ought to search for more satisfactory reasons for existence. We shall find little solace in our frantic preoccupation with rational inquiry, and less still in the frantic preoccupation that many have with the spurious forms of rational inquiry that characterize the world of psychics and parapsychology. [p.79]

SKEPTICISM AS A PROFESSION

Have psi phenomena been proved to occur? It is the repeatedly stated editorial position of the *SI* that the answer is negative. The editor has said (5[2], 3-4): "Despite 100 years of enthusiastic claims that scientific proof of ESP was just around the corner, that proof is just as elusive now as it was way back then." And again (9[2], 100) "The very word *psychic* implies the existence of paranormal powers never scientifically demonstrated."

Most of the parapsychology-related material appearing in *SI* has little relevance to proof of occurrence and, as presented, serves only to create prejudice against the field. Only rarely does CSICOP give space to the better experiments upon which the case for psi primarily rests. It is these rare instances that reveal explicitly the nature of *SI*'s interest in parapsychology.

One class of experiment that is regarded by many parapsychologists (including me) as conclusively proving the occurrence of psi is the "random number generator experiments" in which electronically selected multiple-choice targets are recorded along with a subject's guesses at those targets. These experiments were brought to a high state of technical sophistication by physicist Helmut Schmidt and have since been widely replicated (Radin, May, & Thomson, 1985).[8]

SI published two consecutive papers on Schmidt's experiments, the first by F.C. (1981) and the second by F.D. (1981). These may be the most important papers ever published by *SI* with regard to the question, "Have psi phenomena been proved to occur?" Together, they not only show that these two CSICOP Fellows will never answer that question affirmatively regardless of the quality of the empirical evidence presented to them, but they also illuminate the basis of CSICOP's editorial behavior.

---

[8] Because of the special interest of this meta-analysis of 332 experiments of this kind that were performed between 1969 and 1984, its *Abstract* is reproduced as appendix *B* to this chapter.

Two other classes of experiments widely regarded as independently proving the occurrence of psi phenomena are those under "ganzfeld" conditions and those involving "remote viewing." As chapter appendix *C*, I have included the abstract of a meta-analysis (Honorton, 1985) of 28 ganzfeld experiments by ten different research groups. As appendix *D*, I quote the abstract of a report of some 300 remote perception trials carried out by the Princeton University Engineering Anomalies Research Laboratory (Dunne, Jahn, & Nelson, 1983).

It is not necessary for me to expose the arguments employed by F.C.; for that is done by F.D. in his following article:

> . . . we are in the same camp. Neither of us believes that a scientific case has been made for the existence of psi . . . . [p.34]
>
> Before I continue . . . I should point out that F.C. and I are not responding to the same set of experiments. For some unexplained reason, F.C. confines his critique to the first two years of Schmidt's program . . . . My evaluation of Schmidt's work is based on experiments conducted by him and others over a ten-year period. The fact that other experimenters have claimed varying degrees of success with machines of the Schmidt type, for example, changes the import of some of F.C.'s criticisms [p.35].
>
> F.C., as a critic, feels called upon to provide alternative explanations for results. He restricts his search for alternatives completely to deliberate trickery . . . . The parapsychologists, of course, see F.C.'s position for what it is—a dogmatism that is immune to falsification . . . . Even if one assembles all the world's magicians and scientists, . . . I could always insist that, of the infinite number of variables not explicitly taken into account, . . . many of them—ones still unknown to us—could leave loopholes for a form of trickery we have not yet discovered. In practice it would be impossible even to take into consideration all of the known variables that could allow some form of deception . . . . I do not think it is necessary or wise to feel that we must always provide an alternative explanation for alleged paranormal claims [p. 39].
>
> [As] to Schmidt's work, I think the wise course is to wait. The work is in its preliminary stages. The generators have been neither standardized nor debugged. [I do not know what is meant by "standardized," but the equipment was thoroughly "debugged" by Schmidt as that word is used in electronics. —RAM] The research paradigm is still fluid and far from scientific. The results are provocative but far from lawful, systematic, or independently replicable. We have no need to try to explain or account for any of this now. Only when the parapsychologists settle upon a standardized paradigm, tidy up the procedures, demonstrate that the results follow certain laws under specified conditions, and that these results can be duplicated in independent laboratories, will we have something that needs "explaining" [p. 39].

The category "psi," even among parapsychologists, covers a number of existential possibilities. Some talk about a category of phenomena that are independent of any physical laws now known or conceivable. Others see new types of phenomena and forces that were hitherto unknown but entirely compatible with modern physics. We even find some parapsychologists arguing that, when properly understood, psi phenomena result from the operation of already known forces, such as extremely low frequency waves. And fraud ranges from deliberate, conscious cheating to various psychological aberrations and self-delusions. But in between these complex alternatives is a vast array of other alternatives involving the operation of statistics of rare events, subtle subject-experimenter-environment interactions, improper but nondeliberate manipulations of data, and many, many other possibilities. Among these alternatives could very well be new sorts of biases or ways for experiments to go wrong that we don't know about [p. 40].

The accusation that F.D. brings against F.C. applies as well to himself; for his is "a dogmatism that is immune to falsification." How strange that F.D. did not notice that it does not matter methodologically whether the critic dismisses psi by choosing counter-hypotheses from an infinity of available possibilities (F.C.) or dismisses psi without choosing any *because* there is an infinity of such possibilities (F.D.).

A psychological clue to F.D.'s behavior may be found in the same paper (p. 39): "The drawback of my position is that it counsels patience . . . . But the alternative . . . leads to the inevitable shrill claims, on the one side, that here is proof of psi and, on the other side, that cheating must be going on." These are uncomfortable pickets for a professional fence sitter.

F.D. rejects repeated observation by professional scientists as a sufficient criterion for the reality of phenomena unless those phenomena "follow certain laws under specified conditions," i.e., until we have theoretical understanding that will allow control. Until then, F.D. says that he prefers to "wait."

What F.D. does not say is that being able to "demonstrate that the results follow certain laws under specified conditions" is the goal of scientific research, not the beginning. Theory (law) implies control or prediction. In the tradition of Western science the formulation of a useful theory (model) is not the primary criterion for the reality of a phenomenon. That criterion is sufficient observation.

F.D. is a member of the Executive Council of CSICOP. For unknown personal reasons, he cannot simply "wait," as he promises. He engages continually in the hypercriticism of the best of parapsychological research. He personally eschews suggestions of experimental fraud; for that would be socially degrading to him in his role as a dispassionate arbiter of scientific parapsychology. Instead, he draws his exotic counterhypotheses from what he describes as "a vast array of other alternatives involving the operation of statistics of rare events, subtle subject-experimenter-environment interactions, improper but non-deliberate manipulations of data, and many, many other possibilities." [p. 40]

What he fails to tell his readers is what he has let slip in the article here under discussion, namely, that (along with occasionally legitimate criticisms) his objections to the best research in parapsychology are the sophistries of one who lives in a world where sensory experience is inferior to its symbolic representation.

F.D. is entitled to choose his own reality. What is reprehensible is that he joins forces with the vituperative opponents of parapsychology in confusing the scientific world as to the empirical status of parapsychological phenomena and thereby discourages research support.

I have repeatedly stated that in my judgment the reality of ESP and PK has been conclusively proved by observation despite our total lack of physical and physiological understanding and our inability to produce these phenomena dependably upon demand. I have also repeatedly said that (1) I do not expect anyone to base their beliefs upon my judgment in this matter, and that (2) since there is no scientific consensus upon it, anyone who takes a stance, one way or the other, is ethically obligated to examine beforehand the best available evidence and to be confident of his own technical competence to judge that evidence.

JUDGMENT AND CHALLENGE

What CSICOP's clientele chooses to ignore is that it is an advocational and not a scientific organization even though it shields its activities behind a list of sponsoring scientists. I have illustrated the tactics of its leaders, which are shameful by the customary standards of scientific intercourse. In my thinking I go further and assert that among the members of CSICOP who write critically about parapsychology there is no evidence of intellectual competence for the task they have undertaken. I base this judgment upon their performance in criticizing or, as the case may be, in failing to comment at all upon those better experiments by which the field of parapsychology must be judged.

Every experiment can be criticized—if only for not being some other experiment that the critic would like to have seen done instead. There are, however, a few experimental reports with positive findings in parapsychology whose conclusions cannot reasonably be denied. These experiments the leaders of CSICOP ignore, ridicule, or simply toss off with the comment, "There must be something wrong even though the report appears complete and correct."

One such study may be chapter 4 of this book. Another may be a paper by Schmidt, Morris, and Rudolph (1986) in which three well known parapsychologists collaborated to produce fraudproof evidence of a psi phenomenon.[9]

I have estimated that the *Skeptical Inquirer* is making a profit of a quarter-million dollars a year. May I offer a modest proposal to the philosopher who runs CSICOP: If you are spending that money on pep rallies and perquisites for your faithful followers, why not, instead, seek out front-rank scientists who are competent in all of the revelant techniques and pay each one to criticize the conclusions of one of the best papers in parapsychology.

The papers could be chosen by the Parapsychological Association. What is needed is not criticism of the field as a whole, nor of these research reports as reports, but an explicit, detailed analysis of the soundness of the conclusions that each paper reaches.

The critics you select would have to be courageous men of great stature who value their reputations in the future history of science, who claim an open mind toward parapsychology, and who are not yet in their dotage. It is essential that they act as individuals and not as members of a committee and that they understand that their criticism is to be directed to the research and to the body of the report only in so far as these may bear upon the soundness of the conclusions presented in the report.

---

[9] Although ESP and PK have been classically conceived as "transmission" phenomena (McConnell, 1983, p. 3), the experiment of this paper has a flavor of "connectedness" that is surprisingly similar to the EPR paradox. (See appendix *B* of chapter 3.)

I have one name to suggest: Richard Feynman, the Nobel laureate in physics who, after "doing his homework," gave a well-balanced, dinner address at the Annual Meeting of the Parapsychological Association at Dallas in 1984, and who, more recently, was willing to speak frankly (Marshall, 1986) to the nation about the causes of the Challenger space-shuttle disaster.

Broadly, the question to be answered, is not, "Does ESP or PK occur?", but whether there is strong evidence for the occurrence of physically unexplainable connections between the behavior of some people and certain events in the physical world. In the words of the late J. B. Rhine: "What is the reach of the mind?"

Chapter Appendix A

AREAS OF AGREEMENT BETWEEN THE
PARAPSYCHOLOGIST AND THE SKEPTIC[10]

Does ESP occur? The answer is either *yes* or *no*. Whichever the answer may be, it will be the same next year and 1000 years hence—if mankind lasts that long. If the answer is *yes*, if ESP is a reality, then it is important that we learn that fact as quickly as possible by the only method that can give dependable answers, that is, by the logical-empirical method of science.

Why is it important that we learn the truth about this question? Because, if ESP is a real ability, it will change our outlook and our ways of behaving more radically than any discovery in the history of science—even more than the discoveries of Galileo, of Darwin, and of Einstein. This is what I believe, and it is what some skeptics fear. If ESP is a true phenomenon, it is the most revolutionary discovery of all time.

Every scientist who has taken the trouble to look into the matter agrees that there is evidence favoring the reality of ESP. Where differences of opinion arise, is on the question: How good is that evidence?

I am here as the guest of your instructor. I have high regard for his work on the physiological measurement of taste. He and I have large areas of agreement about what constitutes good scien-

---

[10] Guest lecture given by RAM on 25 February 1976 in an antiparapsychological course at the University of Pittsburgh. Shortened from the *Journal of the American Society for Psychical Research*, Volume *70*, pp. 303–308

tific research, but we are in disagreement as to the excellence of the evidence for extrasensory perception and psychokinesis.

When he offered me the opportunity to speak to you, I decided to try to give a lecture on certain aspects of parapsychology about which he and I agree. I do not know whether I shall succeed. If I fail, I trust that your instructor will tell you later where he thinks I am wrong.

Considered Opinion is Not Authority

Does ESP occur? Unless you have trained yourself in psychology, physics, and the sociology of science, you probably cannot reach a competent, final decision about the quality and conclusiveness of the experimental evidence for parapsychological phenomena. The best you can do is listen to what others say who claim to have studied that evidence—persons like your instructor and me.

However, if you expect to depend upon authoritative opinion, I must warn you that, within parapsychology, there are no authorities. In all of science the word *authority* has no meaning except in so far as there exists a body of opinion supported by a consensus of interested scientists. Unfortunately, in the case of extrasensory perception and psychokinesis there is no such consensus.

If you believe public opinion polls, there is a substantial and growing number of psychologists who accept the reality of ESP as probable or certain, but the size of that group is hard to ascertain.

There are many other psychologists—and they are in a clear majority—who are strongly skeptical about ESP. Moreover, there are some psychologists—I do not know how many—who have studied the evidence for ESP and who are willing to say in the classroom or in public that they find that evidence so weak that they regard the topic as a waste of time.

One such person is your instructor. Because he has said that the evidence for ESP carries no conviction for him, I am especially grateful that he is giving his course. If ESP is a reality, that fact will become generally known only if persons like him are willing to discuss the evidence. I take this opportunity to express the hope that he will give his course next year and in the years thereafter, as long as there are students wanting to take it.[11]

Biographical Snapshot

I am convinced that both ESP and PK do occur. I did not reach that opinion until many years after I became an experimental physicist. One day, I saw a newsmagazine account of some laboratory research supposedly showing the occurrence of PK. Out of curiosity, I went to the library and began to read the original research papers. After four years of investigation, including a summer devoted to extended visits with those who were skeptical about this research as well as those who were actively engaged in it, I entered parapsychology professionally. That was 29 years ago.

I had never taken a classroom course in psychology. I decided at the very beginning that, if I intended to do research in parapsychology—which is a subfield of psychology—I needed to know what and how psychologists think. Much of my time since 1947 has been devoted to the private study of psychology. If your instructor wants to tag me as a "physicist," he is welcome to do so, but I have actually spent more time in the study of orthodox psychology than I did in the study of physics, in which I obtained my doctoral degree.

I think it is a remarkable fact that we have here at the University of Pittsburgh two persons, your instructor and myself, who have looked at the same evidence and come up with opposing judgments as to its meaning. Our disagreement is both scientifically important and intellectually challenging. I believe it is more immediately important and challenging than ESP itself. Consequently, the question I wish to discuss with you today is this: How can we explain the fact that two trained scientists have examined the same evidence and come to opposite conclusions about it?

---

[11] This lecture was given while I was still unaware that Dr. D had only a superficial familiarity with the literature of parapsychology.

Scientists Prefer Their Own Beliefs

As a starting point, perhaps the most important thought I can offer is that scientists are human—ordinarily human—when it comes to believing nonsense.

As you know, people have been believing strange ideas at least as long as recorded history. The most familiar examples of strange beliefs are to be found in the area of religion. I am not about to tell you which religious beliefs are correct, but no one can successfully deny that they are mutually contradictory. The religious beliefs that have existed and do exist over the face of the earth are so divergent that most of them must be false. Nevertheless, people by the millions have supported the killing of others because of religious beliefs, and, odder still, people by the thousands have been willing to die rather than change their religious beliefs.

Scientists do not differ from other people. Unless they are forced to do otherwise, they will hold whatever beliefs suit their fancy, and they will defend such beliefs passionately. They will prove the correctness of their own views, to their own satisfaction, by appeals to observation and logic, with the same ingenuity, sincerity, and finality that have been used throughout history by persons with opposing religious beliefs (Polanyi, 1958).

What am I saying? Am I telling you that there is no such thing as scientific truth on which scientists can agree? *Yes*—and *no*. In physics, for example, there are no serious long-lasting disagreements over what is known. Once a theory is fully accepted, although it may later be found inadequate in a new situation, it is not likely ever to be judged totally false.

By way of contrast, in the biological sciences, including psychology, there are many fundamental disagreements among eminent scientists. And in what are called the social sciences, such as economics, it is no exaggeration to say that there is very little agreement on what is scientific truth and what is mere political opinion. How can we explain this difference between, say, physics and sociology? The difference is not in the scientists who study these two fields, but in the fields themselves. More specifically, it is the conditions existing within a particular field of science at a given time, that determine whether a consensus on truth develops.

Never Trust an Expert

Scientists sometimes reach a consensus, but only because the situation in that particular field, not only allows, but actually forces them into agreement. When, as in parapsychology, those special conditions necessitating agreement fail to exist, there will be no consensus. Worse than that, in such a situation, no one's opinion can be trusted. No matter how famous and clever he may be, no matter how convincingly he appeals to logic and experience, to reason and evidence, a scientist's opinion cannot be trusted in parapsychology.

That applies to me just as much as to your instructor. Both of us may have our emotions concealed, but we each feel strongly about parapsychology. I would not have given up a career in physics to enter parapsychology if I did not firmly believe that ESP is real and important. Your instructor would not have interrupted his research on taste to prepare and give this course unless he felt a strong need to correct certain mistaken ideas about ESP. You are too clever to believe either one of us if we tell you that it is a simple love of abstract truth that has led us to take opposing views on this subject.

What you are seeing in this classroom is a human drama of a kind that each of us may play at some time in his life, but that is rarely performed in public on a university campus. I have bet my life's work that I am right. Your instructor has bet his reputation that he will not be forced some day to backtrack and say that he was wrong in his judgment. One of us is going to lose. Your task is to discover which one it will be.

Chapter Appendix B

PSI EXPERIMENTS WITH RANDOM NUMBER GENERATORS: META-ANALYSIS PART I

Dean I. Radin
Edwin C. May
Martha J. Thomson

SRI International
Menlo Park, California

ABSTRACT:[12] A meta-analysis of 332 psi experiments involving binary random number generators is described. The combined binomial probability for data reported in 56 references published between 1969-1984 has a p of about 10^{-43}. A "filedrawer" analysis reveals that over 4500 additional, nonsignificant, unpublished or unretrieved studies would be required to bring the overall result down to a nonsignificant level. Using a novel approach, we estimate the actual size of the "filedrawer" to be 95 studies. Adding the equivalent of 95 nonsignificant studies to the existing data results in a p of about 10^{-18}, while a meta-analysis of 98 reported control studies results in a p of about .78. An analysis of variance indicates that experimenters' mean z scores are significantly different from each other. We discuss an approach and propose criteria for performing a quality-weighted analysis on the existing data. We conclude that the *prima facie* evidence supports the notion that observers' intentions can affect the statistical properties of truly random number generators.

Chapter Appendix C

META-ANALYSIS OF PSI GANZFELD
RESEARCH: A RESPONSE TO HYMAN

by Charles Honorton

Psychophysical Research Laboratory
Princeton, New Jersey

ABSTRACT:[13] In response to Hyman's (1985) critique of psi ganzfeld studies, an evaluation is reported that eliminates multiple-analysis problems. The evaluation is restricted to 28 studies (of the 42 considered by Hyman) that reported the number of direct hits. A uniform test (Z score associated with the exact binomial probability) is applied to a uniform index (proportion of direct hits). The mean Z score is 1.25 (S.D. = 1.57) with .76 as the lower bound of a 95% confidence interval estimate of the true population mean. The composite (Stouffer) Z score for the 28

---

[12] Quoted from Radin, May, and Thomson, 1985.

[13] Quoted from Honorton, 1985.

studies is 6.6 (*p* less than 10^{-9}, and 43% of the studies were independently significant at the 5% level. Six of the ten investigator groups reported significant outcomes, and the cumulation [of all experimenters, by groups] yields a composite Z of 6.16; the significance of the psi ganzfeld effect does not depend on any one or two investigators.

A number of considerations mitigate against selective reporting bias as a viable explanation of these findings: (a) publication policies and practices in parapsychology show that null findings are frequently reported, (b) a large number of the studies under consideration do report null findings, and (c) Rosenthal's "file-drawer" estimate of the number of fugitive null studies needed to jeopardize the known results requires 15 fugitive studies for each one known.

Contrary to Hyman's claim, no significant relationship is found between study outcomes and measures of study quality (cue control and method of randomization). Hyman's "procedural flaws" analysis is discussed; ambiguities in the flaw criteria are noted, and examples of inconsistent or inappropriate assignment of flaw ratings are given.

Chapter Appendix D

PRECOGNITIVE REMOTE PERCEPTION

B. J. Dunne
R. G. Jahn
R. D. Nelson

Engineering Anomalies Research Laboratory
Princeton University, Princeton, New Jersey

ABSTRACT:[14] A data base of some 300 remote perception trials has been accumulated, largely in the precognitive mode, ranging over geographical separations of up to 11,000 miles, and over times of precognition and retrocognition of more than 48 hours. The degree of anomalous information acquisition implicit in this data base has been evaluated by analytical scoring techniques based on a sequence of 30 binary descriptors in terms of which all

---

[14] Quoted from Dunne, Jahn, & Nelson, 1983.

targets and perceptions are encoded. Each of these methods is capable of establishing the statistical merit of any individual perception by comparison of its score with a distribution of chance scores derived empirically from 42,000 mismatched permutations of targets and perceptions. The overall statistical results are internally consistent, vary little from method to method, and are consistent with more impressionistic assessments. By any method applied, over any of several subdivisions of the data base, the results imply significant anomalous information acquisition via this experimental protocol. None of the parameters explored has been found to influence substantially the yield of such experiments. In particular, no systematic dependence on the spatial separation of the percipient from the target, or on the degree of precognition, is apparent over the range of these data.

REFERENCES

Child, I.L. (1985). Psychology and anomalous observations: The question of ESP in dreams. *American Psychologist, 40*, 1219–1230.

D. (1976). ESP in the psychology curriculum. *Teaching in Psychology, 3*(2), 66–69.

D. (1983). *Experimental Psychology*. Belmont, California: Wadsworth.

Dunne, B.J., Jahn, R.G., & Nelson, R.D. (1983). Precognitive remote perception. *Technical Note PEAR 83003*. Princeton, New Jersey: Princeton University Engineering Anomalies Research Laboratory.

F.C. (1981). A critical analysis of H. Schmidt's psychokinetic experiments. *Skeptical Inquirer, 5*(3), 26–33.

F.D. (1981). Further comments on Schmidt's PK experiments. *Skeptical Inquirer, 5*(3), 34–40.

Honorton, C. (1985). Meta-analysis of psi ganzfeld research: A response to Hyman. *Journal of Parapsychology, 49*, 51–91.

Kammann, R. (1982). The true disbelievers: Mars effect drives skeptics to irrationality, Part I. *Zetetic Scholar*, No. 10, 50–65.

Marshall, E. (1986). Feynman issues his own Shuttle report, attacking NASA's risk estimates. *Science, 232*, 1596.

McConnell, R.A. (1968). The ESP scholar (letter to the editor), *Contemporary Psychology, 13*, 41.

McConnell, R.A. (1973). Parapsychology and the occult. *Journal of the American Society for Psychical Research, 67*, 225–243.

McConnell, R.A. (1983). *Introduction to Parapsychology in the Context of Science*. Pittsburgh, Pennsylvania: Author.

Polanyi, M. (1958). *Personal Knowledge*. Chicago: University of Chicago Press.

Radin, D.I., May, E.C., & Thomson, M.J. (1985). Psi experiments with random number generators: Meta-analysis part I. *Proceedings of the Parapsychological Association 28th Annual Convention*, Volume I, 201–233.

Schmidt, H., Morris, R., & Rudolph, L. (1986). Channeling evidence for a PK effect to independent observers. *Journal of Parapsychology, 50*, 1–15.

Targ, R., & Harary, K. (1984). *The Mind Race: Understanding and Using Psychic Abilities*. New York: Villard Books.

13

A WILD CARD
AGAINST THE ACE OF SPADES

In 1982 the Parapsychological Association and the (British) Society for Psychical Research held a joint convention at Cambridge University to celebrate the 25th and 100th anniversaries of those two organizations.

As the founding president of the Parapsychological Association, I had been invited to give a talk on the early history of our organization. Instead, I offered to speak about the future of parapsychology. My offer was accepted.

For most of my life I have had a piecewise awareness of the crumbling of Western civilization. I welcomed this speaking engagement as an opportunity to examine jointly all of the major problems of the world and to speculate where parapsychology might fit into the future.

After intensive study of journals and books I emerged with a total picture that was far worse than I had expected, and that has permanently changed my outlook toward the future.

The resulting sixty-minute lecture was delivered under the title, "Parapsychology, the Wild Card in a Stacked Deck: A Look at the Near Future of Mankind."[1] The applause for my talk was barely polite. No one offered a congratulatory comment. Two days later, attending the farewell banquet in the Great Hall of Trinity College, I was seated in candlelight beneath a towering portrait of Henry the Eighth and opposite the Scottish President of the Parapsychological Association. It was the kind of century-spanning occasion of which the British are fond—a fitting opportunity, I thought, to probe for an historic opinion about the future of parapsychology. What, I asked in a lull in the conversation, did our leader think of my lecture? His curt reply closed the subject: "It was not what I expected."

---

[1] This talk has since been published as chapter 7 in my *Parapsychology and Self-Deception in Science*.

Although it is customary to publish in full in *Research in Parapsychology* all invited lectures to Parapsychological Association conventions, the governing Council of the Association judged my talk to be too long. The following abstract was accepted:

> [In my lecture I summarized] the probable course of world events between now and A.D. 2000 on the basis of the first and second laws of thermodynamics and the present states and rates of change (and possible, higher-order rates of change) of the following global factors: energy production, arable land, food production, available fresh water, acid rain, atmospheric carbon dioxide, forested area, metallic ore reserves, population growth, Third World debt, genetic deterioration, and moral degradation in the industrialized countries.
>
> I said that, in my view, the end of the Age of Heroic Materialism marks the beginning of an age of world poverty. I concluded on the basis of U.S. Government-published projections that there will be half a billion deaths caused directly or indirectly by starvation before A.D. 2000.
>
> I offered specific, speculative, political, military, and parapsychological predictions and suggested two broad areas, namely, military and philosophical, where parapsychology might affect the course of history.
>
> With the major powers now reduced to nuclear stalemate, parapsychology may provide the future weapons of choice. On the other hand, by leading toward a scientific understanding of the spiritual nature of man, parapsychology might conceivably trigger a moral revival such has not been seen in several centuries.
>
> I believe that Cartesian dualism and its philosophic offspring, upon which our present civilization is built, are incompatible with present knowledge of parapsychological phenomena and that, in time, it will be shown that people have psychic connections that imply new concepts of moral responsibility.

RE-ASSESSMENT—1987

Since I wrote in 1982, we have progressed one-quarter of the way toward the year 2000. To what extent are my logical expectations being fulfilled? I am not pleased with the answer I must give, and I implore the skeptic who reads these pages to tell me where I may be wrong. What follows is a collection of ideas offered as a supplement to the systematic analysis described above.

* * * * *

In 1982 I failed to appreciate the scope of business corruption made inevitable by the leverage of technology. I now believe that the present abuses of power by our business leaders foreshadow the end of private capitalism as we have known it. I shall mention two examples in which the scale of management's misbehavior is such as to destroy all confidence in the system. Without moral self-restraint by its leaders, a free society cannot long survive.

- The purchase of large, successful, high-book-value corporations by other large corporations, paid for by kited securities, to give money and power to corporation officers, often, or usually, without regard for economic consequences.

- The poisoning of customers by adding methyl (wood) alcohol to cheap wines by vintners of Italy, an established practice brought to public notice only when greed overreached itself, causing the prompt death of at least 20 Italians. According to a preliminary report, 65 wine producers were suspected of involvement and Italian wines had been banned from several European countries (Jenkins, 1986).

* * * * *

Although there have been favorable as well as unfavorable social developments since 1982, I regret that I have no reason to soften my evaluation of the prospects for a sustainable, civilized way of life for the human race. For example, with regard to the drug addiction problem in the USA, the good news is that marijuana is now the largest cash crop in the state of California. The bad news is that cocaine has largely supplanted marijuana as the "recreational drug of choice" both among "young urban professionals" and for people at the bottom of the economic heap.

* * * * *

Because of the new realism of the Russian leaders, the USA might be able to come to terms with the USSR as it has with the People's Republic of China. Instead, we are continuing to devote a substantial part of our national budget to something called "Strategic Defense Initiative."

In March, 1983, the idea of "Star Wars," as it is popularly known, was presented to the American people by their president as a space-based defense that "would render nuclear weapons impotent and obsolete." This deceived the layman, but the program was promptly judged by nearly all professionally uncommitted scientists and engineers from relevant disciplines to be practicable only for first-strike support, i.e., for offensive use (Bowman, 1985; Broad, 1985; Carter, 1984; Hiatt, 1986; Myers, 1986; Parnas, 1986; Smith, 1985; Thurow, 1986).

Four years later, every well-informed person knows that defense of the general population against intercontinental ballistic missiles is impossible. The goal of "Star Wars" is now argued by its Pentagon proponents to be "enhancement of deterrence" by the military control of outer space (Tirman, 1986).

The Russians have said that they want to end this madness. Through President Reagan we have proclaimed that we do not. Unless we change our collective mind, the final outcome will be as foreseen by physicist Louis Ridenour (1946) in his "Pilot Lights of the Apocalypse."[2]

I do not doubt the president's sincerity in advocating Star Wars. As our leader chosen by popular vote, he represents the common denominator of American culture. His special skill is in manipulating people, not ideas. His faith in the magic of technology is unencumbered by technical understanding. To a striking degree in this and other areas, he has exhibited the mental illness that afflicts us all: a will to believe whatever we find most satisfying.

* * * * *

Because of its growing Arab population, Israel will find it increasingly difficult to be both Jewish and democratic, and, as a consequence, Israel may be immersed in civil war before the year 2000 if it does not destroy itself sooner by runaway inflation. When this stabilizing country crumbles, the Middle East may become the opening field of Armageddon.

The cultural apartheid that preserved the identity of the Jewish people throughout the centuries and made possible their

---

[2] Rereading this in 1987 was well worth my trip to the library. The thought has since occurred to me that this one-act play would make an exhilirating high school production.

preeminent contribution to Western thought may once again lead to slaughter and Diaspora. This time the outcome could be different. The physical and biological sciences, in which Jews are leaders, are compatible with religious superstition by mental compartmentation. The scientific study of the human mind is not separable from religious belief and, ultimately, will destroy the glue that holds the Jewish people together. This is already evident in the rift between orthodox and liberal Judaism in Israel.

* * * * *

Unrecognized before mid-1981, Acquired Immune Deficiency Syndrome may eventually have demographic importance. If no vaccine is discovered and if the present estimated doubling time of the number of infected heterosexuals persists in several regions of the earth, AIDS may begin to relieve world population pressure by 2000 A.D. Like nuclear war, this worst-case scenario cannot be dismissed as impossible.

We are reminded of the prophetic words of Raymond Cattell (1972, p.277): "Let us set aside [our] lingering illusions and, turning to the vistas of the astronomer and the biologist, frankly recognize the enormous magnitude of the adaptations to catastrophe that may at any moment be demanded collectively of mankind."

Regardless of the ultimate effect of AIDS on population size, we can already be sure in 1987 that its spread will have greater social significance in this century than Alamogordo or Apollo Eleven. Worldwide, the sharp knife of death will separate the educable from those who are not. In the industrialized countries, organized superstition will give way to a search for sexual realities.

Unless a vaccine is discovered, we have seen the end of romantic love but not of sexual crime. Extrapolation suggests that within the next decade perhaps eighty percent of certain strata of society will be carriers of the AIDS virus. At that point we may expect the slow murder of women by rape to become commonplace. Perhaps even sooner, for protection against anal rape, laws will be passed requiring that all male prisoners be detained in separate cells. If so, the present penal space shortage will seem trivial by comparison.

* * * * *

It is encouraging to report that there is a growing awareness concerning environmental problems. In 1982, I had to dig information for my lecture from relatively obscure technical publications, as listed in my end notes thereof. Since then, television and the better newspapers have carried documentary analyses of most of the environmental threats to national and world survival. However, the two basic problems of humanity that are crucial to the solution of all others are still universally ignored. Those two are the genetic inadequacy of the population and the need for a morality based upon science.[3]

Worldwatch Institute began in 1984 the publication of an annual volume titled *State of the World*, and there has been an increasing number of "doomsday" books. Among the most recent of these are *Megatraumas: America in the Year 2000* (Lamm, 1985) and *The Immigration Time Bomb: The Fragmenting of America* (Lamm & Imhoff, 1985). The significance of these two books lies, not so much in their content, which is not new, as in the fact that Richard Lamm, in his third term as a highly successful governor of Colorado, placed facing reality at the top of his agenda. That takes a combination of intelligence and courage rare in a politician.

In the Congress of the United States there has been much talk about environmental problems but little action. In the Executive branch, on the other hand, there has been action—but of a disastrous kind, as I shall describe below.

THIRD WORLD HUNGER

When mass starvation in Ethiopia was brought to world attention by British television, what was the public response?

On July 13, 1985, several hundred million well-fed people joined in a day-long, worldwide television celebration by watching professional rock-and-roll entertainers wail and writhe in obscene contrast to the reality of starvation. This largest real-time show in the history of television was billed as a means for raising money for the hungry.

For both entertainers and entertained the purposes of the show were to reduce the horror of starvation by associating it with

---

[3] Critics of eugenics often fail to acknowledge that genetic inheritance largely determines all aspects of the personality and physique of each of us and not simply our "intelligence."

plcasureable activities and to relieve guilt feelings by pretending that effective help was being sent to those dying of starvation. The amount of money raised was an estimated $56 million, which could feed the starving Ethiopians for several weeks. By this bit of psychological legerdemain the well-fed people of the world escaped the need to consider the causes and magnitude of the hunger problem. It must be acknowledged, however, that through this show some learned that a hunger problem exists.

The world is over-populated, including even the USA, if the goal is an indefinitely sustainable quality of life comparable to that now enjoyed by the average American. In sub-Saharan Africa and in the Himalayan watershed, not only the quality of life, but life, itself, is being destroyed on a massive scale by malnutrition. Before 2000 A.D., barring unforeseen changes, the same will be true in southeast Asia, in much of Central and South America, and in most of Africa.

Paradoxically, between now and 2000 A.D., food surplusses produced by high-cost energy in many parts of the world will foster an illusion of perpetual abundance. Meanwhile, the cancer of an unsupportable population will continue to grow.

Despite this grim picture, which represents the consensus of population scientists, the President of the United States had his representative proclaim at Mexico City (United States Policy, 1984) that poverty in the Third World does not result from excess population but from government interference with business. He won the gratitude of his Roman Catholic and fundamentalist religious supporters by refusing to allow USA financial assistance to any international agency that promotes birth control by abortion or coercion (Finkle & Crane, 1985).

I have condensed the controversial sections of the "Introduction" from the *Policy Statement of the United States of America at the United Nations International Conference on Population* (United States Policy, 1984), which was prepared by the U.S. Presidential staff for the conference held in Mexico City, 6–14 August 1984.

> The Third World population boom since World War II was an opportunity for progress which was converted to a crisis by two negative factors: governmental control of economics and "an outbreak of anti-intellectualism, which attacked science, technology, and the very concept of material progress" (page 577).

> Population control cannot substitute for free private enterprise, which can lead to prosperity and fewer children without governmental intervention.
>
> The second factor, anti-intellectualism, as expressed, for example, by the authors of the so-called *Global 2000 Report*, disregarded past human accomplishments and the sophistication of our scientists, and led to unjustified pessimism and to opposition to the rapid and responsible development of our natural resources.
>
> The Reagan Administration rejects the *Global 2000 Report* prepared by the previous, Carter Administration and looks to technological advance and economic expansion as a solution to Third World problems.

President Reagan believes that the poorer nations can industrialize themselves by hard work and capitalism. The consensus of environmental scientists, on the other hand, is that Third World countries "are forever trapped behind the closed door of the Age of Cheap Energy" (McConnell, 1983, page 131).

Reagan misrepresents the *Global 2000 Report* as opposing the "rapid and responsible development of natural resources" (ibid., page 577). In a footnote characterizing that report (McConnell, 1983, page 144), I said:

> Perhaps the most regrettable feature of the *Report* is its implicit recommendation, based upon an implied assumption. The recommendation is that we should consume all we want between now and 2000 A.D. The implied assumption is that on that date God will send space ships to carry us off to a new planet. To future historians this hope may be known as "the white man's cargo cult."

Far from appearing too pessimistic, the editors of *Global 2000* lead the hasty or nontechnical reader to underestimate the gravity of the situation. The editors eliminated starvation on paper by a 24-year, straight-line extrapolation of world grain yield per hectare, which they based on hoped-for seed improvements and on an assumed ever-growing availability of pesticides, fertilizer, water, and fuel.[4]

The last three items are especially energy dependent. Before 1910, farms were without electricity, gasoline, and chemical fertilizers. Today, in the USA, it takes 10 calories of outside energy

---

[4] Figure 1 of the summary of the *Report* (United States, 1980, page 8).

to produce one food calorie (Steinhart & Steinhart, 1974). That 9-calorie subsidy has been coming from fossil fuels, whose labor and capital extraction costs will be increasingly prohibitive in the decades ahead.

President Reagan based his prediction of a rosy future upon our glorious past. His make-believe optimism appealed to average citizens, who understand neither technology nor history, and led to his re-election in 1984.[5]

DEATH OF DEMOCRACY

In a true democracy, government reflects the desires of the majority. Is the majority of any nation capable of governing itself?

People are often to a degree incompetent in their thinking and improvident in their planning. Nevertheless, egalitarians hold to the pleasant belief that in every country of the earth the majority is capable of governing at least well enough to ensure the continuation of individual freedom.

They point to the fact that populist self-government has succeeded rather well in capitalist USA and Europe for more than a hundred years. We are told that this is because we have freedom to be selfish, which makes us industrious and ingenious.

This is true as far as it goes. However, those with scientific training believe that the most important reason for Euro-American prosperity and for the more recent prosperity of a few other countries has been the application of technology based upon science. By knowledge of nature we have been able to exploit fossil fuels, mineral resources, and the natural fertility of the earth.

Alas, in so doing, we have expended the irreplaceable and despoiled the maintainable without regard to the future. Like the citizens in an oil-rich sheikdom, every Westerner with even a modicum of competence and ambition has been rich beyond the

---

[5] The effects of overpopulation pervade human living and can be insidious or catastrophic. Because of air pollution, for example, before 2000 A.D. I believe it probable that maple syrup will no longer be found on the shelves of American grocery stores (Sugar maple, 1986) and that 100,000 people will have been killed by a one-week air-temperature inversion over Mexico City (Mexico City, 1986).

wildest expectations of the rest of the world. Union workers and capitalist managers alike have said to themselves: "This is what we deserve, and tomorrow we want MORE."

That is all over now. Sometime in the last twenty years the Age of Heroic Materialism reached its zenith. From now on, the long-term economic trend for mankind will be forever downward as the cost of energy and raw materials rises.

Be of good cheer, however. This is also the Age of High Technology, with an insatiable demand for intellectually superior workers and rejection for most of those who cannot handle symbolic complexity. The middle class will grow poorer, while those at the top of the competence pyramid will continue to gain economic ground for yet awhile. In this way, our country will be divided for the first time into two distinct economic classes: the intellectually well-endowed and the serfs of the "service economy."

No amount of transfer payments can reverse this trend. Governmental charity in lieu of jobs is destroying the self-respect of the unemployables and will result in their alienation.

How can one be certain that democracy will not solve its problems? Surely all of them could be ameliorated by self-discipline. But will they be? The following considerations support the proposition that democracy is not sustainable in our culture.

Throughout much of the Free World, but not in the USA, monetary inflation is strangling economic production by vitiating long-range planning. Despite the American people's unwillingness to balance the national budget, up to now we have been able to minimize inflation by borrowing cash and consuming capital.

When we have exhausted our credit and have nothing left to sell, our budgets must thereafter be balanced and our accumulated deficits must be paid with interest. The only way this will be done is by a national repudiation of debt, i.e., by printing paper money.

Meanwhile, we are becoming increasingly a part of Japan's colonial empire. Like Third World countries, our businesses are being managed (and profits sent home) by the nation to which we sold them.

To balance our annual budget and avoid economic servitude would require, among other things, the sharp reduction of unearned entitlements (e.g., in Social Security and Medicare) and of military expenditures, as well as a heavy sales tax on luxury goods. It is a political fact that the majority of Americans lack the intelligence and moral fortitude to face this reality. Consequently, long before 2000 A.D., monetary inflation in the USA will resume at an ever-accelerating pace.

There are at least four major reasons for believing that the collapse of our monetary system will be catastrophic rather than gradual:

- The current abandonment of our wealth-producing industry—both light and heavy—will leave us without the necessary plant and skills as the dollar declines in value, foreign imports drop, and we decide it would be wise to put the underclass back to work.

- Our ever-growing gifts to Third World countries (euphemistically called "loans" and largely made by USA "private," i.e., government-guaranteed, banks) have drawn people of these countries from farms to cities, thereby curtailing food production and otherwise leading to dependence on this flow of unearned money. Now we have reached the stage where our giving cannot be ended without precipitating a world explosion.

- Our accelerating and irreversible drift into a two-class society is bringing social instability, which will preclude rational adjustment to economic pressures.

- The technical complexity of our computer-managed economy renders our country vulnerable to social disorder as compared with our position before World War II.

Social disorder, which is already widespread, will either progress to chaos or be arrested by a change to totalitarian government. Already in our large cities the collapse of cultural values has progressed to the point where murder is not only for money and revenge but often simply for entertainment. Since our problems exist worldwide, it seems certain that democracy will disappear before 2000 A.D. from most of the present Free World and be replaced by anarchy or dictatorship.

Those who yearn for a workable egalitarian society might look to the distant future when, by eugenics and bio-engineering, the character of mankind will have been improved and when an enduring and compelling morality will have been found through science.

SURVIVAL OF CIVILIZATION

In the evolution of a civilization there are always opposing trends that obscure the true state of affairs and that seem to allow us to predict what we please for the future.

Two opposing trends in our civilization are from obliviousness to awareness and from superstition to disbelief in moral order. The first encourages optimism about the future. The second is cause for despair.

The trend to awareness is shown in our increasing concern for those less fortunate than ourselves. We feel sympathy for all who suffer in natural disasters, or at the hands of others, or from personal accidents, or who are born with physical or mental defects. Child and wife abuse, for example, are probably no more prevalent today than a century ago, but we are increasingly willing to acknowledge evil and misfortune, and to offer what immediate help we can.

Awareness extends beyond calamity. We are discovering ourselves and our universe, not only in a formal sense through science, but in a diffuse, cultural, subjective, and personal sense. In their own way, our children are wiser and more sensitive than we.

This is a hopeful progression, but in our thinking it can mask another and ominous trend, namely, that toward moral lawlessness.

In the dawn of history, rules for living, embedded in religious belief, were created as a means to survival. In every civilization this matrix of ethical values has evolved and then decayed. In Western civilization, with the passing generations since the Renaissance, the obligating prescriptions of religion have weakened. Because the rules of behavior drew their authority from revealed religion, it is not surprising that, as superstition waned, immorality has increased in various contexts.

Almost inevitably, in the anonymity of the corporation, amoral self-interest translates into social immorality. On the other hand, the businessman who lived by Christian love alone would soon be bankrupt. We are unwilling to admit this dilemma and to begin the search for principles of rational compromise.

At an interpersonal level, the pursuit of amoral sexual pleasure becomes immoral unless restrained by disciplined concern for the wellbeing of self and others. The Ten Commandments were meant for tribal life and are of little help in dealing with exceptions in a complex world.

In the public arena, the social clothing of our civilization is being ripped away, strip by strip, for profit. We intellectuals destroyed the authority of old-time religion. Now, mesmerized by our commitment to individual liberty, we stare uncomprehendingly, day after day, as our cultural values are destroyed by the advertising and entertainment industries. To be saleable, vicarious sex and violence must be titillating but not alarming, i.e., they must be always just a little more daring than yesterday. Human degradation proceeds inexorably because we have lost our absolute standards of behavior and have no understanding of the process we are witnessing. The resulting distortion of affect in the younger generation signals a brutalizing of the spirit to which we are resolutely blind.

The survival of our civilization may depend upon conceiving a transcendent morality to replace that which was suited to more primitive living conditions. Past civilizations did not survive. Often, as they crumbled, there was a regression to superstition in preparation for the next civilization. This is what we are seeing today.

This self-destructive cycle might be broken by the construction of a new morality based upon science. This advice was offered in an exploratory book by Raymond B. Cattell (1972), who was professionally admired as an outstanding psychometric psychologist but altogether ignored as the most original social thinker of our age. Others of intellectual eminence have made the same proposal, but none so incisively. (See, for example, Nobel laureate, Roger Sperry, 1983.)

Cattell did not say so, but I believe that the seeds of a new morality based upon science will eventually be found in parapsychology, which seeks to relate consciousness to the physical world. Progress in that pretheoretical field has been real but slow.

Meanwhile, the common man grows impatient. In the USA as well as in the Middle East, the forces of irrational religious fundamentalism are gathering strength to do battle with the Great Satan, reason.

I see no hope for a rational morality within our present cultural framework. Our conception of what we are, of what we want, and of how we are going to get it, must change.

We have covered the fertile land with people, and we have stripped the richest of our natural resources. For these reasons it appears probable that ours will be the last civilization.

If civilization disappears, it is probable that scientific knowledge, along with our artistic triumphs, will be lost and never reconstructed in a subsequent, irreversible, worldwide social chaos of the kind now descending upon Africa (Meredith, 1984).

Even assuming there is no nuclear war, some of the factors that, taken together, are seemingly incommensurable with the rebirth of civilization are these:

- The inability of the earth to support but a tiny fraction of its present population without science and technology.

- The impossibility of preserving science and technology in the presence of any primitive superstitious religion that might be capable of restoring morality and a workable society.

- The absence of isolated, resource-rich spaces in which a new civilization might evolve despite chaos elsewhere.

From history we infer that, as symbol-manipulating beings, we need to share a time-binding vision of ourselves before we will cooperate with those yet unborn. I see a hope, however small, that parapsychology may catalyze the development of a new philosophy that will provide such a vision and pave the way for the preservation of human knowledge.

REFERENCES

Bowman, R.M. (1985). Star Wars and security. *IEEE Technology and Society Magazine, 4*(4), 2–13.

Broad, W.J. (1985). *Star Warriors.* New York: Simon & Schuster.

Carter, A.B. (1984). *Directed Energy Missile Defense in Space—A Background Paper.* Washington, D.C.: U.S. Congress, Office of Technology Assessment. OTA–BP–ISC-26.

Cattell, Raymond B. (1972). *A New Morality from Science: Beyondism.* Elmsford, New York: Pergamon Press.

Finkle, J.L., & Crane, B.B. (1985). Ideology and politics at Mexico City: The United States at the 1984 International Conference on Population, *Population and Development Review 11*, No. 1 (March, 1985), 1–28.

Hiatt, F. (1986). 6,500 college scientists take anti-SDI pledge. *Washington Post,* 14 May, p. A3.

Jenkins, L. (1986). Poisoning scandal rocks Italian wine export business. *Washington Post,* 9 April 1986, page 1.

Lamm, Richard D. (1985). *Megatraumas: America at the Year 2000.* New York: Houghton-Mifflin.

Lamm, Richard D., & Imhoff, G. (1985). *The Immigration Time Bomb: The Fragmenting of America.* New York: E.P. Dutton.

McConnell, R.A. (1983). Parapsychology, the wild card in a stacked deck: A look at the near future of mankind. Pages 117–145 in R.A. McConnell(Ed.), *Parapsychology and Self-Deception in Science.* Pittsburgh, Pennsylvania: Author.

Meredith, M. (1984). *The First Dance of Freedom: Black Africa in the Postwar Era.* New York: Harper-Row.

Mexico City. (1986). In Mexico City: Good visibility, bad pollution. *New York Times, 136*, No. 46981(December 7), p. 19.

Myers, Ware. (1986). The Star Wars software debate. *Bulletin of the Atomic Scientists, 42*(2), 31–36.

Parnas, D. (1986). Why I quit Star Wars. *Common Cause Magazine*, May / June, 32–35.

Ridenour, L.N. (1946). Pilot lights of the apocalypse. *Fortune, 33*(January), pp. 116,117,219.

Smith, R.J. (1985). New doubts about Star Wars feasibility. *Science, 229*(26 July), 367–368.

Sperry, R.W. (1983). *Science and Moral Priority.* New York: Columbia University Press.

Steinhart, J.S., & Steinhart, C.E. (1974). Energy use in the U.S. food system. *Science, 184*, 307–316.

Sugar maple. (1986). Sugar maple faces extinction threat. *New York Times, 136*, No. 46981(December 7), p. 69.

Thurow, L.C. (1986). The economic case against Star Wars. *(M.I.T.) Technology Review, 89*(2), 11 and 15.

Tirman, J., (ed.) (1986). *Empty Promise—The Growing Case Against Star Wars.* Boston: Beacon Press. (From the Union of Concerned Scientists.)

United States Council on Environmental Quality and the Department of State. (1980). *The Global 2000 Report to the President: Entering the Twenty-First Century, Volume 1: The Summary Report.* U.S. Government Printing Office: S / N 041–011–00037–8.

United States Policy Statement for the International Conference on Population. (1984). *Population and Development Review 10*, No. 3 (September, 1984), 574–579.

INDEX

f = "and on the following page."
n = "in footnote."